VERSE SATIRE IN ENGLAND

VERSE SATIRE IN ENGLAND BEFORE THE RENAISSANCE

BY

SAMUEL MARION TUCKER PH.D.

AMS PRESS, INC.
NEW YORK
1966

AMS PRESS, INC.
New York, N.Y. 10003
1966

Manufactured in the United States of America

TO MY MOTHER

PREFACE

This essay is concerned with the historical study of literature and the evolution of literary types. For such a study the comparative method forms the only sure guide. This point of view has made necessary the general treatment here followed: a survey of satirical literature in several languages, with an attempt to trace the influence of foreign satire upon the English. So wide a survey is open to criticism on many grounds, but it is hoped that the material here brought together and the conclusions here reached may prove not without value for future investigations.

The difficulties under which the work has been done have been considerable. There are no satisfactory terminology or criteria that might serve as a basis for the treatment of the Satire as a genre. Such terminology and criteria Chapter I of this book attempts to establish. Again, the very subject-matter with which the author has had to deal was found chaotic and widely distributed, some of it hardly accessible. An effort has been made to render this confused mass in some degree more coherent and significant.

The amount of critical work on the Satire and on satirical literature in general, in the shape of books, essays, magazine articles, etc., is enormous. Yet, either through their merely popular character, their restricted point of view, or their desultory method, the vast majority of these studies was found unsuited to the purpose of the present work. Furthermore, no treatment of the evolution of the Satire as a genre in English has yet been attempted. Professor Alden's book, to which I gladly acknowledge my indebtedness, is an able and scholarly treatment of one period—that of the Elizabethan Satire. The present study in some measure leads up to Professor Alden's work, since it essays to trace the development of satirical verse in England from its beginnings down to the close of its first period, in 1540.

Since this essay is in truth merely an introduction to the study and history of the English Satire, its first chapter, giving the theory of the Satire, may seem disproportionately long. This chapter was indeed planned to serve as an introduction to the study of the English Satire as a whole down to the time of Byron. It has been allowed to remain as originally written, in the hope that it may prove suggestive to other students.

The historical point of view has been maintained throughout this essay. Only in its relation to life can the greater part of such matter as is here treated be of any significance or value. If we accept the work of Chaucer, of the author of *Piers Plowman,* and some of the best work of the Renaissance satirists in England, we must confess that very little satire of any great literary value was produced in England before the Age of Elizabeth. Hence such a product becomes of account only in its relation to contemporary life, in the illustrations it gives of English history in the broader sense, and, from the evolutionary standpoint, in its gradual development into something higher.

I am under obligations to the authorities of the Library of Columbia University for many courtesies through years of study. To Professor W. A. Neilson, of Harvard University, Professor G. P. Krapp, of the University of Cincinnati, Professor Brander Matthews and Professor J. B. Fletcher, of Columbia University, I am indebted for many excellent suggestions. My friends, Miss M. P. Conant, Professor of English Literature at the Woman's College, Frederick, Md., and Mr. S. L. Wolff, of New York City, gave me the benefit of their advice in regard to the style of this book; my friend and colleague, Dr. B. C. Bondurant, Professor of Classics at The Florida State College for Women, revised my treatment of the Classical Satire. To Professor A. H. Thorndike and Professor W. W. Lawrence, of Columbia University, I am immensely indebted for help in matter, method, and style.

Above all, my grateful acknowledgment is due my friend and former teacher, Professor W. P. Trent, of Columbia University, at whose suggestion this study was undertaken, and without whose kind and continual assistance and encouragement it could never have reached a conclusion.

TALLAHASSEE, FLA.,
January 19, 1909.

CONTENTS

Chapter I. Introductory 1

Chapter II. From Walter Map to Langland 35

Chapter III. From Langland's Imitators to Chaucer 80

Chapter IV. From Lydgate to the Renaissance ... 118

Chapter V. Henryson, Dunbar, Skelton, and Barclay 134

Chapter VI. Social Satire, 1520–1550; Satire of the Reformation 168

Chapter VII. Sir David Lyndsay and the Satiric Play 197

Chapter VIII. Summary and Conclusion 221

Bibliography 228

Index 235

CHAPTER I

INTRODUCTORY

Great English satirists.—Difficulty of tracing the development of the English Satire.—Triple meaning of the word " satire."—The term " satirical poetry."—Varieties and schools.—Five epochs in the history of satirical poetry in England.—Foreign influences.—Terminology and criteria.—Nature and working of the satirical spirit.—Catalogue of satirical genres.—Elements of the satirical spirit.—Stimuli of the satirical spirit.—Instruments of the satirical spirit.—Satire in prose and in verse.—Distinction between the two forms.—Why satire is not poetic.—The two chief methods of the Satire.—The classical Latin Satire.—The Epigram.—Relation of the Epigram to the Satire.—The nature of burlesque.—Parody and travesty.—The Mock-Heroic poem; its varieties.—The satirical Mock-Epic; its relation to the Satire.—Greek burlesque.—Roman burlesque.—Medieval burlesque.—The Beast-Epic.—The *Roman de Renart*.—The Beast-Fable.—The satiric Allegory.—Difference between the Satire and all other genres.—Four varieties of the Satire.—The Personal Satire.—The Political Satire.—The Moral and Social Satire.—The Literary Satire; " Parnassian " poems.—Summary.

The story of verse-satire in England is long, for it begins with the twelfth century and has not yet ended. It is also a varied story, for not only does it cover the rise, decline, and fall of many a minor satirical genre, but centers as well about the names of great satirists who have differed widely in form, in subject-matter, and in spirit. Walter Map (or whoever may have been that " Bishop Golias " of evanescent personality), Langland (or whoever may have been the author of *Piers Plowman*), Chaucer, Skelton, and Lyndsay; Wyatt, Hall, and Donne; Cleveland and Butler; Dryden, Pope, Swift, Young, and Churchill; Cowper, Canning, Gifford, and Byron —such are some of the great names that serve to mark the rise and progress of English satirical verse.

Thus, for over seven centuries, the stream of English satire has been flowing with a varied course, time and time again deflected by cross currents from abroad. For these reasons and others that will appear hereafter, it is perhaps more difficult to trace the history of the Satire than that of any other poetical genre. The Ode, the Elegy, the Lyric, are far more limited in scope and more clearly defined. If it be admitted that the verse-Satire reached its full development in the work of Dryden, then, in order to understand this consummate product, we must go far back to the very beginning. Up to the Elizabethan era, at least, we shall find it necessary to disregard any strict definition of the Satire, and take into consideration verse that is not only largely informal, but even deficient in satirical quality. Furthermore, we shall constantly trespass on the domains of other genres, such as the didactic poem and the ballad. And all of this we shall find written in three languages, Latin, English and Anglo-French, each of which might be termed a vernacular. While very little of this considerable medieval product conforms to any strict definition of the Satire, it is still significant as exhibiting tendencies that finally resulted in a perfect form, and that therefore deserve our attention, despite the difficulty of giving them consistent treatment.

Again, it is not easy to see that the genre underwent any well-marked evolution. The term "evolution" has now become popular, and is too often loosely applied. Strictly speaking, it would scarcely be demonstrable to say that the English Satire is a product of distinct evolution. Still, it must be apparent to any student that this genre has indeed been the result of a long process of growth. Its three different elements, Form, Subject-matter, and Tone, have by degrees gained in richness and scope as the nation has developed. The form has gradually grown more artistic and individual; the subject-matter has become more comprehensive; the tone has learned to run the gamut from grave to gay, has grown more expressive of the individual writer, and has gained a larger sense of the ludicrous.

Furthermore, any study of satirical poetry in England is at the very outset rendered difficult by a confusion of terms. A source of this confusion lies in the really triple meaning of the word *satire*. As given in the dictionary, *satire,* in one sense, is an abstract term cognate with ridicule; as when we say, "*Satire* has accomplished revolutions." A second meaning refers to a literary form that has for its object destructive criticism, as when we say, "Butler's *Hudibras* is a *Satire* on the Puritans."

There is in this double meaning no confusion too great to be simplified by the mere use of a capital letter when the word "satire" is used to denote a literary form. But, unfortunately, a double meaning lurks in the first and more abstract signification of the word as given in the dictionary. Here two things are confused: the *satirical spirit,* an intangible, abstract something that underlies and inspires what we commonly call satire—or ridicule—or invective; and *satire* itself, which is merely the concrete manifestation of the satiric spirit in literature. This distinction may seem fanciful; certainly it can be justified and made clear only through discussion and illustration. But let it be borne in mind that throughout the following account of the nature of satirical verse in general and the history of the English product in particular, the term *satirical spirit* always refers to a point of view; the word *satire* to a concrete but general embodiment of that point of view in literature; and *Satire* (capitalized) to the literary form or genre, as well as to any particular example of that genre. Thus, we may say, "The *satirical spirit* is unenthusiastic"; "Butler's *satire* is directed largely against the Puritans"; "Butler made an important contribution to *the Satire*"; "Butler's Hudibras is *a Satire* in the burlesque method." From the double use of the capitalized form there should arise no ambiguity, the meaning being apparent from the context. In this perhaps inadequate way we shall at least have taken a step toward a clearer and more definite terminology.

The confusion, however, is not merely verbal. English satirical poetry is not one genre alone, but is an inclusive term covering a number of genres more or less clearly defined. To be sure, the English Satire *par excellence* is indeed a distinct genre, with a form and traditions of its very own. Though this genre is in origin that of the classical Latin Satire, yet its growth and development in England from its first beginnings in the Satires of Sir Thomas Wyatt in 1540 to the Satires, say, of Gifford at the close of the eighteenth century, have been so definite as to justify the proposition that this particular form of English satirical poetry has been actually evolved.

But aside from this, its most significant and clearly-defined variety, satirical verse in England includes several other varieties and schools. The Goliardic Latin satire of the twelfth and thirteenth centuries; the troubadour[1] and trouvère product of the same period (the *sirvente*); the satiric Eclogue of Barclay, Googe, Spenser, and Gay; the Elizabethan and Augustan Epigram; the satiric Fable of Gay and of Prior; the satirical Mock-Heroic—all these are varieties in themselves—and all are satirical. Beyond these, we find *schools* of satiric verse: the Anglo-Latin Satires of the twelfth century—the work of Wireker and his contemporaries; the Songs against the French and Scotch by English gleemen through the reigns of the first three Edwards; the Lollard Satire in Latin and in English, *pro* and *con,* of the early fifteenth century; the allegorical Satire, from the *Speculum Stultorum* to the *Satyre of the Thrie Estaitis*; the Satire on Woman; the peculiar politico-satirical ballads of the fourteenth and fifteenth centuries, in which noblemen are referred to by their cognizances; the Satire of the Reformation; the productions of Skelton and the Skeltonic school; the "Fool Satire" from Wireker to Skelton; the "Satire on Rogues," of the early sixteenth century; the satirical ballads of the Civil War and Protectorate; the work of Cleveland and his imitators; the Satires of the Hudibrastic school; and the "Parnassian Satires" of the seventeenth, eighteenth, and nineteenth centuries—from Suckling to Lowell.

The rise and progress of verse-satire in England, in all these and other kinds, from 1200 to 1800, from Walter Map to Byron, is roughly divisible into five great epochs. The first period of development begins with Goliardic satire and satire in Anglo-French, and ends with the consummation of medieval satire in the work of Lyndsay, 1540. With the birth of the formal genre, in the classical Satires of Sir Thomas Wyatt, begins a second epoch that ends with the decadence of

[1] The troubadour *sirvente* was connected with the English dominion in France; see *infra,* p. 48 f.

this classical Satire about 1628. The satire of the Civil War and Protectorate, of Cleveland and Butler, marks the third period. A fourth begins with the revival of the Classical Satire by Dryden and ends with its decline in Gifford. Out of this fourth epoch grows a fifth, which begins with the satire of the *Anti-Jacobin,* and culminates in the masterly work of Byron, perhaps the greatest of English verse-satirists.

Foreign influences, emanating chiefly from France and Italy, have again and again through its history affected English satirical verse. The Goliardic poetry was probably a French importation; the *sirvente* was French and Norman; Anglo-Latin satire was perceptibly affected by the classics. The *Roman de la Rose* certainly exercised an influence upon Langland and Chaucer; while the latter was clearly indebted to the method of the *fabliau* for some of his best satirical work. Wyatt drew from the Italians; the Elizabethan formal satirists, from both the Italians and the classics. Butler gained at least his framework from *Don Quixote*; the great satirists of the Restoration and Georgian eras were profoundly influenced, first by Boileau, later by La Fontaine. Gifford fancied himself a follower of Juvenal; while Byron was not without his debt to the Italians.

To the history of the English Satire, the present volume can be regarded only as introductory. For the *form* does not take shape until 1540; and we can here concern ourselves only with the largely formless medieval product that found its close and consummation in the work of Barclay, of Skelton, and of Sir David Lyndsay.

Our purpose being to treat satirical poetry as distinct from all other poetical forms, we must establish a certain terminology and certain canons of criticism whereby to determine what shall and what shall not be included in our treatment. It is possible, first, to differentiate satirical poetry from all other forms through the fact that it is *destructive* in its criticism, while all other forms are *constructive.* This peculiar and individual tone sets satirical poetry apart.

But this individual tone is not alone characteristic of satire in *verse;* it is shared by a great mass of satire in *prose.* We have, then, at the outset, four important things to do; first, to ascertain the nature, the *stimuli,* and the working and mode of manifestation of the spirit that gives to this body of prose and verse what is called its "satirical tone"; second, to distinguish between prose and verse satire; third, to describe and illustrate the two great methods of the Satire, and to show the relation of the formal verse-Satire to certain kindred and also to certain subordinate genres; finally, to differentiate between the Satire and all other genres of poetry, and to describe its different varieties.

I

In the first attempt—to ascertain the nature and the working of the satirical spirit—there would be less difficulty were satirical literature in itself homogeneous. But apparently its range of tone is quite commensurate with its enormous extent. What, then, may be the essence of the informing spirit that can stamp as *satire* each distinct production in this great body of prose and verse? Surely, if the product itself is so diverse, the spirit animating it must be complex and multiform.

Yet this spirit must also possess certain constant elements, however variable its incidental characteristics. It is possible, indeed, to obtain some knowledge of the nature of this satirical spirit, but only after forming a general idea of what may be included under the head of satirical literature. Then it at once becomes evident that, whatever its minor characteristics, this spirit is eternal and perennial, and has constantly found expression in European literature since the days of Homer. In order to indicate in a general way the field covered by this satirical product, it may be well, even at the risk of stating commonplaces, to make a diagram of the various forms that the satirical spirit assumes, giving for each form, as far as possible, at least one great typical example. The catalogue, though far from exhaustive, may still serve for illustration.

It is easy to see the kinship between Aristophanes, Lucian, Ulrich von Hutten, and Rabelais; but it is a far cry from Horace, Erasmus and Addison, through Dryden, Pope and Boileau, to Juvenal, Swift and Churchill. Yet all these, according to the universal verdict of criticism, are satirists.

Prose

- The formal (professed) prose Satire: *The Praise of Folly,* by Erasmus.
- The Dialogue: The *Dialogues* of Lucian, of Ulrich von Hutten.
- The Play: The satiric prose comedies of Molière.
- The Novel: *Gulliver's Travels,* by Swift.
- The Tale: *Candide,* by Voltaire.
- The Essay: The satiric *Essays* of Addison.
- The satiric Burlesque of any prose genre: The *Don Quixote* of Cervantes, the *Gargantua* of Rabelais (parodies of the Romance of Chivalry); The *Sermon Joyeux* (parody of the Sermon).

Verse

Direct method.

- The formal verse-Satire: *Satires* of Horace, Juvenal, Ariosto, Boileau, Pope.
- The Epigram: The *Epigrams* of Martial.
- The Lampoon or Pasquinade: Lampoons by Defoe.
- The satirical Ballad and Song: The Ballads of the Civil War and Protectorate in England (1630–1660); the *Songs* of Béranger.

Indirect method.

- The satirical Mock-Heroic: *La Secchia Rapita* of Tassoni; *Le Lutrin* of Boileau; *Hudibras* of Butler; *Don Juan* of Byron.
- The satiric Tale: The satiric *Fabliau;* Chaucer's *Friar's Tale.*
- The Beast-Epic: *Roman de Renart.*
- The satiric Play:[2] The Plays of Aristophanes; *The Alchemist* of Ben Jonson.
- The satiric Fable: *Fables* of Marie de France; *Fables* of LaFontaine; *Fables* of Gay, of Prior, etc.
- The satiric Burlesque of any poetic genre: (Parody) The *Morgante Maggiore* of Pulci; (Travesty) The *Virgile Travesti* of Scarron.

What, then, is this satirical spirit that is said to bring all these great writers under the same category? Is it not, in the first place, as we have said, essentially the spirit of adverse or negative criticism, the spirit that prompts *attack?* Negative criticism destroys. Yet this, if the chief and essential quality of the satirical spirit, is still but one of its elements, and varies greatly in degree. Alone, it would not form the satirical spirit in its entirety. Negative criticism unalloyed may produce in-

[2] The German Fastnachtspiel, though embodying much incidental satire, can scarcely be termed a satiric genre (see Creizenach, *Geschichte des neueren Dramas,* I, 416–420). The French Farce and Sottie, though often dealing in very effective satire, are, as genres, humorous rather than satirical (see Creizenach, I, 439–442; Lenient, *La Satire en France au Moyen Age,* ch. XXII).

vectives, sermons, didacticism in many forms, but not *satire*. The truly satirical spirit includes other elements that vary in degree with the individual satirist; for the satirical method of Horace is not that of Swift; and that of Byron or of Berni is not that of Juvenal. These other elements consist, on the part of the satirist, in a sense of superiority, a sense of the ludicrous, a tendency towards exaggeration, and a reformatory purpose.

The critical spirit implies a feeling of superiority, which, as the concomitant of adverse criticism, is always in some degree present in satire, but increases as the criticism grows more bitter, *e. g.*, from Horace to Juvenal. It is found even in Horace, who delighted to include himself among the objects of his own ridicule. And such an attitude is possible, for the personality in these cases is objectified, and the Satirist becomes superior to the Man.

Since the spirit of satire is negatively critical, the tendency of satire is of course destructive. It always attacks to destroy, not, primarily, to reform the object of its criticism. Still, though there is little expression of reformatory purpose in ideal satire, the satirical spirit must by implication construct where it has torn down; but not avowedly, else the satire drifts into mere didacticism. From this the truly satirical spirit is distinguished not only by its destructive tendency but also by its sense of the ludicrous. The destructive element it has in common with invective. But pure invective is totally lacking in humor, which presupposes sympathy either real or assumed. Humor the satirical spirit has in common with the mighty mass of purely uncritical humorous literature, the aim of which is only to amuse and the method of which is positive; and though, in its simpler manifestations, the satirical spirit may be identical with pure humor in so far as humor depends on the perception of incongruities, it is dissimilar in that it must attack these absurdities made evident by humor and reduce them to harmony. Obviously, humor and the satirical spirit grow more and more unlike as the latter becomes increasingly antagonistic and bitter and loses the mere sense of amusement in a feeling of indignation.

There are certain elements of the satirical spirit that must vary in inverse ratio to one another. Even the spirit of censure that prompts adverse criticism, though ever-present, is a variable element in that it grows more pronounced as the satirist becomes more earnest and indignant. Though essentially unsympathetic, yet in its lighter moods the satirical spirit may be tempered by humor, which is thoroughly sympathetic, or by a sense of contemptuous pity, which is partially so. But these qualities are eliminated, as the criticism, at first leavened by a large sense of genuine amusement, passes through the intermediate stages of a more stringent, less sympathetic criticism, and finally becomes direct and severe rebuke, unmitigated by any sense of the ludicrous. What was at first mild and even laughing criticism, has become bitter invective; what was amusement, has become unspeakable contempt and scornful disgust. In its more genial manifestation, the satirical spirit worked to make its object merely ridiculous; finally, it strives to render its object absolutely loathsome. Thus, as the adverse criticism grows more severe, the sense of humor decreases, and at once with this decline of sympathy, the earlier and more kindly attributes yield to scorn and contempt, though the moral earnestness apparently gains in depth.

The tendency toward exaggeration that marks every manifestation of the satirical spirit is perhaps rather a result of its working than an essential quality of its being. And yet exaggeration is so omnipresent in satire that it is easy to regard it merely as a varying element of the satiric spirit itself. Undoubtedly it often results from the satirist's desire to heighten the effect of those incongruities which he professes to feel so keenly. This, of course, is that conscious method of which Horace is an excellent exemplar. If, on the other hand, the exaggeration is unconscious and inevitable, it must result from some exaggerated—*i. e.,* distorted—view of life on the part of a satirist who does not "see life steadily and see it whole." Such a satirist narrows his vision down to the objects of his attack, removes these from their surroundings, fails to see them in their right relations, and exaggerates their importance. Of this class were Juvenal and Swift.

But this tendency toward exaggeration is not the only quality of the satirical spirit that is but questionably an essential attribute. A certain stock definition of the Satire invariably refers to its "reformatory purpose."[3] This seems highly questionable. The desire to reform is rather an incidental than an essential quality. Half of the satire in literature has sprung from no apparent reformatory purpose, though such a spirit has undoubtedly inspired some of the world's greatest satirical masterpieces. The satirist may not be animated by any such high motive, as we shall see later. It is true that the result of all genuine satire would inevitably be reformatory, irrespective of the author's motive, were the condition surrounding its reception entirely favorable to that end. Social satire, for instance, reforms only when it gives expression to a popular desire for reform—in other words, when the satirist is merely, consciously or unconsciously, the people's voice in some great movement. This spirit of reform may utilize satirical genius, but so also may the spirit of pure malice. These, of course, are the two extremes. But granting that in many cases the reformatory purpose is predominant, this spirit seems to increase with the earnestness and vigor of the criticism. Yet not necessarily so, for certainly some of the milder satirists, such as Erasmus and Addison, were actuated by this high motive; and many of the most severe, as Swift, Churchill and Oldham, seem to have been inspired more by malice than by any desire to reform.

So much for the elements of the satirical spirit, whether essential or incidental, variable or constant.

We must not confuse the *elements* of the satirical spirit with those *stimuli* which are external to it. These *stimuli* are furnished, first, by a sense of incongruity, inconsistency, and excess, either general or personal, in the social, political, and literary worlds; and, secondly, by a sense of injury, or a feeling of dislike or hatred toward an individual, institution, or class. The first cause results in the more general, the second

[3] Stock phrases of this character are usually immature generalizations from a few standard examples—principally those furnished by the classical Latin Satire; *e. g.*, Juvenal's *Satires,* VIII and XIV.

in the more personal, satire; but the former produces perhaps the more typical variety, as personal satire too easily degenerates into invective. Obviously, we find at times these *stimuli* working together so closely that it is impossible to say which preponderates. The animus itself may have been somewhat malicious and personal, and yet, as in Dryden's *Mac Flecknoe,* the resulting satire may be that of the higher and more general order.

A discussion of these external *stimuli* forms a natural connection between that consideration of the essential nature of the satirical spirit which has already been undertaken, and some discussion of the instruments or weapons through which that spirit works and manifests itself in literature.

It is obvious that as the satirical spirit grows more intense, its instruments must change accordingly. There is, to be sure, no sharp line of demarcation as the tone changes. One satirist alone may in turn use many weapons. Even Horace does not confine himself to lightest raillery; no more does Juvenal always fight by means of bitter invective. Still, it is safe to say that the weapons employed by a satirist of the milder type are sharper and lighter, though not necessarily less effective, than those used by satirists of the more severe order. Light raillery, slight exaggeration, an abundant sense of the ludicrous, playful wit, and a certain amount of gentle sarcasm, are characteristic of all so-called "Horatian" satire. As we pass through the second class, of which Dryden and Pope are good exemplars, the light and even laughing raillery is lost, and the humor decreases, though the wit is constant; the exaggeration is greater, the sarcasm grows more cutting, and the ridicule more obvious. When we reach the third class, that of Juvenal, of Swift, and of Gifford, the sarcasm is most bitter, the ridicule, if there be laughter at all, is unspeakably scornful, humor has been mainly displaced by invective; and, finally, gross exaggeration is everywhere evident.

We have seen that the satirical spirit, using these weapons, finds expression in a vast literature. Its perennial life has been apparent in European literature, at least, since the days of Archilochus—or perhaps Homer. Its expression may be thoroughly unliterary, but still very much alive. It may persist in this form from the Fescennine verses of the Romans down to the modern political street-song; it may occur in the popular Ballad, and in almost any literary form of the Middle Ages. It may seek formal expression in the Satire proper, the Epigram, the Burlesque, even in the prose Fable, and may find less formal expression in any genre of both prose and verse;—in prose, the Play, the Novel, the Essay; in verse, epic, lyric, and dramatic poetry in all their sub-varieties of Ode, Sonnet, Elegy, Verse-Fable, Epistle, and the rest.

The Satire, then, never really dies, but changes shape, when it rises into literature, and adapts itself to prevailing genres. Both formal and popular satire are animated by the same spirit, but the Satire assumes superior form and becomes literature under the same conditions that affect the state of literature in general; and this is true, although in certain epochs when highly imaginative literature is eclipsed, the purely classical Satire flourishes. Such was the case in the so-called "Augustan Age" of English literature. By this time the formal Satire had been completely evolved, and can be considered as an independent product. But up to this period—the period of Dryden and of Pope—the unliterary satire, including all that immeasurable mass of prose and verse making no pretension to literary worth, often showed a tendency or in some way affected the purely literary product. Such was undoubtedly true of the verse-satire of the early and middle seventeenth century in England. Hence, until the time of Dryden, any consideration of formal satire in England must be supplemented by some reference to the unliterary product with which it was so closely allied.

We have attempted in the preceding pages to determine the nature and the working of the spirit that gives a distinguishing tone to the great mass of literature we term "satirical." Now we can undertake some differentiation between the part of that satirical literature which is written in prose and the part which is written in verse.

II

When we consider the formal Satire, we find the broad division into prose and verse-satire most convenient. Prose-satire divides itself into two great groups: first, the meditative Satire in essay form, with its variations; and, secondly, the imaginative and creative forms, such as the Dialogue, Play, Tale, and Novel. Under verse-satire we find, first, the classical Satire, meditative and realistic; secondly, burlesque poetry, including every form of parody and travesty.

Satire in prose is almost incapable of classification, as it is Protean in its shape, and invades the domain of many genres. The professed or "formal" Satire in prose, such as *The Praise of Folly* of Erasmus, is rare. Prose-satire has in the main proved ineffective except when disguised.[4] But under the disguise of other genres it has, for obvious reasons, made a much wider and more effective appeal than the Satire in verse. Its material is of far greater scope, and includes not only the vagaries and follies of the upper classes, which have proved so prolific a source of material to the verse-satirist, but also embraces all the varied interests of human society. The prose-Satire, too, has been more polemic, more reformatory in its purpose, and more efficient in working out its reformation. It has made a more popular appeal by means of more popular material and a more popular style. It is the Satire of action rather than of reflection, aimed at society at large rather than at classes. Its form is less restricted by precedent than that of the Satire in verse, which consciously follows literary models and has its tone, form, and choice of material more or less influenced by such precedent. This distinction, however, would apply rather to the classical Satire and classical Mock-Epic than to burlesque verse-satire, which in material and method approaches more nearly the scope and power of the prose Satire. Both in literature and in life prose-satire has played the larger part. In addition to its greater scope of material, it has offered a wider field to the imagination through

[4] Even *The Praise of Folly,* since its method is really indirect, wears a thin disguise. The piece is in truth a glorified *sermon joyeux,* and thoroughly ironical.

its freedom from metrical restrictions. Lucian, Erasmus, Ulrich von Hutten, Fischart, Rabelais, Cervantes, De Foe, Swift,[5] Voltaire, are perhaps the greatest names in prose-satire, though in different spheres. To equal these in creative genius, verse-satire has scarcely a name to offer except that of Aristophanes.

For the satirical spirit is anything but idealistic in its treatment—it is realistic; it deals, in the main, with sordid aspects of life and character, not with those higher and more beautiful phases with which pure poetry concerns itself. Hence this spirit finds its natural expression in prose. Certainly there are cases in which this very material has been transmuted into something truly poetical by the force of the satirist's emotions. The satires of Juvenal at times exemplify this fact; and in *Mac Flecknoe* Dryden has actually raised his Shadwell into something universal and poetical. But, in the main, it must be acknowledged that the Satire in verse is not essentially *poetry*. The satirist is scarcely animated by emotions "that voluntary move harmonious numbers." When he has written in verse, from Horace to Pope, he has chosen this method of expression on account of its conciseness and its opportunity for epigrammatic point. But this choice has determined the form of what we call preëminently *The Satire.*

Now that we have ascertained the nature and the working of the satirical spirit, and have distinguished between satire in verse and satire in prose, we can proceed to carry out the third part of the program outlined on page 6. This leads first to some discussion of the two chief methods employed by the verse-Satire.

III

The verse-Satire, whether the form be that of Horace or that of Butler and of Byron, has in general two methods of expression: the direct, and the indirect or dramatic. These two methods are fundamentally distinct and usually exist separately, but, as may appear later, are occasionally found in com-

[5] The satiric pamphlet of the early eighteenth century in England, handled so brilliantly by Defoe and Swift, furnishes perhaps the best examples of effective prose-satire in our literature.

bination. The direct method is that of the pulpit—hortatory, reflective, expository, didactic. Possibly this was the earlier method, for satire in its origin was certainly largely personal. In pure literature the classical Latin type is the chief exponent of this direct method.

The development—or evolution—of the Latin Satire, from its faint beginnings in Ennius, through its treatment by Lucilius, to its perfect form in Horace, Persius, and Juvenal, has been traced so often and so thoroughly that there is here no need of such a history. What remains to be done is to treat specifically the exact form of this Latin Satire in its Roman period, and to determine the influence of Horace, Persius, and Juvenal upon the formal English Satire of the Elizabethan and Augustan eras. Such a treatment, however, would be out of place in a work that ends its study with the year 1540, at the very appearance of the classical Satire in England. Still, in order clearly to show how utterly the medieval English satirical poetry differs from this classical product, we must here attempt a general characterization of that very clearly defined and formal genre, the classical Latin Satire.

The Satire of Horace, Persius, and Juvenal was as separate and distinct a literary genre as any in literature. Though running a certain gamut in tone and even undergoing certain changes of form from Lucilius, through Horace and Persius, to Juvenal, it still retained its unique character. It was clear-cut, definite, precise. Hence, despite these changes of form and tone, it may still be possible to frame some comprehensive description that shall serve as a test for any imitations of this type:

The classical Satire is written in a dignified and uniform meter, and, at its longest, is a comparatively short poem. It is not characterized by any fixed organism, but is remarkable for an extent of ideas which somewhat compensates for this lack of definite structure. It may utilize various methods of expression, such as those of direct address, narrative, or dialogue; but remains largely a subjective poem depending for its formal details entirely on the personality of the individual satirist. Thus it drifts naturally into self-revelation. It deals largely in personalities to illustrate its teachings. Its purpose is mainly that of destructive criticism,—the objects of its attack range from the smallest breach of good-taste in the social or the literary worlds to the grossest crime against morality; and its weapons, consonant with its subject-matter, vary from the lightest raillery to the bitterest invective. Finally, this classical Satire is purely formal and arises from the writer's reflective turn of mind rather than from any polemic or reformatory motive. Its emphasis is entirely on private evils and it is devoid of political or distinctly religious coloring.

This same classical species has appeared again and again, since the beginning of the Renaissance, in Italy, Spain, France, England, and Germany. It has always risen as the work of scholarly, or would-be scholarly, poets, under direct classical influence. Often dry, pedantic, and dull, but still occasionally with something of native flavor and force, it rises at its best into the inimitable work of Boileau and of Pope. This type, which above all others deserves to be called the Satire, is easily recognized. Its range is limited, and of all genres it is perhaps the most self-conscious and purely formal. Arising in England with Wyatt,[6] it was later utilized by Hall, Donne, and others; again in a more favorable age by Pope and Young, and finally by Gifford. It is significant that the classical Satire adopts the great national verse of its vernacular and rarely appears in any other form: in Italy and Spain, the *terza-rima*; in France, the Alexandrine; in England, the heroic couplet.

Just here it may be well to notice briefly a genre, by modern consensus termed satirical, which has always closely associated itself with the formal Satire, and which by preference employs the direct method. This genre is the *Epigram*. Despite innumerable popular articles on the subject, there yet remains to be written a thorough and consistent treatment of the history of this most variable and ill-defined form. The Greek epigram was not often satirical—though among the

[6] See *infra*, p. 227.

later epigrams of the *Anthology* occur a few—by Lucian, Lucilius, and others—that point the way toward Martial. The Latin Martial, epigrammatist *par excellence* of all literature, was, though satirist by preference, yet not always satirical. In his case it was perhaps rather the nature of the writer than the demands of the literary form that made his epigrams satirical. Martial's influence, however, pervading all the subsequent history of the genre, has practically identified the Epigram with satire. The medieval Latin epigrammatists were his followers—Godfrey of Winchester and Henry of Huntingdon[7] among the English writers, for instance; and so were the Latin epigrammatists of the Renaissance, such as Bembo, Scaliger, Buchanan, and More. In English, came the vast flood of Martialian epigrams in the time of Elizabeth, beginning with those of John Heywood, and in a later period the golden age of the English epigram under the seventeenth-century poets, with Pope at their head. The Epigram of Ben Jonson—Greek rather than Martialian—differs so widely from that of Pope, for instance, that it would seem impossible to obtain any satisfactory description of a genre including products so diverse. For the Greek epigram meant almost anything—a short poem on an occasion, real or supposed—verse, style, matter, tone, varying *ad libitum.* The epigram of Martial and his imitators is usually satirical in intent, but differs from the Satire in something more fundamental than in length. For the typical satirical epigram must be not only comparatively short, but *complete*; not only witty, but *concrete*; not general, but *specific, occasional.* Moreover, it gives but one glimpse, one side, of the object attacked. Such is the truly satirical Epigram through all its history, from Catullus down to the present day.

What is the chronological place of the Epigram in English satire? Except for the school of Anglo-Latin satirists of the eleventh and twelfth centuries, no place at all until the Renaissance, and then no place as a vernacular form until the Elizabethans. When the Epigram assumes the rank of a leading

[7] Not treated in the present volume; their Epigrams, scholarly imitations of those of Martial, form "an isolated phenomenon."

genre and vies with the Satire itself in depicting contemporary manners, a fuller treatment of its nature and history will be necessary. In the history of English literature, such is not the case until the age of Elizabeth.

The purely classical variety of the Satire, interesting and important as it is, has yet never been the prevailing, most characteristic, or most effective type of its own genre. The narrative burlesque of Italy and the Mock-Epic have preponderated. Almost all of the great satire in Italian literature employs the indirect method of pure burlesque. Indeed, the second great method employed by the Satire—the method that has already been termed *indirect* or *dramatic*—is chiefly exemplified by *Burlesque.*

Burlesque is either pictorial or literary. The pictorial burlesque—called caricature—consists in the selection of characteristic features of an original and the exaggeration of those features with ludicrous effect. When this exaggeration transcends the bounds of the possible, the *burlesque* passes into *grotesque* caricature. The difference is one of degree, not of kind.[8] So it is with the literary burlesque, which is also essentially caricature. The grotesque in literature is the further exaggeration of the burlesque. The motive remains the same: the grotesque Satire is the burlesque Satire carried into the realm of the impossible.[9]

The grotesque has found its highest expression in prose. Its masters have been such writers as Rabelais, Fischart, and Swift. In poetry it appears in the mock-heroic *Orlandino* and *Maccaronea* of the Italian, Teofilo Folengo, parodist of Ariosto (1491–1544); and in the *Morgante Maggiore* of Pulci (1432–1487). The grotesque has not flourished in English poetry, though traces of it appear in Butler's *Hudibras*; but the burlesque poem is splendidly exemplified by the work of Dryden, of Pope, and of Byron. The English comic imagination, with the exception of Swift, who was of the train of Aristophanes and Rabelais, has not achieved that broad gro-

[8] See Schneegans, *Geschichte der Grotesken Satire,* p. 46.
[9] *Ibid.,* Einleitung, p. 33.

tesque style so loved and so magnificently handled by the great continental masters. This grotesque method has always carried with it a certain peculiar style, free from restraint, often gross, shaking with large laughter. The grotesque writer laughs at conventionalities; his colossal figures stride easily over these petty things; his style runs past restraint. An Englishman like Swift achieves it; other Englishmen have been incapable of it.

Instead of the open rebuke and immediate attack of the direct satirist, the burlesque writer, not necessarily less earnest and determined, works more effectually by means of irony.[10] For, in such a case, the contrast between the satirist's ethical ideal (Ethos) and the picture he paints is complete and convincing.[11] Again the method of the stage asserts its general superiority; for, as the burlesque approaches dramatic form in speech and action, it undoubtedly gains in power and effectiveness. It leaves farther behind the method of the pulpit, and adopts that of the stage, its home.

In respect to form, burlesque poetry is roughly divisible into *travesty* and *parody.*

The travesty is a comparatively rare variety, for its range of subject-matter and form are limited. It consists in the degradation of elevated material through inferior form.[12] This subject-matter of the poetic travesty has usually been drawn from various mythologies; not invariably, however, for any superior material, ideas, institutions, and so on, may be travestied. In the mythological world, Scarron's travesty of the *Æneid* is perhaps the most famous and successful of its kind. Of this kind English literature has a host of examples —"Scarronides," "Homerides," etc., which vary from mere insipidity to rank vulgarity, but agree in their common lack of literary merit. The usual satirical range of the travesty is narrow; but for Scarron's satire there was ample scope: at the court of Louis XIV the sublime grew irksome. The great Greek satirist Lucian (c. 165 A. D.), and his imitator, the

[10] See Schneegans, p. 495.

[11] *Ibid.*, p. 495.

[12] The travesty occurs very rarely in England before the Renaissance; but is exemplified in *On the Council of London;* see *infra,* p. 87.

German humanist and reformer, Ulrich von Hutten (1520), though writing in prose, used the travesty as a most effective vehicle for satire. Yet, in the main, humanity prefers that the truly sublime remain on its lofty pedestal; hence the use of the travesty for satirical purposes has never been very general or successful.[13]

The parody,[14] more frequently encountered, is the reverse of the travesty. It consists in the use of dignified form for inferior material, with intentionally burlesque effect.[15] Every poetic species, from the Epic to the Sonnet, suffers this parodic ridicule. The burlesque may be intended to degrade the form merely, to render the subject-matter ridiculous, or to effect both purposes at once. The first purpose is illustrated by the *Batrachomyomachia*; the second by Pope's *Dunciad*; both together by *La Secchia Rapita* of the Italian poet Tassoni.

Parody of the form usually follows the decadence or the abuse of any poetical genre; such as, in Italy, the Sonnet in the sixteenth,[16] and the Epic in the seventeenth, century. This is well illustrated by the burlesque Sonnets of Francesco Coppetta (1510–1554), who parodied Petrarch; and the Mock-Epics of Teofilo Folengo and of Tassoni, who ridiculed the Epic poets. Such, also, are the parodies of the Fable, Elegy, and Eclogue, in the England of Pope, when a great mass of parodies, mainly in ridicule of the form, marks the exaggerated use of each of these genres in the early eighteenth century. These parodies appear at their best in the work of John Gay (1688–1732), such as *The Shepherd's Week* and *Town Eclogues,* parodies of the Pastoral; *Trivia,* in ridicule of the

[13] For an interesting account of the travesty with ample illustration, see Babuder, *L'Eroicomica e Generi Affini di Poesia Giocosa-Satirica,* p. 36 f.

[14] Parody is here used in its narrow sense as the burlesque of a literary *form.* Burlesque has another species of parody—that of ideas, habits of thought, speech, action,—which is broader and more significant.

[15] Wireker's *Speculum Stultorum* may be termed a parody; see *infra,* p. 43.

[16] Other poets who used the sonnet for satirical purposes, but perhaps not in parody of the form, were Domenico Burchiello (1400–48); Francesco Berni (1497–1535), who used the form for violent personal satire, as did Matteo Franco, his contemporary, who wrote two hundred and eighteen Sonnets against Aretino! Another contemporary, Pulci, follows the tradition of Burchiello. To parallel these, we have in Spanish literature the burlesque Sonnets of Gongora (d. 1626).

prevailing didactic poetry; *Elegy on a Lap-Dog*; parody of the Elegy; and the *Satirical Fables.*[17]

The double purpose of ridiculing both form and matter is illustrated by Canning's famous *Knife-Grinder* (1797),[18] in which Southey's dignified sapphics are rendered absurd, and the material is in its turn satirized through the superior form it is made to assume.

From all this it should be evident that the satirical spirit may so utilize any poetical form that the piece practically becomes a Satire. Still these formal parodies are complex in their nature, for they share the characteristics of another genre—the genre that they parody. The result is satire in the form of an elegy, an ode, a sonnet, etc.; and though many a one of these is purely satirical, yet to avoid confusion, it is better to admit that each genre has its mock- or parodic-variety, which may be used for satirical purposes, but does not rise into formal satire. Thus may be treated a great mass of confusing material that would highly complicate any attempt to differentiate the Satire from other genres of poetry.

But that parody on the epic genre that is called the Mock-Epic is a genre in itself. Its dignity is far greater than that of any other parody, and it occasionally rises to the height of creative literature. It has existed side by side with the epic since the days of the imitators of Homer. The exalted character of the epic form in burlesque affords the best imaginable contrast between manner and matter; and hence the poetical burlesque is here at its best—either in the true Mock-Epic or in the narrative burlesque poem of the Italian school. These two varieties constitute what is loosely called the Mock-Epic, but more correctly the mock-heroic poem in general.

The mock-heroic poem is a parodic form and may well be treated under the present head. Its first variety, the true Mock-Epic, is in itself of varied character, yet is always a parody of the epic form, whether its original be the epic of

[17] Further illustrations are furnished by the *Art of Love* and *Art of Cookery,* of William King (1663–1712); and *Art of Preaching,* by Christopher Pitt (1699–1748).

[18] *Poetry of the Anti-Jacobin,* ed. Edmonds (1890).

Homer or of Ariosto. However, the truly classical Mock-Epic, such as *The Dunciad* of Pope, has been the chief English type. A second variety is that of the burlesque narrative poem of Italian origin—an admirable vehicle for satire. Of this type, Byron's *Don Juan* is perhaps the greatest English example. Butler's *Hudibras,* though vastly different from *Don Juan* in character and in origin, is also to be classed here. In these narrative burlesques, not epic in the strictest sense, the indirect method is frequently exchanged for the direct, the narrative framework is forgotten, and the satirist speaks *in propria persona.* Such is rarely the case in the true Mock-Epic.

All mock-heroic poems fall into two general classes: those written primarily to amuse, in which satire is merely incidental; and those which are primarily satirical, and claim the rank of professed Satires. The first class would include such poems as Boileau's *Le Lutrin* and Pope's *The Rape of the Lock.* The second, and far more comprehensive, class would include, in English literature alone, Pope's *Dunciad,* Cambridge's *Scribbleriad,* Dryden's *Mac Flecknoe,* and Byron's *Vision of Judgment.*

We are concerned, however, only with those mock-heroic poems that are professedly satirical. Of these, those that are mock-epic are parodies of the epic form; while the mere narrative burlesques are parodies of the heroic narrative poem or "metrical romance." Hence consistency requires that this satirical and mock-heroic poetry, in so far as it is actually *parody* and therefore complex in its formal nature, should be treated as the parodies of the minor poetical genres, and declared outside the pale of the *Satire.* But the Satire has adopted this mock-heroic form as its own in a sense in which it has accepted no other parodic form, and made it the principal vehicle for the indirect method. As has been said, the length and general dignity of the mock-heroic differentiate it from other and less pretentious parodies and render it a distinct genre. Finally, an excellent argument lies in the fact that to exclude the mock-heroic poem would be to refuse recognition to some of the greatest of our English Satires, such as *Mac Flecknoe, Hudibras,* and *Don Juan.*

This burlesque treatment is no new method. If we consider the classical Latin Satire alone, which has been taken as a model of the *direct* method, we find it but a step from Horace's Appian Bore[19] and Juvenal's Domitian and the Mighty Turbot,[20] to the more elaborate and conscious exaggeration of the pure burlesque. The germ, the possibility, lives even in the Latin Satire. But its origin is still more remote than this. To find how ancient the burlesque method is, and how the mock-heroic particularly has served as a vehicle for satire, we must go back to the Greeks, who utilized the burlesque centuries before Lucilius became the first great exponent of the direct method.

Among the Greeks the satirical spirit undoubtedly found its first literary expression in burlesque. The direct and personal Satires of Archilochus, Hipponax, and Simonides of Amorgos, came later. They were never the typical Greek form, if ever they rose into sufficient dignity of length and tone to be considered as Satires. Whatever may have been the exact form and content of the Homeric *Margites* (700 B. C. [?]), it was very probably a burlesque Satire—"the first Dunciad," Flögel calls it, with apparent propriety.[21] This same epic form was assumed later by the pseudo-Homeric Mock-Epic, the *Batrachomyomachia* (150 B. C. [?]), which ridicules the Epic by making frogs and mice engage in mighty combat in the true heroic manner.

Parodies and travesties seem to have been numerous. Hegemo Thasius, who lived during the Peloponnesian war, burlesqued the Sicilian expedition. Eubeus of Paros, a contemporary of Philip of Macedon, wrote four books of parodies on the Homeric war. All these are of course in epic style. The dramatic burlesque was represented in the plays of the earlier comic dramatists. Epicharmus the Sicilian (470 B. C.) described the nuptials of Hercules and Hebe in travesty; and

[19] Horace, *Ser.* I, IX.

[20] Juvenal, *Sat.* IV.

[21] See Flögel, *Geschichte der komischen Litteratur,* Vol. I, p. 345.

Cratinus (423 B. C.) travestied the intrigues of Zeus and Leda.[22] In *The Frogs* of Aristophanes we have both parody and travesty; the former in the literary satire on the work of Euripides; the latter in the burlesque representation of gods and heroes.

Later, during the Alexandrian decline, come the famous *Silli,* of which the two most distinguished writers were Xenophanes of Colophon and Timon of Phlius (c. 300 B. C.). From the few fragments of the *Silli* that have come down to us we judge them to have been parodic poems, in which the heroic verses of great poets were perverted to satirize current philosophical dogmas.[23]

From these typical illustrations it is evident that Greek satire mainly employed the method of burlesque, and particularly of *parody.* Aristophanes occasionally uses the formal parody, but he prefers that more subtle and effective parodic method that does not necessarily parody the literary form of an original, but burlesques the habits of thought and speech of the object to be satirized. It caricatures so effectually that the satire becomes immediately apparent, and the thought and action satirized become their own refutation. This form of parody is that characteristic of the stage in all ages, and renders the satiric comedy from Aristophanes, through Molière, to the present day, the most effective vehicle for satire.[24] When great imaginative genius speaks in satire it utilizes this dramatic method.[25] The formal Satire after the classical Latin type, which satirizes existing social conditions, seems never truly to flourish in a great creative age; for in such an age, satire speaks through the drama or by the general dramatic method. When Aristophanes spoke from the stage, no work was left to be done by the formal satirist of the classical Latin type. This formal Satire, however, may not necessarily be the product of a society thoroughly settled and apparently immutable. We notice that Juvenal, who feels himself writing

[22] See Babuder, pp. 6, 7.
[23] See Müller and Donaldson, *History of the Literature of Ancient Greece,* Vol. 2, pp. 462–3.
[24] Cf. *infra,* p. 220.
[25] In England, for example, the satirical comedies of Ben Jonson. Cf. *infra,* p. 220.

in an age of decay, makes his whole protest against the passing of the old, and what he affirms to be the better, order. But such a school of satire is certainly, at its best, the product of a non-dramatic period. Greek society could have furnished ample material for the Horatian Satire. For this, on the one hand, the age of Aristophanes was not too troublous, nor society too homogeneous on the other. But the imaginative genius of this period found its expression in the drama—from the tragedies of Æschylus to the satiric comedy of Aristophanes and, later, of Menander.

From the *Margites* to the *Silli,* we may infer the broad scope of Greek satire, with its literary, social, personal, and political elements. It was epic in the *Margites* and *Batrachomyomachia*; lyric in the personal invective Satires of the Archilochian school; dramatic in the plays of Aristophanes; didactic in the *Silli*;[26] but, excepting the lyrical satire, always in some form of burlesque, and chiefly that of *parody,* either of form or of subject-matter.

While the Old Comedy of the Greeks may have influenced Lucilius and have given a dramatic touch to the work of Horace, yet, in the main, Greek satire was without influence on the Romans. The burlesque and indirect method of the Greeks was quite distinct from the direct and individual satire of the Latin writers. Very little of this burlesque satire survived till the Renaissance, and the Latin type became the model for extensive imitation.

The burlesque method, however, is perennial. It was largely prevalent in the Middle Ages, when some of the Greek burlesque satire was paralleled—though without a trace of classical influence. At this period parody was frequent, and obeyed the law of its being in satirizing the prevailing genres. Parodies of the *Chansons des Gestes* were abundant.[27] One mock-heroic parody of the Romance of Chivalry satirized the Flemish burgers.[28] Another, one of the *Dit d'aventures,* of

[26] See Flögel, 2, 17 f.

[27] See Lenient, *La Satire en France au Moyen Age,* Ch. VII.

[28] Schneegans, p. 88.

the thirteenth century, is a grotesque Satire on the romance of adventure;[29] and Chaucer's own *Sir Thopas*[30] is of this type.

Here, too, must at least be mentioned the *Beast-Epic* of the Middle Ages—a form which, if not truly parodic in its nature, employs the indirect satirical method, and so connects itself with the satiric allegory and the mock-heroic. This, one of the most important and characteristic satirical forms of the Middle Ages, rises at its best into the vast *Roman de Renart,* in which, with its companion pieces, is concentrated the satirical genius of its age. In its allegorical form this beast-epic probably satirizes feudal society, and so is closely connected with the supposedly satiric beast-fables, such as those of Marie de France. Concerning the satirical import of the *Roman de Renart* and its analogues, various opinions are advanced—some critics even maintaining that the story has no double meaning at all. The weight of opinion, however, distinctly favors the affirmative.[31]

The *Roman de Renart* is not a mock-heroic in the ordinary sense, nor is it truly parodic, since it is quite innocent of any attempt to ridicule the epic genre. This fact, as well as its allegoric form, sharply differentiate it from the *Batrochomyomachia,* which, though a beast-epic, has no double meaning. The *Roman,* finally, with its series of disconnected adventures, lacks the heroic diction, and the high burlesque and machinery, of the true Mock-Epic. It is interesting to see both the classical and the medieval beast-epic combined in the *Froschmeuseler* of Rollenhagen, the German satirist (1595).

The medieval beast-epic is in itself a vast satirical genre. According to Lenient, the cycle of Reynard alone comprises over 118,000 lines—beginning with the Latin poems of the eleventh and twelfth centuries and culminating in the *Renart le Contrefait,* about the middle of the fourteenth century. But

[29] See Lenient, pp. 129–30; Schneegans, p. 93 f.

[30] See *infra,* p. 118.

[31] See Thoms, *The History of Reynard the Fox,* Percy Soc. Pub., Vol. 12; Wolff, *Reinke de Vos und Satirisch-didaktische Dichtung;* Lenient, p. 131 f.; de Julleville, *Histoire de la Lungue et de la Lit. française,* Tome II, 2, pp. 14–55.

there is no end to these beast-epics. Through Italy, Spain, and Germany the genre spread itself, being finally galvanized into activity by Goethe himself. There is here no place in which adequately to trace its history; for, while so vigorous on the Continent, it did not appear in England—excepting, of course, Caxton's prose translation—until the appearance of Spenser's *Mother Hubberd's Tale.*[31a] A full treatment of the beast-epic would be in place only in connection with Elizabethan satire.

Closely related to the beast-epic is another allegorical form, the *Beast-Fable,* in prose and in verse. The *fable* is not necessarily satirical; indeed it may be doubted whether the true fable is ever satirical. From its origin in the Hindoo *Pantcha Tantra,* through its peregrinations in the Arabic, Persian, Hebrew, to the Greek Æsop, the Latin Phaedrus, and a host of other ancient fabulists, it was moralistic and didactic. Under medieval influences it became satirical. The greatest of medieval verse-fabulists, Marie de France, was certainly a pungent satirist: the beast in her fables always concealed a man. And then follows the modern and almost innumerable group, with La Fontaine, the inimitable master, forever at their head—chiefly satirists pure and simple; though the German Lessing reverted to what he considered the pure and original Æsopic type of sheer didacticism. But the Fable is also in itself a distinct genre, and far too vast a subject for discussion here. A host of commentators, Lessing, Deslongchamps, Fischer, Taine, have treated it from various points of view. LaFontaine's influence on the verse-Fable of the Georgian era in England was incalculable and, should we consider that age and that genre, an elaborate discussion of the origin and history of the Fable would be necessary. Just here, however, such a treatment would be superfluous. Robert Henryson, the Scotchman, the only satirical verse-fabulist included in our era,[32] is satirical in but one or two of his famous

[31a] That early *fabliau, The Fox and the Wolf,* and the *Nun's Priest's Tale* of Chaucer, while based on the beast-epic, do not reach "epic" proportions.

[32] The work of Marie de France does not properly belong to the history of English satire; see Lenient, pp. 92–6.

beast-Fables; and these will be considered in their chronological order.[33]

The satiric Allegory might perhaps be termed a parodic, hence a burlesque, form; but in no true sense, for here the satirical intent never concerns the allegorical form itself. Moreover, the satiric Allegory is at best a rare species, and certainly could not assume the dignity of a genre. Nigellus Wireker's *Speculum Stultorum*[34] is certainly an Allegory, and satirical, yet of a kind altogether different from such an Allegory as Jean de Meung's *Roman de la Rose.* The *Vision of Piers Plowman*[35] cannot be called truly satirical, since in it satire is subordinate to didacticism. But Chaucer's *House of Fame*[36] is both an Allegory and a Satire,[36a] and so must stand as the supreme representative in English of the satiric Allegory in verse.

However, in not one of these cases is the allegoric form itself the object of ridicule; hence the product is in no sense parodic. The allegorical form is merely a vehicle, usually a heavy and cumbersome one, for satirical subject-matter.

Of the two methods employed by the Satire, we have seen that the first, the direct method, is best illustrated by the classical Latin Satire; the second by the different varieties of the Mock-Heroic. Obviously, these two methods are often combined. The burlesque appears even in the classical Satire; the direct address even in the Mock-Heroic, when the burlesque method is not well sustained. The abandonment of the indirect or burlesque form produces the effect of direct satire. In such a case, as at times in Butler's *Hudibras* and very often in Byron's *Don Juan,* there is no real characterization. The character is merely a mouth-piece for the direct satire of the author.

We have now described and illustrated the two methods

[33] See *infra,* p. 134.
[34] See *infra,* p. 43.
[35] See *infra,* p. 70.
[36] See *infra,* p. 114.
[36a] This still remains true, even though neither the allegory nor the satire be held to bear any personal application to Chaucer.

employed by the Satire, and have indicated the relation of this genre to those kindred and subordinate genres, the Epigram, the Beast-Epic, the Beast-Fable, and the satiric Allegory. It still remains to carry out the fourth and final part of the program outlined on page 6, namely, to distinguish the Satire from all other genres, and to describe its different varieties.

IV

With these methods classified, and the Satire distinguished from minor satirical poetry that partakes of the nature of other genres, it now becomes merely a question of the tone and spirit characterizing any production under discussion as to whether or not it shall rank as a member of the professed genre of the Satire. For this purpose we have attempted to describe the nature of that satirical spirit that must give its tone to every true Satire. The Satire in the direct method always tends toward didacticism on the one hand and invective on the other. Many such poems, bearing the name of Satire, are really either didactic verse or mere invective. Many other poems, with every characteristic of the genuine Satire, go under other names: such are, for instance, the *Epistles* of Pope. The mere name "Satire" is significant as usually indicating a conscious imitation of the classical Latin Satires; but apart from this it may mean nothing at all. Such being the case, we must ascertain the real nature of the Satire—its tone, subject-matter, form, and purpose—and, by this criterion, reclassify our material.

After the Satire has been set apart by itself, we see that it differs, in a very significant way, from all other genres of poetry. This difference does not lie merely in the fact that any genre possesses an individuality of its own, and that each, including the Satire, has a characteristic tone which distinguishes it from all other forms. This is true enough, and yet not the whole truth; for the Satire, in a very essential fashion, stands by itself, apart from all other genres of poetry. The distinction is fundamental:—the Satire is destructive: other genres are constructive; the Satire is realistic; the others are idealistic. All other genres of poetry have their enthusiasm and faith, their elevated diction, their more or less attractive subject-matter. The Satire, on the other hand, has a tone ironical and unenthusiastic, a diction characteristically prosaic, subject-matter often sordid, sometimes positively ugly and revolting. Hence it follows that the Satire stands apart from all other forms, and must depend largely upon its *style* to perpetuate material in itself more or less ephemeral and unattractive.

Employing methods and forms so various, with frequently so little of organic form and methodical structure, the Satire, unlike the Ode, the Elegy, the Lyric, etc., cannot possibly be classified as a distinct genre of an individual and characteristic form. Still, we can differentiate the professed Satire from these other genres, even from didactic poetry and the lesser parodic forms. This done, we yet find a great mass of interesting material that remains to be considered.

This material is roughly divisible into four more or less clearly defined groups. Each of these has individual characteristics, but often mingles with the other varieties.

Personal Satire, in which the primitive satirical spirit finds expression, and which gave birth to all other kinds, is common to every age and literature.[37] It is scarcely a variety in itself, for it easily passes into its kindred kinds. In such cases the personalities are used to point the moral and adorn the tale of social, political, or literary satire;[38] but the personal Satire, as a distinct variety, only too easily becomes invective, the product of hatred or of malice, unrelieved by humor. Such invective may still by force of genius be lifted into the domain of literature, as for instance, the vitriolic sonnets that the Florentine poet Berni hurled at the head of his crafty enemy, Pietro Aretino, the Venetian. But these are not true *satire*. The interest afforded by invectives is largely antiquarian, and must depend on the personality of the contestants. To this class belong the Greek lyric Satires, since their poisoned darts

[37] For primitive satire among the Lapps and the Greenlanders, see Flögel, I, 319–20.

[38] Such is usually the case in England before the Renaissance; *e. g.*, the *sirventes* against King John, *infra*, p. 48; the satire against Suffolk, *infra*, p. 126 f.; against Wolsey, *infra*, p. 149 f.

were winged solely with malice, and their purely personal attacks voiced no general need or desire. Where humor is entirely lacking, where malice breathes in every line, there is no *satire*. The usual result of rage is not satire, but abuse.

Something universal must first find expression through this personal element, before such a "Satire" can attain a high place in literature. Berni's magnificent sonnet is literature, because the personality of Aretino is merged in the poet's scorn for the eternal type of the hypocrite.[39] Ulrich von Hutten wrote a prose Satire called *Phalarismus* against the infamous Duke Ulrich of Würtemberg. It is edged with violent personal rancor; but in the Duke, Hutten, with infinite humor, satirizes the eternal type of the tyrant. Thus the dialogue rises into great literature and, more narrowly, into the true Satire. Dryden's *Mac Flecknoe* is also an excellent example. It is personal in its target, yet Shadwell represents the eternal poetaster. Here the satirist's personal feeling toward the object of his attack is lost in the qualities that mark the highest type of satire—the presence of the ludicrous and the possibility of a broad application. The *Dunciad* is great despite many bitter and foolish personalities, for at its best it corresponds to *Mac Flecknoe*. It has humor as well as wit; and where there is true personal satire, there must be laughter. This laughter may be scornful and contemptuous enough, as in the Satires of Swift, but the satirist's attitude must be one of *amused* superiority. Personal malice there may be, but it must not dominate the tone. The satirist may hold his enemy up to public ridicule, may caricature him, but he must do this with a sufficient sense of the ludicrous.

The political Satire is essentially a product of free political conditions, and may exist apart from any other variety. Scarcely existent in the literature of Rome, hardly more so in that of Italy and of Spain, only to a limited extent in that of France, the political Satire is characteristically English.[40] It is obvious that in periods of revolution, of change and stress,

[39] So with Skelton's satire against Wolsey, who typifies the tyrant and royal favorite; see *infra*, p. 152 f.

[40] It begins early, and never dies; see *infra*, *passim*, and especially ch. IV.

the political Satire will flourish.[41] An extensive satirical literature has accompanied every great political revolution of modern times.[42] Such satire has been a growth as the people have gained in ability to govern and to express themselves. Lampoons, squibs, political ballads, furnish the more popular and degenerate dress of the spirit that occasionally attains such expression in literature as Dryden's *Absalom and Achitophel.*

Political satire is essentially ephemeral. Its illustrations are drawn from transient conditions; its localisms in time become obscure and lose their pristine flavor. This evaporating process may at last leave the political Satire a lifeless thing, of interest only to the special student. But however ephemeral, it is in its day by far the most effective variety of its genre. The political satirist appeals to the heart of the people and can be at once both popular writer and literary artist.

The personalities characterizing this variety show its love for the argument *ad hominem.* It points its moral by means of some familiar name, and like the personal Satire is apt to utilize invective.[43] Though its prosaic material offer little for the fancy to play upon, it may still become great literature, as in the masterpiece of Dryden.

The most characteristic and formal, yet perhaps the least effective variety, is the Moral and Social Satire. It rises into greatness in the work of a Horace or of a Pope, yet the horde of satirical poetasters who exercise themselves on this social material, are terribly fond of inane generalization, didacticism, and dullness.[44] These small aspirants have wandered off into mere generalities and attacked in vague meaningless terms the follies and crimes common to every age.[45] Certainly this is one way of gaining "universality." Such satirists attain

[41] Did it originate with Æsop's fable of King Stork and King Log, which he told to those Athenians who resented the tyranny of Peisistratos?

[42] The great satirists of the Reformation, such as Murner, Luther, Hutten, Fischart, Lyndsay, and Buchanan, were necessarily political to a certain extent, where the question of the Pope's temporal sovereignty and political influence was concerned.

[43] *E. g.,* the politico-personal Satires of Skelton, see *infra,* p. 149 f.

[44] Only too prevalent in medieval England; see *infra, passim.*

[45] Such generalized subject-matter forms what has aptly been termed "satirical commonplace."

the universal well enough, but through lack of imagination, fail to re-embody it in the concrete material afforded by the characteristic life of their own times.

The classical Latin Satire, though not lacking in personalities and in literary elements, is still of this general type.[46] It has served as a model for all subsequent satire of its kind, and we find everywhere the Social Satire betraying the greatest classical influence, the most rigorous form. When genuine and indigenous, it is always the product of a highly organized and complex society, in a time of peace. Such a society has both desire and leisure to study itself. This highly sophisticated and self-conscious variety of the Satire is both the result and the mirror of these conditions.

But the Satire on literary subjects is perhaps an even more sophisticated variety.[47] Existing side by side with the Moral and Social Satire, it is often absorbed into these more comprehensive types. Really beginning with Aristophanes, it is continued by Horace. Juvenal, too, amuses himself with literary pretenders; and since his time, the Satire on literary themes has furnished a play-ground for every writer of the formal Satire. It has proved a handy and effective weapon in literary quarrels, and under these conditions has usually flourished; as witness *Mac Flecknoe, The Dunciad, English Bards and Scotch Reviewers,* to mention only a few representative poems of a type whose exemplars are legion.

A pleasant sub-variety of this purely literary Satire is that of what might be termed the "Parnassian" poems. This fashion was set in Italy by Cesare Caporali, with his *Viaggio in Parnaso,* and *Vita de Meccenate*; and continued by Boccalini in his *Ragguagli di Parnaso.* In Spain, Cervantes followed with his elaborate *Viaje al Parnaso* (1615); while in England the tradition has been preserved successively by Suckling, Wither, Lady Winchelsea, Sheffield, Swift, and Leigh Hunt.[48] The series is continued in America with Lowell's *Fable for Critics.*

[46] See *supra,* p. 15.

[47] This variety is very rare in England before the Renaissance.

[48] Goldsmith's *Retaliation,* though its subject-matter is somewhat more inclusive, really belongs to this class.

We have now, however inadequately, finished the four divisions of the analytical program outlined on page 6: first, to ascertain the nature and the working of the satirical spirit; second, to distinguish between satire in prose and satire in verse; third, to describe the two methods of the Satire and to indicate the relations of the Satire to certain minor genres; and, finally, to differentiate the Satire from all other genres of poetry and to set forth its different varieties. It still remains to be seen how the product in England before the Renaissance bears out and illustrates the foregoing analysis.

CHAPTER II

From Walter Map to Langland

Absence of satire in Anglo-Saxon poetry.—Possible reasons for same.—Revival of literature under Henry II.—Three schools of satirical verse: Goliardic; Anglo-Norman; Anglo-Latin.—The *sirvente.*—The Goliards.—Walter Mapes.—Themes and methods of Goliardic satire.—Anglo-Latin satire.—*Apocalypsis Goliae.*—*The Confession of Golias.*—Other Goliardic Satires.—General character of these productions.—The *Speculum Stultorum.*—Alexander Neckham's *De Vita Monachorum.*—John of Salisbury's *Polycraticus;* his *Entheticus.*—Goliardic satire in the reign of King John.—Anglo-Norman *sirventes* against John.—Satires in the reign of William II.—The Barons' War.—*Richard of Cornwall.*—*A lutel Soth sermun.*—The Visions of Heaven and Hell.—*The XI Pains of Hell.*—Satire under Edward I.—Social satire.—*The Owl and the Nightingale.*—Attacks on the clergy.—The friars.—*The Order of Fair Ease.*—*The Land of Cokaygne.*—Political satire.—Robert Manning's *Handlyng Synne.*—Richard Rolle's *The Pricke of Conscience.*—Satire under Edward II.—Its subject-matter.—*A Poem on the Times of Edward II.*—Rise of class-satire.—Causes of same.—Satires on Piers Gaveston.—Satire under Edward III.—Satire against France.—*Prophecy of John of Bridlington.*—*The Vision of Piers the Plowman.*—Its subject-matter.—Its relation to the *Roman de la Rose.*—Its allegorical form.—Its various methods.—Its satire against abstractions; against classes.—Its didactic element.—Its humor and realism.—Langland's advance beyond his predecessors.

I

Neither in Anglo-Saxon poetry nor in the Latin writings of the Anglo-Saxon period can we find a trace of satire. Pictures of the Last Judgment, debates between the Body and the Soul, sombre invective in the Blickling homilies and in the homilies of Wulfstan, form the nearest approach to the satirical that this first period of English literature has to offer us. We need not seek far for the reasons. One lies, perhaps, in the serious temper of a race lacking in humor and in lightness of touch; a race, too, bound by heroic traditions, serious and high in purpose; a homogeneous race, finally, and a society in which objects for satire either political, literary, or social were largely wanting. Even the ecclesiastical body, for centuries afterwards a prime object of attack, while by no means immaculate at this period, had still not sunk into the corruption that subsequently rendered it the target for universal reproach; and social and political conditions in general were certainly not such as to foster satire of any description.

After that century of civil war following the Conquest, a century during which not merely literature but society itself was in a deplorable condition, there came an intellectual revival. The Gallic spirit was already operating beneficently on the sombre and exhausted Saxon genius. Comparative leisure and peace had succeeded the unspeakable ravages of Stephen's reign, and even John's political follies could not prevent a renascence of literary life in the monasteries and some attention to contemporary affairs on the part of monastic writers. At this period, the close of the twelfth century, after the establishment of the universities with their greater attention to literature, and after the fusion of Saxon and Norman elements in the nation under the rule of Henry the Second, we discern the first trace of the spirit which was destined, almost five centuries later, to find its consummate expression in the masterpieces of Dryden and of Pope.

The first impulse came from abroad. The racial effect of the Conquest give birth to English satire: it made a heterogeneous people; it finally directed English students to the University of Paris. From this foreign influence sprang the poetry of the Goliards and of the Anglo-Latin satirists and epigrammatists.

Throughout the first two centuries of its history, English satirical poetry divides itself into three principal schools. During the twelfth century we find the Goliardic Latin rhymes, the Anglo-French *sirventes*,[1] the more formal satire of the Anglo-Latin writers. In the thirteenth century, the Goliardic poetry used not only Latin, but Anglo-French and English as its vehicle; the *sirvente* of the trouvère and troubadour passed into the satirical song of the English gleeman; the Anglo-Latin passed into the nondescript ecclesiastical satire in Latin, in Anglo-French, and in English. So we have to deal not only with three classes but with three languages.

[1] Not strictly Anglo-Norman, but referring to any *sirventes* written either by trouvères or by troubadours which refer to England or to English affairs.

The *sirvente*[2]—sometimes called the *sotte chanson*—originated toward the end of the eleventh century, perhaps in Picardy, but soon became the common property of both trouvères and troubadours. It was at first a mere personal challenge, often outrageous in its tone; afterwards it became more general. But it was always daring, witty, satirical, varied in its subject-matter, and abounding in personalities. Bertrand de Born, one of the greatest of the troubadours, was its chief exponent; but it had already found its way into England shortly after the Conquest. It was essentially lyrical: Béranger's *Songs* were its lineal descendants. Transplanted into England, the *sirvente* has come down to us in a few isolated examples in Anglo-French; but it soon left its Anglo-French and its personalities for English and nationality; and, in the reign of Edward I, became the song of the English gleemen. It was specific and definite in its subject-matter, hurled itself at kings like John and Henry III, then at the Scotch; finally turned against its own ancestral people and ridiculed the French themselves. The comparatively few satirical songs that have survived merely hint at the vast number of these light and winged satirical occasional poems that must have perished while scarcely off the gleeman's tongue.[4]

Far more abundant than the *sirventes* is the Goliardic product of this period. The term "Goliardic" is usually restricted to Latin rhyming verse, but at least one authority would include poems in both Anglo-French and English.[5] Who were the "Goliards"? A literary question more difficult could scarcely be raised. In the great age of the University of Paris, clerks, students, scholars, thronged to France. They were far-travelled and sharp sighted; satire was their natural weapon. Some one (was it Walter Map, the Englishman?) began the rhyming Latin satirical verse, to be known as "Goliardic." Critics disagree as to the origin of the name.

[2] *Sirvente* comes from Latin *serviens,* by allusion to the *suivant d'armes* charged with the cartel in the name of his master.

[3] See Lenient, pp. 21–22.

[4] The lyric satire of the *sirvente* was paralleled by the political and personal satire in the songs of the minnesingers (c. 1200).

[5] See Haessner, *Die Goliardendichtung, passim.*

Who impersonated Bishop Golias, type of the immoral prelate that satirized monachism, women, and public morals, and praised wine and song, with such gusto and facility? Was Bishop Golias one man or a thousand? Did the name derive from *gula,* the gullet, or from Goliath of Gath? When did this peculiar and influential form of verse originate, and where?

France was probably the birthplace, and the early twelfth century perhaps the time.[6] The genre was already decaying when it passed into England, carried by the young students from Paris. It is impossible to say how many Goliardic songs originated in France. Goliardic poetry is usually lacking in any personal or local allusions that may stamp its origin. Of the poems included by Wright in his *Latin Poems Commonly Attributed to Walter Mapes,* some were probably of French authorship. But the name of "Walter Mapes" has been attached to Goliardic poetry by the tradition of many centuries. The variety of his literary activity, his fame as a wit, his known hatred of the Cistercians, may have foisted upon him the parentage of the whole Goliardic genre. At best, he was the author of but few of the poems ascribed to him—perhaps of none. The two elaborate Goliardic Satires to which his name is inseparably attached will here be treated as his, however; for neither exact time, locality, nor authorship, is of great import when considering Goliardic poetry.[7]

This Goliardic satire persists in England through the later twelfth century, through the entire thirteenth, and even down to the reign of Edward III. At first written exclusively in rhyming Latin verse, it passes into Anglo-French; finally, with an effort on the part of its authors to popularize it, even into English. Its most characteristic themes are the decadence of the age, the immorality of the ecclesiastical orders, and woman; and these themes, at first international, develop in

[6] *Die Goliardendichtung, passim.* But cf. Chambers, *The Mediaeval Stage,* Vol. I, p. 61, who gives the order issued by Gautier of Sens in his *Constitutiones* (913 A. D.): "Statuimus quod clerici ribaldi, maxime qui dicuntur de familia Goliæ . . . etc." This would set back the date two hundred years!

[7] See Haessner, pp. 150–1.

England distinctly national traits, and even become political. The Goliards, liberal in politics, can occasionally speak with the freedom, vigor, and bitterness of the trouvères. Their method is both direct and dramatic; their tone infinitely varied. Independent of tradition, without classical influences, the Goliardic poetry was entirely the product of its time.

Clearly distinct from this Goliardic satire, but also indirectly emanating from the University of Paris, is the Anglo-Latin satire of the twelfth century. This passed, as did the trouvère and the Goliardic, through Anglo-French into English. Beginning about 1200 A. D. with the prose works of Walter Map and others, for example the *De Nugis Curialium*, it sprang from reformatory tendencies in the Church itself. The elaborate compositions of Nigellus Wireker, John of Salisbury, and Alexander Neckham, are succeeded in the following century by a mass of nondescript satire in English, sometimes by monks, perhaps by parish priests. The subject-matter is frequently ecclesiastical or social, the tone severe, the style free from allusions of any kind. But it may run to the opposite extreme—if we include *The Land of Cockaygne* and *The Order of Fair Ease*. Indeed, in every respect its range is so extensive, its product so often almost nondescript, that its ecclesiastical authorship and academic style alone serve to distinguish it from the satirical product of Goliards and of gleemen.

II

That order of Benedictine monks, which, under Augustine, converted England from paganism, had long since declined from its pristine spirituality into the numberless corruptions that make the staple theme of medieval satire. In an attempt to reform the Benedictines, about 1132 A. D., several new orders were introduced into England. Among these orders were the Cistercians, who were soon to become, through their extensive wool industry, the wealthiest body in the realm. But not half a century passed before the reformatory impulse of the new orders was exhausted, and they themselves had sunk into the same low spiritual condition as those very Benedictines whom they had come to reform.

These depraved ecclesiastical conditions formed a favorite Goliardic theme. Among these Goliardic compositions are two, as has been said, that were perhaps the actual work of Walter Map.[8] The first of these two poems is the *Apocalypsis Goliæ,*[9] an elaborate composition of over four hundred lines in rhyming quatrains.

Through a miraculous revelation, which is in form a parody[10] of the Revelation of St. John, the sins of the clergy, from pope to parish priest, are revealed to the poet. The entire hierarchy is summoned before the Throne of Judgment. Pope, Bishop, Archdeacon, Dean, Abbot, and Monk, are infected with vice—false shepherds, blind leaders of Christ's flock! The poet's epithets are of unsparing severity, and his rebuke is as direct and overwhelming as any that could well be delivered. A more severe indictment against the whole ecclesiastical hierarchy does not exist in the satire of England. The attack, if made by Walter Map, emanates from one of their own order, a critic who knew both Church and world; not a cloistered monk, but a man of action. The satirist perhaps feels too keenly the degradation of the priesthood to indulge in any humor. His tone is throughout bitterly severe, so much so as to become invective rather than satire; for though the verse at times gives a ludicrous effect, there is no intentional burlesque, and the frequent word-plays are not to raise a laugh, but to carry a point.

The Confession of Golias, though in subject-matter largely identical with the *Apocalypse,* is yet in form and tone widely dissimilar. The *Confession* is burlesque in form,[11] and at first richly humorous in tone, but finally didactic.[12] Bishop Golias, type of the immoral prelate, confesses his various enormities to the Bishop of Coventry. In the course of this "heart to

[8] Only *perhaps;* there is reason to believe *The Confession,* at least, of Italian origin. See Symonds, *Wine, Women and Song,* p. 60.

[9] *The Latin Poems Commonly Attributed to Walter Mapes,* ed. Wright, Camden Soc. Pub., Vol. 16, pp. 1–20.

[10] See *supra,* p. 25.

[11] See *supra,* p. 18 f.

[12] The *Latin Poems,* etc., p. 71 f.

heart talk," he admits that he loves the tavern and the wine-cup:

> " Meum est propositum in taberna mori,
> Vinum sit appositum morientis ori;
> Ut dicant cum venerint angelorum chori,
> Deus sit propitius huic potatori "—

but he professes himself sincerely repentant and promises to reform. Certain parts of this burlesque confession have been adopted as a drinking song of universal celebrity, and have led to the wholly unwarranted supposition that the author of the poem was himself a toper.

Among these supposedly English Goliardic poems are many of a very general character, such as lugubrious wails over the depravity of the age, the state of the church, and the approaching destruction of the universe. Of this kind are the *De Mundi Miseria,*[13] and the *Prophecy of Golias,*[14] which is a general call to repentance; while the medieval attitude toward woman finds expression in a violent attack on the sex entitled *Golias de Conjuge non Ducenda.*[15] This unmitigated libel rehearses, in a fashion both gross and dull, those perennial charges that have been the property of the ages since the time of Simonides. This particular poem, however, seems to have had a certain popularity; and it exercised some subsequent influence, as is witnessed by an English paraphrase of the fifteenth century.[16]

But Goliardic humor, though lacking in these more serious attempts, is at times exuberant. In several poems on the universal sovereignty of money, a humorous perception of social incongruities finds expression in very effective, albeit rather bitter, irony. Such is the *De Cruce Denarii,*[17] in which is celebrated the omnipotence of the penny and the magical transformations effected by that modern worker of miracles. Nothing more effective than the Penny, cries the poet, in the

[13] *Ibid.,* p. 149 f.
[14] *Ibid.,* p. 52 f.
[15] *Latin Poems Commonly Attributed to Walter Mapes,* p. 77 f.
[16] *Ibid.,* p. 295 f.
[17] *Ibid.,* p. 223 f.

palace or the consistory courts! And this, too, is the complaint of the author of *De Nummo*,[18] which is of the same type, and was afterwards imitated in French, Latin, English, and Scotch; becoming, with others of its class, the founder of a great family of such poems throughout medieval Western Europe.

It could not have been at a much later date that some "Goliard" expressed himself vigorously on the subject of a French education and French vices.[19] "Those barons who send their sons to be educated in France," declares the satirist, "are responsible for the introduction of foreign vices into England." Another, against "The Social Parasites" (the "ribalds"),[20] addresses itself most seriously to Bishops and Abbots, warning them to be liberal, but not to squander their wealth on these parasites who thrive upon the life-blood of society. Illustrated by Biblical examples, but largely unquotable, the poem hints at unspeakable conditions of society—as do others of its kind. Still another, *A General Satire on all Classes of Society*,[21] concerns itself with subject-matter less objectionable, and hits chiefly at the condition of the Church. Its frequent intermixture of Norman words would seem to indicate an attempt to popularize the Goliardic satire.

Still more humorous, though unfortunately highly indecorous, are the two burlesque poems that purport to be accounts of sacerdotal convocations in which the monks have assembled to discuss the decree of Pope Innocent III (1215), condemning the wives or concubines of the clergy.[22] These are fairly good examples of an undoubtedly humorous, though rather crude, form of burlesque.[23]

These various Goliardic poems, with a multitude of others of like form and tenor, all written at about the same period (1175–1250?), are characteristically devoid of personal and

[18] *Ibid.*, p. 226.
[19] *Anecdota Literaria*, ed. Wright, pp. 38–9.
[20] *Ibid.*, pp. 40–2.
[21] *Anecdota Literaria*, pp. 43–4.
[22] *Latin Poems Commonly Attributed to Walter Mapes*, pp. 171, 180.
[23] See *supra*, p. 18 f.

local allusions that might enable us to fix their time and place with any degree of certainty. Though without individuality, they probably represent the attitude of a large body of thoughtful people of their period. This fact renders them in some degree a genuinely popular expression, evoked by existing conditions, whether in England or on the Continent.

Far more academic than the Goliardic satire in both form and treatment is the *Speculum Stultorum* of Nigellus Wireker (fl. 1190), precentor in the Benedictine Monastery at Canterbury, and friend and protégé of that able but mischievous prelate, William de Longchamps, Bishop of Ely. In this instance the criticism comes entirely from within the fold, and shows the monastic bodies as they seemed to one of their own more faithful and spiritual brethren. The poem is also the product of that purer Latin style and love for classical imitation, which, introduced into England by the Normans, resulted in an interesting school of satirists and epigrammatists during the eleventh and twelfth centuries.

In the prologue, addressed to his friend William, Nigellus states his purpose in writing and his conception of the nature of satire. His motive for writing is that professed by the satirist in every age; but his idea concerning the form and treatment of the Satire is strangely Horatian. "There are to-day in the world," he says, "many hypocrites; there is no art or order in which there is not some deceit. Professors of the arts simulate knowledge; the religious orders simulate virtue." Recognizing these unfortunate conditions, he proposes to reform by jocosity what cannot be effected by rough rebuke; "for many are the diseases which yield more readily to unguents than to caustic."[24] True enough for a general theory of satire; but the good monk was wrong in thinking that his unguents could effect what only the caustic method of wholesale disestablishment accomplished some three centuries later.

[24] *The Anglo-Latin Satirical Poets and Epigrammatists of the Twelfth Century,* ed. Wright, Vol. I, pp. 3–145.

In this same prologue the monastic satirist gravely explains the allegorical features of his work, as if apologizing for its delightful humor by emphasizing its reformatory and didactic purpose. Fortunately his explanations of the ass, the tail, the prescription in its fragile glass bottles, are confined to the prologue, and do not affect the humor or the conduct of the story, which would be sufficiently effective in itself without the allegory.

Burnellus, the ass, represents the whole monastic body, greedy for gain, eager for change. Burnellus ardently desires a longer tail. He consults the physician Galen, who, after expostulating with him upon the folly of his desire, gives him an absurd prescription that is to be filled at Salerno and brought back in glass bottles—typifying thereby, as we have learned from the prologue, the monk who runs after vanities both costly and frail. On his journey toward Salerno, Burnellus is cheated by a London merchant, and on his return trip meets with a variety of mishaps that arise mainly from the malice of monks of other orders. (Burnellus is a Benedictine.) A Cistercian brother, near Lyons, sets upon him four mastiffs who bite off half of his tail and break his medicine bottles; but the final issue is disastrous for the Cistercian, since the ass incontinently and gleefully drowns him in the Rhone, singing upon his demise a Canticle of victory:

> "Cantemus, socii! festum celebremus, aselli!
> Vocibus et votis organa nostra sonent."

Burnellus, unwilling to return home with his mangled tail, proceeds to the University of Paris. He is ready to study and does not fear the rod. But, after spending seven years in close application, he cannot even remember the name of the city where he has been toiling; so he leaves in disgust and resolves to enter a monastic order. After this resolution is formed, he reviews without satisfaction the various religious bodies, with rather severe criticism of each. The vices both of monks and nuns are dwelt upon—Cistercians, White Friars, Templars, Carthusians, Regular Canons, and others. The ass is disgusted with all, and determines to form a new order for himself which shall unite the best characteristics of the others. He meets Galen, describes his plan, and invites his coöperation. But at this juncture Bernardus, his old master, appears on the scene, claims his property, and leads Burnellus away to his original condition of servitude.

In this form we find a singular union of burlesque and allegory, ordinarily two most incompatible elements. On the face of it, the story is merely a burlesque on monachism and on university life at Paris. The general idea of the ass as a representative of the monastic body; and, in particular, Galen's absurd prescription for lengthening Burnellus' tail, and Burnellus' song of triumph over the drowned Cistercian brother, are all examples of burlesque. But best of all is the plan for the order of monks, which the ass proposes to establish, to be known as the "novus ordo Burnelli."

"I shall found a new order,"[25] he says, "that shall perpetuate my name. My order shall take the best from all the others. From the Templars we can learn to use softly-stepping horses, that my monks may be pleasantly seated; but the right to lie at all seasons, also peculiar to the Templars, I shall deny to every one but myself. The monks of Cluny will teach me how to enjoy rich feasts on the six holidays of the week—the other brethren can live on my scraps. I commend the Gradimontanes for their excessive loquacity, and shall imitate them; and the Carthusian brethren ought to be followed in certain of their customs. Let us also imitate the Black Canons in their habit of eating flesh, lest we be termed hypocritical; and the Præmonstratenes will teach us how to wear soft clothing. From other orders we learn how desirable is a female companion; for this, the first order was instituted in Paradise, and should be perpetually maintained." And so on. But apart from these burlesque features are the allegorical elements as Wireker expounds them in his prologue. In all this allegory, however, are no personified ab-

[25] "The Order of the Ass" later became common satirical property on the Continent.

stractions such as became popularized through the *Roman de la Rose* less than a century later. The two have absolutely nothing in common, though, as we shall see later, the *Roman de la Rose* was not without its influence on English satire.

The *Speculum Stultorum,* with its attack on ecclesiastical corruption, and its incidental satire on university life, seems to be the work of a man who knew his material at first hand. Though obviously an academic product, Wireker's Satire has the vitality and significance of a work evoked by contemporary needs, and having an earnest purpose. It is written in fairly good Latin elegiac verse and is, as has been said, a product of the purer Latin style introduced into England by the Normans. That it is deficient in the higher qualities of poetry goes almost without saying; yet its rich humor of theme and expression may well atone for its lack of poetical merit. The " Novus Ordo Burnelli " soon became common satirical property and exercised a perceptible effect on subsequent satire. It forms, in fact, the first member of a long series of " fool Satires," which were to appear again centuries later in the work of Barclay and the less elaborate efforts of Lydgate, Skelton, and others.

But Nigellus Wireker, though by far the greatest, was not the only Anglo-Latin satirist. His contemporary, Alexander Neckham (1157–1217), Abbot of Cirencester, besides his elaborate scientific treatises in prose and in verse, and other works, wrote in elegiac verse his *De Vita Monachorum.*[26] Admonitory, serious in intent, in no true sense satirical, this elaborate didactic poem exhorts the monks to lead pure lives, upbraids the rich and powerful, bitterly bewails the decadence of manners, reproaches the female sex. This last note connects itself with the Papal edict on celibacy, which evoked such widespread controversy.[27] Neckham emphasizes the danger of marriage and the necessity of celibacy. Sincere enough, doubtless, and greatly needed, certainly, *De Vita Monachorum* is still dry, didactic, and dull.

An early contemporary of both Wireker and Neckham, John

[26] *Satirical Poets and Epigrammatists,* 2, 175–200.
[27] Haessner, *passim.*

of Salisbury, Bishop of Chartres (1120–1167), in addition to his famous *Polycraticus* and his letters, wrote "a satirical poem in six books, supporting scholastic philosophy against the courtiers."[28] This work is entitled *Entheticus de dogmate Philosophorum.* Knowing the scarcity of real satire among Anglo-Latin productions of this period, and how prone the good clerks were to sheer didacticism without a saving grain of humor, we may well doubt the satirical tone of the *Entheticus.*

But the *Speculum Stultorum* and *De Vita Monachorum* by no means exhaust the religious satire of this reign. Other, and very minor, productions, couched mainly in Goliardic Latin verse, appeared but a few years later, in the early thirteenth century, when King John and Pope Innocent III disagreed over the appointment of an Archbishop of Canterbury. In 1207 the king sent large sums of money to Rome to bribe the advisers of the Pope, but failed to prevent the appointment of that Stephen Langton who was soon to embarrass John so seriously at Runnymede and elsewhere. The papal interdict had followed upon the King's refusal to receive Langton as archbishop, and this uncomfortable state of affairs continued for five years. Within this period we find some clerk, aroused by the miserable condition of the country, inveighing bitterly against papal aggression. He writes in Goliardic Latin rhyme, and his text is the avarice and venality of the Roman court.[29] "Rome is a market where all is offered for sale," he cries. "The highest bidder wins, and the poor man, pleading without the eloquence of money, though he have on his side Justinian and all the canons of the saints, cannot prevail." In one stanza the poet indulges in those characteristic Goliardic puns that appear in the poems attributed to Walter Map, and that are constantly employed in religious satire until they show themselves finally in Gower's moral diatribes two centuries later:[30]

[28] Morley, *English Writers,* III, p. 181.

[29] *Political Songs of England from John to Edward II,* ed. Wright, p. 14 f.

[30] The translations given here are in some cases revisions and condensations of those furnished by Wright; but for the accuracy of these and all other translations in the present volume the author alone is responsible.

> "Solam avaritiam Roma novit parca;
> Parcit danti munera, parco non est parca;
> Nummus est pro numine, et pro Marco marca,
> Et est minus celebris ara, quam sit arca."[31]

Growing more directly out of the papal controversy, and far more specific and personal in its character, is a virulent attack in rhyming Latin verse in seven-line stanzas, on the bishops of Bath, of Norwich, and of Winchester, who sided with the king.[32] This constitutes our first extant Political Satire.[33] The invective is preceded by some general remarks before the writer reaches his true theme, and is followed by a eulogy of Rochester and Ely, who favored the Pope.

But the beginning of political satire in the reign of King John is not confined to this Latin product. It is also exemplified in more popular Anglo-French songs[34] against the king's foreign policy. At Richard's death, Normandy, long restive under foreign rule, was lost to England, but there still remained among the Normans a faction devoted to the English cause as against Philip of France, the new ruler. Soon after the Siege of Thouars, in 1206, some Norman trouvère reproaches the English king for leaving the Bordelois, laments the separation from England, and beseeches Savary of Mauleon not to fail the cause.[35] But far more pointed and bitter is another *sirvente,* a personal attack on the king, written probably in 1214, after the loss of Poitou and Touraine, by the younger Bertrand de Born, and also addressed to Savary de Mauleon.[36] The poem is short, but vitriolic. "King John," says the troubadour, "has lost his dominions over sea, but he does not care. He cares but for hunting hawks, greyhounds, and ease!"—

[31] "Penurious Rome knows only avarice. She spares the gift-giver, but is not sparing to the penurious man. She prefers money to God and a mark to St. Mark. Her altar is less celebrated than her money-chest."

[32] *Political Songs,* p. 6 f.

[33] See *supra,* p. 31 f.

[34] For other examples of this lyric satire, see *infra, passim,* and especially p. 124 f.

[35] *Ibid.,* p. 1.

[36] *Political Songs,* p. 3.

"Mais ama l'bordir e l'cassar,
E bracs e lebriers et austors,
E sojorn."

The reproach was not entirely just, for John did not surrender his French possessions without a struggle. This, however, though relating to England's king, is really a foreign product; as are the two *sirventes* against Henry III, written by Bernard de Rovenac.[37] They would neither have been written nor have been sung in the England of this period. Still these, together with the Latin poem on the bishops, are the only verses that remain to echo the momentous events of John's disastrous reign. The loss of a foreign empire, the domestic struggles against Church and baronage, wars with Irish, Welsh, and Scotch, Stephen Langton and Magna Charta—these great events, despite the lack of a common medium of speech, may well have been the themes of singers in songs that have utterly passed away. Domestic turmoil may prevent the rise of a high order of literature, but it cannot hush political satire, which has flourished in every such troubled period of English history.

Nor have we much more surviving from the stormy half century of Henry III's rule. Intolerable papal extortion, royal oppression, unsuccessful invasions of French territory, and, most significant of all, the prolonged struggle between king and baronage, have scarcely survived in polemic verse. King John's servile submission to the Pope, and the resultant papal taxation, resented so bitterly by the English people, were followed in the reign of John's immediate successor by the culmination of papal tyranny in England—a tyranny that finally grew so intolerable as to lead in the latter part of Henry's reign to utter and successful revolt. With the authority of the Pope, the king compelled the clergy to contribute one-tenth of their goods to enable him to carry on his unfortunate foreign wars. It was probably at the period of the Sicilian expedition, in aid of the Pope (1257), that some eccle-

[37] *Ibid.*, pp. 36, 39.

siastic uttered in Anglo-French his bitter protest against this intolerable tax.[38] The attack on the king is more direct and unsparing than we usually find in these expressions of resentment against the royal policy. "King and Pope plan how they make take from the clergy their gold and silver"—

> "Li roi ne l'apostoile ne pensent altrement,
> Mès coment au clers tolent lur or e lur argent."

The use of Anglo-French in this protest might seem to indicate something of an appeal to the secular governing classes. But we find a somewhat similar complaint, in Goliardic Latin rhyme, directed against the avarice of the prelates.[39] And another goes still farther, including the king and his nobles in the indictment.[40] "No one is truly esteemed in this degenerate age unless he has sufficient cunning to deceive the simple. The rich are avaricious, and the poor are oppressed."

But these vague and general academic complaints do not exhaust either in spirit or in subject-matter the satire of Henry's reign. The king's imbecile tyranny, his foreign favorites, and his intolerable taxation, led to the baronial league under the great Earl Simon, which achieved its victory of Lewes in 1264. That long historical and eulogistic Latin poem known as *The Battle of Lewes*[41] is supplemented by what for us is a far more significant production. This is a politico-personal ballad in *English*,[42] directed chiefly against the king's brother, Richard, Earl of Cornwall, King of the Romans, who was the object of much popular hatred. After the battle of Lewes, he fled to a windmill, which he garrisoned and tried to hold against the baronial army. This incident

[38] *Political Songs*, p. 42.

[39] *Ibid.*, p. 44.

[40] *Ibid.*, p. 46.

[41] *Ibid.*, p. 72.

[42] *Altenglische Dichtungen*. ed. Böddeker, p. 98; *Altenglische Sprachproben*, ed. Maetzner, I, 152; *Ancient Songs and Ballads*, ed. Ritson, I, 12; *Political Songs*, p. 69; *Reliques of Ancient English Poetry*, Percy (1847 ed.), p. 89.

was a fruitful source of ridicule, and now some English gleeman embodied it in a thoroughly popular ballad,[43] giving to us for the first time in satire that English speech which had survived under Norman despotism, and now spoke again for English liberty. Richard, upon his return to England in 1259, had attempted to introduce a great body of foreigners; but this was resisted by the barons, and he was compelled to send his foreigners home again. The attempt, however, added to his unpopularity. When the barons were trying to come to an understanding with Henry III, they offered Richard thirty thousand pounds if he could persuade the king to agree to peace on their terms. Henry refused, and the sum was, of course, not paid. But the writer of this ballad maliciously makes it appear that Richard himself demanded the money. Windsor, the king's principal stronghold, was, to the great indignation of the English, garrisoned with foreigners, through Richard's aid. After the battle of Lewes, the Earl of Warren, Henry's partisan, escaped across the sea to France.

"Sit ye still and hearken to me. The King of Almaigne asked thirty thousand pounds to make peace in the country, and so he did more. Richard, though thou art ever a traitor, nevermore shalt thou deceive.

"While Richard was king, he spent all his treasure upon luxury. He brewed evil; let him drink it. He seized the windmill for a castle, brought from Almaigne many a wretched soul to garrison Windsor. He who let the Earl of Warrenne pass over the sea, did great sin.

"Sire Simond de Mountfort hath swore bi ys chyn,
Hevede he nou here the Erl of Waryn,
Shulde he never more come to is yn,
Ne with sheld, ne with spere, ne with other gyn,
to help of Wyndesore."

But such verse as this does not represent the most characteristic satirical product of the age. In order to see what direction the spirit of adverse criticism is taking in the main, how it is producing invective or sombre rebuke rather than satire,[44] we have only to consider *A lutel Soth sermun,* writ-

[43] See catalogue of satirical genres, *supra,* p. 7.
[44] See *supra,* p. 8.

ten, or rather preached, about the middle of the thirteenth century.[45] The poem is only one hundred lines in length, but it is, most significantly, in English, and was probably written by some friar of one of those great bodies, the Franciscans and Dominicans, introduced into England in 1220 and 1224 respectively, and originally instituted to check the corruption of the monastic orders after the Crusades. In England the friars found their work in cities and towns, and among the poorer classes, healing the sick and performing every imaginable office of ministration, at a time when the monastic orders were resident mainly in the rural districts and were making their appeal chiefly to the aristocracy; while the secular clergy were thinking of the income from their benefices rather than of any popular ministration. The friars were the only preachers, and here some good brother is addressing his flock in the vernacular. His subject-matter is entirely social, his tone severe and admonitory, his appeal to the lower classes:

"We know," he says, "how Adam fell from bliss and abode in hell until Christ ransomed him. Into that same hell shall wend all backbiters, thieves, lechers, and whoremongers. But not merely these. Bakers and brewers, who give false measure, make bad bread, and care not if so they get their silver—thither shall they also wend. All priests' wives shall be damned, and

Þeos prude yongemen,
    þat luuyeþ Malekyn,
And þeos prude maydenes,
    þat luuyeþ ianekyn.
At chireche and at chepyng;
    hwanne heo to-gadere cóme—

talk but of illicit love. Yea, even when they come to church on holy-day. Masses and matins concern them not; they are thinking on Wilkin and Watkin. Robin takes Gilot to the ale house, where they talk and drink. He pays for her ale, and in the evening she goes home with him. Though her parents threaten to beat her, she will not give up her Robin."

[45] *An Old English Miscellany,* ed. Morris, E. E. T. S., Vol. 49, p. 187.

The *A lutel Soth sermun* is but one of a multitude of such productions of this age. A Sermon is not a Satire. The most productive literary class, the only class producing anything but the metrical romances and the popular ballads—the clergy—was busily preaching the life to come. The Church was a foe to genuine satire. Her weapon was the sermon.

Hwon holy chireche is vnder uote[46] is but another of this general type, rather more severe and denunciatory, perhaps, than the average. Its thirty-six lines of septenary verse are one lament over decadent ecclesiastical conditions—

> " Nv is holy chireche vuele vnder honde
> All hire weorreþ þat wuneþ ine londe—."

Of course satire finds no scope here, nor in the *Poema Morale,* nor in the dialogue between the Body and the Soul.[47] In the latter the Soul reproaches the Body for its luxurious living, in a tone sombre, heavy, moralistic, but certainly not satirical.[48]

Just here may well be mentioned a peculiar and interesting medieval genre, the *Visions of Heaven and Hell.* This genre is interesting not only in itself, but as culminating in that supreme *Vision,* the *Divine Comedy.* Theological in its origin, it became a powerful instrument in the hands of the clergy with its " threats of hell and hopes of paradise." In France, in the thirteenth and fourteenth centuries, the genre was illustrated in *le Songe d'Enfer* and *la Voie de Paradis* of Raoul de Houdan; and in *Le Pelerinage de la Vie humaine* and *Le Pelerinage de l'ame* of Guillaume de Digulleville.[49] It begins in English literature with the frequent references in the Anglo-Saxon prose of Aelfric and of Wulfstan; takes more formal shape in Bede's *Vision of Furseus* and *Vision of Drihthelm* in the *Ecclesiastical History*; and appears in the Cynewulfian

[46] *Ibid.,* p. 89.
[47] *Altengl., Sprachproben,* I, 92 f.
[48] For a contrary opinion, see Haessner, p. 80.
[49] de Julleville, Tome II, 2, p. 205 f.

poems. The main source of the later English metrical visions, however, seems to have been the *Vision of St. Paul,* in Greek of the fourth century; from which are derived four metrical versions in English. The *Vision of Tundale,* 1149 A. D., an elaborate composition in 2,400 lines, presenting Hell, Purgatory, and Paradise, sums up all preceding *Visions.* Robbers, murderers, and bad clergymen are placed in Hell, but treated sermonically, not satirically.[50] About 1150 A. D., the famous *St. Patrick's Purgatory* continues the form, and within the next fifty years appear two Latin "versions" in prose; *Visions of the Monk of Evesham* (1196), and *The Vision of Thurcill* (1206).

Most important for our present purpose of all the English metrical versions is *The XI Pains of Hell* of the thirteenth century, which, together with two other versions, one by John Awdelay, is a rendering of the early Greek *Vision of St. Paul.* It is given by Morris in his *Old English Miscellany* as two hundred and ninety lines in length, in tetrameter verse, rhyming *a a b b,* with occasional lines in French.[51] In other versions, St. Paul is conducted to Hell by the Angel Michael, while here the sinner returns from hell and narrates his vision of the eleven dreadful forms of punishment. First, he sees burning trees upon which are hanged the souls of those who in this life never went to church. In a heated oven suffer the maker of unjust laws and the unjust judge:

Þer schule þe saulen beo to-drawe.
Þat her arereden vnryhte lawe.

Unchaste women, lovers of usury, suffer in a stinking pen; where also are punished those who ill-treated the innocent and weak and robbed the poor. Those who condemned Christ to death stand forever in a hot pool under a deep gaol. Had a hundred men with teeth and tongues of steel talked from the time of Cain till now, they could not have told all the pains of Hell!

[50] See Becker, *A Contribution to the Comparative Study of the Medieval Visions of Heaven and Hell, passim.*

[51] E. E. T. S., Vol. 49, p. 147.

The Eleven Pains of Hell may be taken as representative of this extraordinary and very vigorous genre. Even where it deals in vituperation or invective it is always quite innocent of humor, most sombre in coloring, didactic in purpose. Satire it is not even in the most remote sense; but can scarcely escape slight mention in any account of English satirical verse, if only by the mere fact that it so clearly shows how intensely practical literature was bound to be in the hands of ecclesiastics, and how incapable of real satire is sheer didacticism. Even *A lutel Soth sermun* in its faint picture of contemporary manners is too earnest to use its picture satirically; while the *Visions of Hell and Heaven,* with their mighty import and dreadful message, could be nothing else but profoundly earnest and didactic. Perhaps more germane to our present purpose is the remote possibility that this genre was parodied in the French fabliau, *li Fabliaux di Cognaigne* and its celebrated English version, *The Land of Cocakaygne.*

There is another side to the picture, however; for some clerk of this period has left us a very light and humorous little poem directed against the tailors.[52] Its subject-matter is very general, without personalities or special local color, but it springs from something more than the ordinary commonplaces. After Henry's marriage with Eleanor of Provence in 1236, the queen's kindred poured into England, introducing foreign customs and fashions of dress. And again, in 1243, the king was followed home from France by a new flood of his mother's kinspeople. Hence this genuine little Latin Satire, beginning with a witty adaptation of the opening lines of the *Metamorphoses:*

> "In nova fert animus mutatas dicere formas
> Corpora, Dii coeptis, nam vos mutastis et illas,
> Aspirate meis."

This bit of sartorial satire is the prototype of a variety that appears again and again in periods of extravagant fashion in

[52] *Political Songs,* p. 51.

dress, such as those of Henry VIII and of Elizabeth. Many years later, toward the close of the century, in the reign of Edward I, this same material is again utilized, but in a very different spirit. The speech is now English, the motive that of the preacher of *A lutel Soth sermun.* In a few lines of savage rebuke, the writer inveighs against the female love of finery in general, and, more particularly, against the disposition, displayed even by women of the lowest class, to follow prevailing fashions in dress.[53]

Not only in such social satire[54] as the preceding, but also in the more elaborate attack on the venality of the judges, this same severity of tone appears. During the absence of Edward I in France, from 1286 to 1290, the public service was badly neglected. Complaints poured in against the judges of the courts at Westminster, who, as the chief administrators of the law, were charged with violence and corruption. Edward returned to punish the offenders severely; but, probably within this period of the king's absence, some very caustic critic has embodied his opinion of judicial venality in some one hundred and fifty lines of rhyming Latin.[55] The attack is direct, but not without its share of rather bitter humor. "There are obviously judges in this land who are open to bribery," he says. "They send their minions, who conclude the financial arrangements; and it is generally admitted that those whose purse-strings are tight will have to wait a long time for justice." This complaint, though characteristically without any revelation of individuality, and lacking in any personalities, was undoubtedly evoked by contemporary abuses. It sounds the now familiar note protesting against the oppression of the poor.

The overbearing ecclesiastical tribunals, known as the Consistory Courts, are also objects for severe attack at this same period. A short poem in English[56] has come down to us, in which some minor criminal is supposed to describe his experi-

[53] *Political Songs,* p. 153.
[54] See *supra,* p. 32 f.
[55] *Political Songs,* p. 224.
[56] Böddeker, *Altenglische Dichtungen,* p. 107; *Political Songs,* p. 155.

ences at an ecclesiastical court in a style at first coarse and finally rankly vituperative.

We must now turn aside for an instant to consider a famous poem whose only claim to a place just here is the fact that it was written within this period, probably about 1250, and perhaps concerns itself with ecclesiastical affairs. *The Owl and the Nightingale,*[57] a *débat* of about eighteen hundred lines in tetrameter couplets, is a spirited poem of the "flyting" type that appeared centuries later in the writings of Skelton and of Dunbar. So great an authority as Professor Courthope sees in this scolding-match an attempt "to present the opposite opinions of the strictly monastic party, on the one side, and of the more latitudinarian among the secular, and even the regular clergy, on the other."[58] To the ordinary reader this is not apparent. Aside from one or two contemptuous references, not a trace of satire appears on the surface of the poem, at least, so general, so free from allusion, is its subject-matter.

Closely related to the Satire on the Consistory Courts is the customary attack on the clergy. In the following instance, the criticism extends beyond the monastic bodies and their luxurious and stately life at the abbeys and monasteries, and includes even the friars, who have now sunk into that same condition of iniquity which but half a century before they had endeavored to reform. This sudden and complete degeneration of the orders of St. Francis and St. Dominic in England is one of the most astounding phenomena in history. As the Franciscans were at first the most zealous and effective of the four orders, so now they seem to be singled out as special targets for attack, and are accused of adding hypocrisy to those other misdemeanors that they have in common with the monks.

Some really witty and satirical critic of contemporary religious conditions has left us an Anglo-French poem of about two hundred and fifty lines, the form of which is obviously an imitation of Wireker's "Novus Ordo Burnelli."[59] This

[57] Ed. Wright, Percy Soc. Pub., Vol. 11; ed. J. E. Wells, *Belle-Lettres Series,* 1907.

[58] Courthope, *History of English Poetry,* I, p. 134.

[59] *Political Songs,* p. 137; for a discussion of *burlesque,* see *supra,* p. 18 f.

master of irony knows his clergy with a degree of thoroughness that must have been galling to the objects of his attack. "The Order of Fair-Ease" is a new fraternity of ecclesiastics, seeking to combine the varied excellencies of all the others. From the Abbey of Sempringham it has adopted the idea of including both brethren and sisters together in one monastery. Beverly has taught it how to eat and drink as long as the candle of eighteen inches' length continues to burn. The Hospitallers have taught the new order to dress elegantly. The Canons, who in self-sacrifice eat flesh in their refectory three days in the week; the Black Monks, who are drunk every day—but for social purposes only; and the Secular Canons, who furnish a good example by their high esteem for ladies, and insist that the brethren and sisters should be constant companions both before and after matins—have all contributed their several admirable characteristics. And so the ironical arraignment continues through the orders of friars, adopting from each brotherhood what is alleged to be its most distinctive trait. This is the first really humorous piece of religious satire since the *Speculum Stultorum.*

Similarly burlesque in tone and belonging to this same period is the highly indecorous but amusing little Satire known as *The Land of Cokaygne,*[60] written in one hundred and ninety lines of English verse. It is directed against the monks and nuns, and describes an imaginary country where conditions are supposedly ideal—where there is plenty to eat and drink, for the abbeys are built of food, and the rivers flow with milk and wine. Best of all, the monks and nuns are afforded unlimited opportunities for intercourse. Unquotable as it is, this little Satire affords an amusing commentary on what was supposed to be the conventual ideal of the period. Is *The Land of Cokaygne* a parody of the medieval *vision genre,* as well as an ironical burlesque[61] on monastic sensuality? However that may be, it derives, without doubt, from the French. *Le Fabliaux di Coquaigne* describes a happy land of feasting and idle-

[60] *Poems and Lives of Saints,* ed. Furnivall, p. 156.
[61] See *supra,* p. 18 f.

ness, where they celebrate Easter and Candlemas four times every year, with Lent only once in twenty years; where the houses are made of turbots and salmon, the beams of sturgeons, and the shingles of sausages; while the spits turn incessantly across the streets between rivers of wine![62]

Just as satirical, but no longer burlesque, and somewhat more severe, is the crude medley of religious and of class satire, which Dr. Furnivall entitles *Of Men Lif that Woniþ in Lond*,[63] written in English about this same time in twenty six-line stanzas. After ironically attacking the friars and monks, the writer turns against the various mercantile classes of his locality—tailors, sutlers, spinners, potters, bakers, and so on, all of whom are inveighed against in turn. Though of Irish origin—for the scene is ostensibly laid in Kildare—the satire applies only too well to the England of its period:

> "Hail be ȝe prestis wiþ ȝur brode bokes
> poȝ ȝur crune be ischaue, fair beþ ȝur crokes
> Ȝow and oþer lewiduen deleþ bot a houue.
> Whan ȝe deliþ holibrede, ȝine me botte a litil
> Sikirlich he was a clerk
> þat wrochete þis craftilich werke."

But the Consistory Courts and the religious fraternities are not the only objects for satirical attack during the glorious reign of Edward I. A short poem of two versions, in Latin and Anglo-French respectively, speaks volumes against the administration of the great law-giver. It is a genuine expression of popular discontent, an indictment against public fraud and oppression. Some learned clerk is feeling very pessimistic over the condition of affairs. He is too much in earnest, too near the objects of his attack, to indulge in superfluous humor, even were he capable of it—which is doubtful.[64] His wail is echoed by another poet in a strange medley of Latin, English, and Anglo-Norman, who laments the oppression of the poor and the general corruption of the age;[65] and by still

[62] See Lenient, p. 92.
[63] *Poems and Lives of Saints*, p. 152 f.
[64] *Political Songs*, p. 133.
[65] *Ibid.*, pp. 251–252.

another, writing more elaborately, and in English, who voices particularly the miserable lot of the peasant:[66]

> "To entredite and amonsi
> Al thai, whate hi evir be,
> That lafful men doth robbi,
> Whate in lond what in see;
> And thos hoblurs, namelich,
> That husbond benimeth eri of grund;
> Men ne schold ham biri in non chirch,
> Bot cast ham ute as a hund."

Though one grant the sincerity of these several productions, he must still in general regard them such as every period produces in greater or less quantity. Far more vital than these, and expressing apparently a popular feeling, is a very interesting poem in English, purporting to be the complaint of a husbandman against inordinate taxation. In order to carry on his wars with France, Flanders, Wales, and Scotland, Edward I was compelled to resort to extremely heavy taxation, actually amounting at one time in the case of the clergy to one-half their income; and in that of the tenantry, to one-fourth. This tax fell most grievously upon the poor. What the wretched peasant perceived was not the glorious issue of the great king's projects, but his own immediate sufferings. This vigorous complaint seems to voice the misery of all the poor in England:[67]

> "Ich herde men upo mold make muche mon,
> Hou he beth i-tened of here tilyynge,
> Gode ȝeres and corn bothe beth a-gon,
> Ne kepeth here no sawe ne no song syng.
>
> "Now we mote worche, nis ther non other won,
> Mai ich no lengore lyve with my lesinge;
> Ȝet ther is a bitterore bid to the bon,
> For ever the furthe peni mot to the kynge."

In general this same protest is again expressed by another

[66] *Ibid.*, p. 195 f.

[67] *Altenglische Dictungen,* p. 100; *Political Songs,* p. 149.

poem[68] in mixed Latin and Anglo-French, which seems to refer to the king's expedition against Flanders. Characteristically, either through loyalty or for fear of the consequences, it blames the king's ministers, though no ruler was ever more responsible for his own actions than was Edward I. The king had, to his great joy, discovered a new source of revenue in fixing a heavy duty of one-tenth on all wool exported from the country. The stress laid upon this grievance might indicate the writer to have been some Cistercian monk:

"A King should not leave his country without consent of the *commons.* Every year the fifteenth penny goes to work this common harm, and the common people must sell all they have to meet the tax.

> "Depus que le roy vodera tam multum cepisse,
> Entre les riches si purra satis invenisse;
> E plus, à ce que m'est avys, et melius fecisse
> Des grantz partie aver pris, et parvis pepercisse.
> Qui capit argentum sine causa peccat egentum.

To the evil counsellor, not the king, should be laid the blame for this. Such taxation is robbery. Let the rich be taxed, but spare the poor."

But while the war with Flanders had no sympathy from the people, that against Scotland aroused their enthusiasm. After the battle of Falkirk, in 1298, some cleric, writing in Latin, mingles together an account of the battles with the Scotch, sneers at the conquered people, eulogy of Edward, and didactic moralizing. He exclaims:

> "Scribo novam satyram, sed sic ne seminet iram."[69]

The defeat of Wallace at Falkirk and the great patriot's execution were followed in September, 1306, by the battle of Kirkencliff, where Sir Simon Fraser was taken prisoner. It is on the execution of this Scottish leader that we have a thoroughly popular ballad in English.[70] Gibes against the Scotch

[68] *Political Songs,* p. 182.
[69] *Political Songs,* p. 160.
[70] *Altenglische Dictungen,* p. 121; *Ancient Songs and Ballads,* I, 28; *Political Songs,* p. 212 f.

constitute its only claim to satire, for it is in effect rather a pæan of victory.

But the political ballad and the general social Satire do not entirely exhaust the satirical verse of Edward's reign. The pride and ostentation of his courtiers meets with a sharp protest in a short poem in English—rather disgusting, but certainly instructive—on the retinues of the great nobles.[71] Far more humorous is an attack on the scholastic studies of the universities, in Goliardic verse, written perhaps by an adherent of that older and broader system of instruction that had been displaced by the rise of scholastic theology under the friars in the early part of the century.[72] Roger Bacon might well have sympathized with, or even written, this remarkably acute and humorous protest. But our cleric led no general revolt, for scholasticism continued to flourish throughout the following century:

> " Circa dialecticam tempus cur consumis,
> Tu qui nullos redditus aliunde sumis?
> Colat qui per patriam natus est e summis,
> Dives agro, dives positis in faenore nummis."[73]

Entitled to a place here, chronologically, at least, are two successors of the Anglo-Latin satirists of one and two centuries earlier. Robert Mannyng and Richard Rolle are not by intention satirists, but didactic writers whose elaborate works very well illustrate the output of their time and class. Yet they deserve mention here, if only to differentiate the *Handlyng Synne* and *The Pricke of Conscience* from any genuine satire.

Robert Mannyng's *Handlyng Synne*,[74] written perhaps in 1303, was a translation into English tetrameter couplets of a

[71] *Altenglische Dictungen*, p. 134; *Political Songs*, p. 237 f.

[72] *Ibid.*, p. 206 f.

[73] "Why do you waste your time on dialectics, you who receive no income from other sources? Let the high-born cultivate it, he who is rich in land and in money laid out at interest."

[74] Ed. Furnivall, E. E. T. S., Original Series, 119 and 123.

didactic work entitled *Manuel des Peschiez* by a certain William of Waddington. The elaborate plan comprises a treatise on the Ten Commandments, various transgressions thereof being set forth by doctrine and illustrated by tales. The Seven Deadly Sins, the Seven Sins of Sacrilege, The Seven Sacraments, are also treated in the same fashion. The whole, while distinctly related to its time, in fact replete with contemporary matter, can lay no claim to satire. It is one of those serious and didactic performances which are really utterly foreign to the satiric temper.[75]

No long interval elapsed between the composition of *Handlyng Synne* and that of Richard Rolle's *The Pricke of Conscience.*[76] The "Hermit of Hampole" lived from 1290 to 1349, and probably wrote his elaborate didactic poem at the very time when Lawrence Minot was so gleefully celebrating the triumphs of King Edward III. The difference between them is the difference between the court and the cloistered cell. *The Pricke of Conscience*—almost ten thousand lines long, in tetrameter couplets—has seven parts—Birth, Life, Death, Purgatory, The Judgment, Hell, and Paradise. The whole is one long sermon without humor or contemporary allusions. Of the two poems, *Handlyng Synne* is superior in human interest. Neither work, however, merits any elaborate treatment in the story of English satirical verse.

III

But if subject-matter for satire was ample in the times of Edward the Law-Giver, it was vastly augmented in the reign of his son and successor, Edward the Second, the unwise and unruly (1307–1327). Bannockburn, with its inglorious defeat, in 1314, followed for many years by merciless Scotch ravages on the Border; in 1315–1316, a terrible famine as a result of the dearth which had begun in 1289; and this followed by so great a pestilence in 1316–1317 that "the living scarcely sufficed to bury the dead"; a dreadful murrain among the cat-

[75] See *supra*, p. 8.
[76] Ed. Morris, Phil. Soc. Pub., 1863.

tle; wheat rising from 3 pence to 10 shillings per bushel:—these were among the disastrous events and conditions of Edward the Second's reign. And all this time lasted the king's contemptible conduct, first with Piers Gaveston, then with the Despensers, which led to a war with the barons in 1322, until finally the queen's treacherous intrigues occasioned the fall both of the wretched king and his ambitious favorites. All through these unfortunate political conditions continued the maladministration of justice; while the corruption of both the monastic and of the secular clergy, from prelate to parish priest, was a conspicuous and growing evil that was rapidly leading to the great reformatory movement under Wycliffe half a century later.

All these various conditions are summed up by an earnest critic, not without a sort of bitter humor, in a vernacular poem of almost eight hundred lines, in every respect superior to any preceding "Satire"—*A Poem on the Times of Edward II,*[77] as it has been styled. This "poem" in its subject-matter, tone, and method, is so typical of its age and of its kind as to merit a somewhat detailed description. It sums up in itself a multitude of minor efforts.

First of all, the *Poem* is social satire in its wail of protest against the condition of the poor, and religious satire in its attack on the clergy. But the political note is lacking—and that in an age so fruitful in matter for political satire. Still, if—as we assume—the poem is a popular production, there are obvious reasons for the absence of this note. The matter of primary interest to the people was their own condition. Famine, pestilence, and the ravages of war were too near to admit consideration of political affairs or perhaps any interest in them. Even granting that this interest existed, the people had scarcely learned how to express themselves. Furthermore, that portion of the clerical body which alone produced the literature of medieval England was not engaged in politics, and, in the main, paid little attention to political affairs; while the baronial class, participating in state affairs and powerful

[77] Ed. Hardwick, Percy Soc. Pub., Vol. 28; ed. Wright, *Political Songs,* p. 323.

enough to express an adverse opinion, produced no literature.

But apart from this absence of the political note, our satirist makes a praiseworthy effort to cover the ground, with a superb disregard for unity of theme, yet with redeeming vigor and sincerity:

"Why werre and wrake in londe
And manslaugt is y-come,
Why honger and derthe on erthe
The pour hath over-nome;
Why bestes beth i-storve
And why corne is so dere,
ȝe that wyl abyde,
Lystyn and ȝe mow here,
With skyl;
Certes without lesyng,
Herken hit ho so wyl."

"Gold will buy honor for a criminal. Archbishops and bishops, who are guardians of men's consciences, are afraid to condemn others, since their own lives are so impious. Archdeacons are open to bribery; simony wins preferment for the unworthy. When a priest has once gained his benefice, he leaves it in the charge of a servant, while he himself goes hunting in a far country. Abbots and priors spend their time in sport. We have religion enough, but no God in it. See how these monks punish themselves for the love of God! They wear socks and felt boots; they are well fed with good flesh and fish, and leave little in the dish!

"Religion was i-maked
Penance for to drye,
Now it is mych i-turned
To pryde and glotonye.
Wer schalt thu fynde
Redder men on lerys
Fayrer men other fatter
Than monks, chanouns, other freres in town?
Forsothe ther nys non aysier lyf
Than is religion."

Friars are selfish and covetous, readily bribed, contemners of the poor, flatterers of the rich:

> "ȝif the rych man deyth,
> That was of grete myȝt,
> Then wol the freres al day
> For the cors fiȝt.
> Hyt is not al for the calf
> That the cow loweth,
> But it is for the gode gras
> That in the mede groweth,
> By my hod!"

Having finished with the clergy, the satirist proceeds to indict the different classes and professions in the usual medieval manner—physicians, lawyers, barons, squires, knights, merchants, sheriffs, judges, statesmen, and others, all of whom thrive by imposing on the poor.

Nothing could be more popular, more alive, in that it draws inspiration directly from existing conditions with which its author was familiar. Here are sounded the three principal notes of the characteristic medieval English Satire—the misery of the poor, the vices of the clergy from Pope to friar, the faults of the various professional and social classes.

This last note is heard now for the first time, and, for a century or over, continues to characterize satirical poetry. Its origin is fairly obvious, but interesting. As a result of wider commercial relations, there grew up in England during the latter part of the reign of Edward I that great burgher class which was later to become the mainstay of the English nation. With the growth of the towns came the working gilds, giving each class its individual dress. These newer trade divisions, together with the classes resulting from chivalry—the knight, the squire; and the ecclesiastical classes—the monk, the friar, the parish priest; form in the early fourteenth century a society of rigid divisions; each trade, art, profession, with its distinctive dress, so significant and easily distinguishable, that our satirist tends to endow the individual class with fixed moral characteristics as marked as its outward habit. Thus men are regarded not as individuals, but as members of a certain order. This lack of individuality, and consequently lack of characterization, in medieval satire, is of course the result of well understood pre-Renaissance conditions of life where the Church and the feudal system helped to merge the individual in his class.

Both in its popular form and in its choice of subject-matter this poem on the bad times of Edward II is what might be expected at this period, when the national consciousness is growing, the voice of the people is making itself heard, and the Anglo-French dialect, with its limited appeal to the court circle, has been supplanted by the English language—the speech of a homogeneous nation.

In October, 1311, Edward II was compelled to yield to the demand of his nobles and grant a reconfirmation of Magna Charta, consenting among many other things to the banishment of his infamous favorite Gaveston. But the king had no sooner escaped from his nobles than he rejoined Gaveston and broke his promises. Based on these circumstances, a political poem of a hundred lines in English, with an admixture of Anglo-French, reproaches the king for his perfidy and inquires into the condition of the kingdom.[81] "The king can make and unmake," says the poet, "but he does so too often for the good of the State. Our Prince of England, by the counsel of his people, held a great parliament at Westminster. He made Magna Charta of wax, as I understand, and very well believe, for it was holden too near the fire and is molten all away."

The king's breach of faith led to the death of Gaveston in 1312. Within a few months the powerful and jealous Lancaster and that Earl of Warwick, whom the royal favorite had styled "The Black Dog of Ardenne," accomplished his ruin. He was captured and, after throwing himself at Lancaster's feet and pleading in vain for mercy, summarily beheaded. Two short Goliardic poems, parodies of hymns in the old Church service, attest the joy of at least the ecclesiastical contingent over Gaveston's fall.[82] While partly elegiac, partly celebratory in tone, these two poems are in effect attacks on the king and his policy.

[81] *Political Songs,* p. 253; for the Political Satire in general, see *supra,* p. 31 f.

[82] *Political Songs,* p. 258 f.

Only two years after Gaveston's execution came Bannockburn. Without the consent of Parliament and apparently also without popular sympathy, Edward met the Scotch and was overwhelmingly defeated. The Earl of Gloucester was among the slain—through treachery, asserts the author of the Latin poem which is at once a description of the battle, an elegy on the Earl, and an attack on the king.[83] The king is charged with bad judgment and weakness in heeding those evil counsellors through whose venom England is poisoned. Bannockburn was lost through treachery, declares the poet, and Gloucester brought to his death by these same wicked men, on whom the remaining nobles should take vengeance.

Although Anglo-French has now been supplanted by English, the vast preponderance of Latin shows that literature is still largely in the hands of ecclesiastics. This does not mean, however, that some Latin poems were not in a sense a popular product. It is necessary to distinguish between Latin productions that are merely academic and poems, such as have just been considered, which are in a measure an expression of the sentiment of the whole people. With the growth of the towns and the rise of the burgher classes came a new order of things, which greatly influenced satirical poetry in the latter part of the fourteenth century. The soldiers and the free population of the towns gained expression for their sentiment. But great multitudes still were silent; and it was very long before the lowest class either contributed anything to this vast body of satirical verse or was affected by it.

IV

It is again in Latin that the next significant satirical verse is written. Twenty years had passed since the melancholy times of Edward II when the brilliant victories at Calais, Crécy, and Poitiers, cemented the English people together by a common national pride. The satire against Scotland is now supplemented by that against France. The songs of Lawrence Minot, the laureate of the French and of the Scottish wars,

[83] *Political Songs*, p. 262 f.

are eulogistic and triumphal pæans, celebrating Halidon Hill, the sea-fight at Sluys, the avenging of Bannockburn, the siege of Tournai, the victory at Crécy. Minot is in reality a gleeman, successor to the older English minstrels, whose songs are in no sense satirical but purely celebratory.[84]

England had long had no love for France, and Edward's pretensions to the French crown increased this customary ill-feeling to an exceeding bitterness that is amply manifested in the two political poems which follow. The first, through some four hundred rhyming hexameter lines, endows poor France with every abominable quality and extravagantly eulogizes Edward. Only a characteristic extract can give any idea of the vigor and the variety of epithet in this patriotic diatribe;

> "Francia, fœminea, pharisæa, vigoris, idea,
> Lynxea, viperea, vulpina, lupina, Medea,
> Callida, syrena, crudelis, acerba, superba,
> Es fellis plena, mel dans latet anguis in herba,
> Sub duce Philippo Valeys, cognomine lippo,
> Amoris nomen famam cognomen et omen—."

The other poem, in but sixty lines of elegiac verse, is a product of the same spirit, though its subject-matter is rather social or moral than political. The Frenchman, in replying to charges brought against his nation by the Englishman, admits that his compatriots are given to excessive care of the hair, to effeminacy, to affectation, but bitterly denies the charge of licentiousness, and, in turn, accuses the English of being boors.[85]

The form of these poems in hexameter and in elegiac verse stamps them as academic productions that are still an expression of popular sentiment, of growing national consciousness and pride. A far more elaborate and very different order of political poem is the long Latin *Prophecy of John of Bridlington,* written about 1370 by some clerk in the service of the last Humphrey de Bohun, Earl of Hereford.[86] This historical

[84] *Political Poems and Songs,* ed. Wright, Vol. I, p. 26.
[85] *Political Poems,* 1, 91.
[86] *Ibid.*, 1, 123 f.

retrospect purports to be the prophecy of John of Bridlington, a popular saint in Yorkshire, who died in 1379. Bale says he had the gift of seeing visions.[87] The poem is accompanied by a prose commentary appended by the supposed editor of the original treatise. The *Prophecy* is an historical narrative of over six hundred lines, with incidental eulogy and satire. Almost the entire reign of Edward III, with its multitudinous events, is passed in review. The character of Edward II is severely handled, and Pope Clement and David Bruce are attacked, while Edward the Third's private character undergoes searching, and by no means favorable, analysis. The author claims that the king's sins are responsible for the evils now coming apace upon the country. Much of the poem is intentionally obscure, and much is tiresomely didactic, but, though in every sense an academic product, *The Prophecy* is yet significant for its interest in public affairs.

V

These various Latin poems utilize but a small part of the subject-matter afforded by their age. They emphasize, in the main, only the brilliant aspect of a reign that was in reality replete with difficult labor problems, with the oppression of the poor, with the corruption and venality of the clergy. A more complete picture was to be painted toward the close of Edward's reign by a genuinely popular satirist[88] who voiced the evils of the times and proposed a remedy for them in his *Vision of Piers the Ploughman.*[89]

To call *Piers Plowman* a Satire is to use the term in the broadest possible sense. The great allegory, through its general lack of humor and particularly its large constructive element, becomes a didactic poem,[90] a fairly complete criticism

[87] See G. P. Krapp, *The Legend of St. Patrick's Purgatory,* p. 57.

[88] We are not here concerned with that perplexing and still unsettled question, the authorship of *Piers Plowman.* In the present discussion "Langland" signifies the author, whoever he may have been, and whether one or several. But cf. Manly, *Mod. Phil.,* Vol. III, no. 2.

[89] *Piers the Plowman and Richard the Redeless,* ed. Skeat, 1886.

[90] See *supra,* p. 8.

of its age, rather than a Satire. Still, aside from the work of Chaucer, it represents all that its immediate period has to offer in place of genuine satirical poetry. For this reason, and because it embodies the main characteristics of previous English satire, it must be considered an important link in the chain binding the earlier product with the consummate form of three centuries later.

Beneath the outward glory of Edward the Third's reign, the bitter humiliation of France, the vast extension of English trade, the glitter of a chivalric court, the famous exploits of the Black Prince, lay a dreadful abyss of misery. One side, the brighter, is portrayed by Chaucer; the other side, the darker, is depicted by the author of *Piers Plowman*. Material for satirical treatment was never more plentiful, from a medieval point of view, than when the first text of *Piers Plowman* was written in 1362. In the three great realms, political, ecclesiastical, and social, there was no dearth of subject-matter. Those ecclesiastical conditions that were soon to lead to Wyckliffe's revolt against clerical corruption and papal tyranny, ever increasing since the reign of John; those political conditions of royal misrule and oppression that were finally to lead to the deposition of Richard II; those social conditions that were to arouse the Peasant's Revolt in 1381—all surrounded this sombre champion of popular rights, and are mirrored in his verse. The subject-matter forming the staple of Langland's theme, though almost inextricably confused, may yet be divided into these three classes. This strange but powerful medley forms the epitome of every Satire of significance that we have yet considered.

Langland's allegorical form of narrative, with its innumerable personified abstractions, perhaps resulted from the influence of the *Roman de la Rose,* at this time highly popular in England. Langland undoubtedly utilizes the satire on beggars and idlers which Jean de Meung puts into the mouth of False-Seeming. The French poet clothes False-Seeming in the garment of a friar, and directs some of his sharpest satire against the Franciscans and other ecclesiastical orders; and perhaps this, too, gave hints to Langland. But the poet of *Piers Plowman* makes no use of that bitter and pitiless satire on women with which the *Roman de la Rose* was so replete as to elicit a reply in the *Champion des Dames* of Martin Franc. Jean de Meung's *Duenna* furnished valuable suggestions to Chaucer, however, and perhaps the whole of the Frenchman's satire against women had its influence in England. It is impossible to say how much of the later English product was influenced by the *Roman de la Rose*.

Langland's form of allegory, closely related to Jean de Meung's, has little in common with that of the *Speculum Stultorum*. It needs no prologue to render a hidden meaning apparent. But while admirable for didactic purposes, it is rather too cumbersome a garment for the swiftly-moving Muse of Satire. This allegorical form becomes effective as a vehicle for satire only when its personifications are genuine characterizations, individuals. Langland has achieved characterization in his pictures of Avarice and of Gluttony, which are so true to nature that they become not merely types of avarice and gluttony, not merely class representatives, but real individuals. Apart, however, from these two lifelike figures, and a certain amount of individuality in that of Lady Meed, there is no life in the abstractions called Falsehood, Conscience, Reason, and others, that stalk through the first few cantos of the poem. From these frequently dull and platitudinous cantos, we pass to something far more vital and interesting. The figure of Piers Plowman has actual vitality; he is a character, not a personified abstraction.

The allegorical form is essentially constructive and didactic, and hence unfitted in its very nature for satirical purposes. It is also too abstract, while satire is essentially realistic.[91] Wherever Langland grows really satirical, he merges abstractions in pictures of actual life with its varied types. His allegorical form springs from prevailing literary influences, and results in a unique adaptation of a very abstract method to very realistic material. In English satire this form is entirely without either precedent or subsequent influence.

[91] See *supra*, p. 14.

In his moral satire, Langland uses two distinct methods. In the first, as has been seen, he personifies some abstraction; in the second, he arraigns society by its *classes*—a thoroughly medieval point of view, already somewhat exemplified in the poem on the times of Edward II.[92]

The first method is perennial, but Langland's use of it is distinctly medieval. The classical satirists habitually inveigh against single vices, yet never against abstractions. They select an individual, real or imaginary, who is supposed to embody some particular foible, and that person is made to live before our eyes. But the medieval satirist either attacks the special vice entirely in the abstract, or attempts to endow it with a kind of factitious life by personification. It has been seen how such personifications, under the touch of genius, may rise into actual characterization, until, indeed, they become the Sir Epicure Mammon and Sir Giles Overreach of centuries later. But in the main Langland's figures are mere names. We have Simony, who is a shame to Holy Church and a vexation to the people, and is of all men most familiar with Lady Meed; and Bribery, personified as Lady Meed, the principal figure in the first four cantos of the poem, who is most splendidly clothed in the finest furs adorned with all manner of precious stones, of ravishing array, and is as familiar in the Pope's palace as Holy Church herself. We have, too, the Seven Deadly Sins. One of these, Sloth, has been priest and parson passing thirty winters, yet can neither sing nor read saints' lives. He can find a hare in field or furrow better than he can construe one phrase in the *Beatitudes*.

But the satire against classes, both ecclesiastical and social, is more elaborate and certainly, in the main, more effective. The idle classes are objects of Langland's severe rebuke. It is part of his ideal social system that such people should be made to work. Hunger will bring them to reason, he argues. And this Hunger does, in a wonderful scene where he seizes and almost destroys the horde of idle vagabonds who are wasting the substance of honest Piers Plowman. Not only the idle

[92] See *supra*, p. 64 f.

classes but those who live by fraud, such as Knights, Clerks, Sizers, and Summoners; Sheriffs, Beadles, Bailiffs, and Brokers of Merchandise; Victuallers and Advocates, are held up to contumely. Summoners, Deans, Archdeacons, and Registrars, are ordered to serve Simony; Friars are drawn in a cart made by Liar. It is asserted that of all men Brewers, Bakers, Butchers, and Cooks most harm the poor people who buy in small quantities. Reason will not have pity till Clerks be covetous to feed the poor; till Bishops spend their money on beggars rather than horses, and on the poor Orders rather than hawks and hounds. Even the Pope is not spared, for he is counselled by Reason to take pity on Holy Church and, ere he give grace, first govern himself. Sergeants-at-the-Bar, who plead only for pence and pounds, never for love of our Lord; Chaplains, who may be chaste, but are withal lacking in charity; Priests, whom avarice hath bound; Pardoners, who by special license from the Pope, sell pardons, but are themselves unchaste; Parsons and Parish Priests, who live away from their cures; Bishops and even Novices, both masters and doctors, who, instead of preaching, praying, and feeding the poor, live in London and take secular occupation for the sake of gain; Friars, who preach for their own profit and have become mere pedlers of articles to please the women; Pilgrims and Palmers, who journey to Rome and Campostella and visit the shrine of every saint save Truth; Hermits who carry their wenches about with them; and Jesters and Jugglers, who behave in an unseemly fashion—all these figures mingle in that motley throng which moves on the plain called Life; that plain lying between the Castle of Truth and the Bottomless Pit, stretching out illimitably in the Dreamer's vision until its distances are lost in mist. Its life is fantastic, yet real. Through it we move as if ourselves in dream. The shapes are sometimes sharply defined, again indistinct in the twilight. The hour is always gray dawn, when the mist has not yet lifted, or near eventide, when it is about to descend from the Malvern hills upon the plain.

But while classes and abstractions are usually satirized each apart from the other, they are often enough associated.

Liar is rescued and welcomed by the Pardoners, desired by the Leeches, housed for a while by the Minstrels, but finally possessed by the Friars. Lady Meed is received at Westminster right royally. She is honored by all, and consoled by some of the Justices, who hasten to her bower. A Confessor, clothed as a Friar, offers to absolve her; though she has poisoned Popes, as Provisors know. Sizers and Summoners praise her; and Sheriffs were ruined without her. She so clothes the Commissary of the Consistory Courts, and his Clerks, that she ever escapes punishment. She installs ignorant Bishops, provides for parsons, permits Priests to have concubines, and corrupts the Justices of the Law with her jewels.

Throughout this satire both on classes and on abstractions, mingled confusedly at every step of the way, are charges against Church, State, and society at large. The Church is criticized through its hierarchy, from Pope to mendicant Friar, among whom Simony reigns supreme. Absentee clergy, and those "provisors," foreigners appointed by the Pope to English benefices, are bitterly assailed. "Corruption," cries Langland, "has pervaded every branch and order of the Church; luxury and power have bred contempt for the poor; heavenly things are neglected for temporal; hypocrisy, sensuality, and greed, have eaten up the ecclesiastical body." But all this is merely an epitome of the charges that previous satirists, since the time of Walter Map, have been urging against the clergy. It shows the state of affairs to be worse than ever—the darkest part of the night before the first faint dawn of the Wycliffian protest.

The State, in turn, is most severely blamed for its corrupt law-courts. Westminster is the supposed seat of justice, but there Meed is the favorite companion of Judges. Under officers of state, Sheriffs and the like, also receive bribes and oppress the poor. Finally, the people, including almost every social order, are infected with manifold vices. The best type of all is the honest farmer, and he is oppressed by the upper classes.

Now the remedy for all these unhappy conditions in Church,

State, and Society, is no revolution in the existing ecclesiastical, political, or social systems; no abolition of the old order in any respect; but only the application of one great righteous principle—Love or Right-Dealing. This is the positive and constructive element in *Piers Plowman.* Langland exposes unsparingly and minutely all the abuses he sees about him, and proposes as the remedy the simple but fundamental precept of common brotherhood. Perhaps the larger part of the poem is taken up with this constructive element, simply didactic, sermonic. By no possible definition could such constructive passages as these be termed in any sense satirical; they are purely didactic, and entirely without humor.[93]

But Langland not only makes an immense step in advance in his wide range of subject-matter and his portrayal of types transcending mere abstractions; he also marks a new era in his brief but graphic pictures of contemporary life. Here and there, throughout the Dreamer's Vision, are scattered those vivid *genre* pictures which seem the only concrete realities amid a world of shadows, and which show a marvelous familiarity with common life and an equally marvelous power in portraying it. The tone is sometimes sympathetic, as when the poet touches upon the plain fare and simple life of the agricultural laborer.[94] Again, we have pictures full of life and color, startling in their realism, as in the description of a London crowd.[95] Sometimes the poet's touch is purely satirical, as in the description of the confession of Gluttony, who on his way to be shriven is thus enticed by Beton, the brewster:

> "'I haue gode ale, gossib,' quod she · 'glotown, wiltow assaye?'
> 'Hastow auȝte in þi purs · any hote spices?'

[93] Among these constructive passages are the speech of Repentance to Avarice (P. 5, l. 276 f.), and to the other sinners; Piers Plowman's instructions to the Knight (P. 6, l. 38 f.); the admonitions given by Hunger (P. 6, l. 215); the conversation between the Dreamer and Holy Church about Truth, Conscience, and Charity (P. 1, entire); the appeal of Conscience to the King against Lady Meed (P. 3, l. 229); and almost the entire eighth *passus.*

[94] *Passus* 6, ll. 282–97.

[95] *Prologue,* ll. 216–30.

'I have peper and piones,' quod she · 'and a pounde of garlike,
A ferthyngworth of fenel-seed for fastyngdayes.' "[96]

Glutton yields. He finds in the shop, Eis the shoemaker, Wat the warrener and his wife, Tim the tinker, and two of his prentices, Hick the hackneyman, Hugh the needle-seller, Clarice of Cock Lane, the clerk of the church, Daw the ditcher, and others, among whom are a fiddle-player, a ratter, a sweeper of Cheapside, and a rope-maker. They hold wassail. Glutton gets dead drunk, is carried home by Clement the Cobbler, put to bed, and wept over by his wife and daughters. In this is illustrated the characterization of Gluttony, already referred to more than once; the picture of contemporary life, and the satire on the vice of drunkenness.

In addition to such contemporary pictures as these, Langland alludes to the pestilences and storms that had recently devastated the country; to the awful visitations of the Black Death in 1349 and succeeding years, and the terrible phenomena preceding them—all of which he affirms to be a punishment for sin.[97] Again, he mentions the sufferings of the English soldiery in the recent Norman campaign, closed by the Treaty of Bretigny in 1360;[98] and, referring to the religious fervor that led

" —folk to goon on pilgrimages
and palmers for to seken straunge strondes
To ferne halwes, couthe in sondry londes—,"

he raises a cry against the money loss to the kingdom resulting from such follies, and has Reason rule that the shrine of St. James be brought from Campostella to where the poor sick lie in prisons and on cots.[99]

Thus in range of subject-matter, in characterization, in attention to contemporary events, in pictures of the life of his time, Langland advances far beyond his predecessors. It is in

[96] P. 5, ll. 310–13.
[97] P. 5, ll. 13–20.
[98] P. 3, ll. 188–207.
[99] P. 4, ll. 126–133.

the final and very vital feature of humor that he is perhaps lacking. The Malvern Dreamer is no humorist. Humor of a certain kind he has—the rather bitter humor of a stern moralist who is half indignant, half sorrowful, but a humor sometimes faintly gleaming through his sombre allegory like glimpses of the sun through the Malvern mist. It springs most frequently from the satirist's perception of the incongruity between practice and profession, and the futility of mere external observances:

"Pilgrymes and palmers · pliȝhted hem togidere
To seke seynt Iames · and seynts in rome ·
Thei went forth in here wey · with many wise tales,
And hadden leue to lye · al here lyf after."[100]

Again, the shaft is directed against social classes, by means of that association with abstractions, already noticed, as when the Summoners are saddled as palfreys for the use of Simony and of Civil;[101] and as when Falsehood flees for refuge to the Friars, Guile is sheltered by the Merchants, Liar is tenderly cared for by the Leeches and the Minstrels.[102]

But the most subtle piece of satirical humor, and also the most genuine satire, in *Piers Plowman,* is the following:

Having made confession, a great multitude were seeking for Truth. After devious wanderings, they met a man in a pilgrim's guise. He bore tokens from Sinai, Rome, and Galacia. They asked him whence he came:

"'Fram synay,' he seyde, 'and fram owre lordes sepulcre;
In bethleem and in babiloyne · I haue ben in bothe,
In ermonye, in Alisaundre · in many other places.
Ȝe may se bi my signes · þat sitten on myn hatte,
Þat I haue walked ful wyde · in wete and in drye,
And souȝte gode seyntes · for my soules helth.'"

"Knowest thou ought of a saint that men call *Truth*?" he is asked. "Nay, so God help me," said the man, "never heard I palmer ask after *him* till now!"[103]

[100] *Prologue,* ll. 46–9.
[101] P. 2, ll. 161–82.
[102] P. 2, ll. 210–32.
[103] P. 5, ll. 518–43.

The Vision of Piers the Plowman represents a period of change, when revolution or reform was imminent in every estate of the realm. The conditions leading to these changes are faithfully mirrored by Langland, though the only reform he would institute is that wrought by love as an active principle. The application of this moral theory introduces into his work that vast constructive element which partly distinguishes the didactic poem from the Satire.[104] The general lack of humor, fatal in a later age to the pretension of any poem claiming to be considered as satirical, is yet so characteristic of English satirical poetry before the Renaissance that the objection in this case cannot well be urged. We have seen something of the nature of Langland's infrequent humor. Such as it is, it yet marks an advance beyond much that has gone before. But *The Vision of Piers Plowman* illustrates a still more striking progress by its faithful and graphic pictures of contemporary life, its few yet admirable character studies, and the vast range of its subject-matter—which sounds every note struck through the two preceding centuries. Beyond this, it is popular, vital, and spontaneous; no result of literary traditions, but the direct and seemingly inevitable product of existing conditions.[105]

[104] See *supra*, p. 8.

[105] The second part of *The Vision—Do Wel, Do Bet, and Do Best*—is rather a tedious piece of work, the good qualities of which all appear in *The Vision* itself. For our present purpose it may safely be disregarded.

CHAPTER III

FROM LANGLAND'S IMITATORS TO CHAUCER

Pierce the Plowman's Crede.—Satire under Richard II.—The Peasants' Revolt.—Its record in verse.—Gower's *Vox Clamantis.*—His *Tripartite Chronicle.*—Lollardry.—The Lollard satire.—*Burlesque on the Council of London.*—*The Complaint of the Plowman.*—*Jack Upland.*—Sir John Oldcastle.—Occleve's poem on Oldcastle.—A later poem on Oldcastle.—" Satirical commonplace " in this reign.—Gower's poem on the reign of Richard II.—His *Confessio Amantis.*—*Richard the Redeless.*—Personal satire in allegorical form.—Satire in the poems of Chaucer.—Distinction between Chaucer and other satirists of his time.—His subject-matter.—His methods.—Satire in the General Prologue.—Social types.—Satire in the interludes.—Satire in the Tales.—The Pardoner.—The Wife of Bath.—*The Monk's Tale.*—The Continental *fabliau.*—*Fabliaux* in England before Chaucer.—Chaucer's *fabliaux.*—*The Nonne Preestes Tale.*—*The Friar's Tale.*—*The Summoner's Tale.*—*The Canon Yeoman's Tale.*—*Sir Thopas.*—*The House of Fame.*—Satire in the minor poems of Chaucer.—Chaucer's unique qualities as a satirist.—His isolated position.

The Vision of Piers the Plowman exercised an immense popular influence that resulted in the adaptation of its name to very different and far inferior productions.[1] Among other imitations, so-called, is *Pierce the Plowman's Crede,*[2] which was written about 1394, fifteen years after the final text of Langland's poem. The imitation is confined mainly to title and metre, but includes also a certain similarity of subject-matter. Though less effective and elaborate, it is the same expression of the common feeling and the same appeal, in turn, to the popular sentiment. In homely speech, a simple countryman describes his efforts to find some truly spiritual man who can teach him his Creed. The theological knowledge at this time demanded of a layman was extremely simple and clearly defined. A knowledge of Creed, Pater Noster, Ave Mary,

[1] *How the Plowman learned his Pater Noster* (*Reliquiæ Antiquæ,* ed. Wright, Vol. I, p. 43) is a humorous *fabliau* without any relation to the *Vision.*

[2] Ed. Skeat, E. E. T. S., Vol. 30.

and Commandments, was indeed imperative; but any further knowledge was resented by the Church.

"May Christ speed this beginning," says the Plowman; "I have learned my Pater Noster and Ave Mary, but not yet my Creed. I seek some good man to teach it me. Many have I questioned diligently, but they are as ignorant as I. First of all, sought I the friars. I went in turn to the Franciscans, the Dominicans, the Carmelites, and the Austin Friars; but all they did was to abuse one another. They knew nothing of religion, and evidently the truth was not in them. Because I had no money, they called me a fool, and bade me go my way. At last I found a poor ploughman and told my trouble. 'Trust not the friars,' said he; 'the devil founded them. They are the kindred of Cain, hypocrites who make great display, but whose father is Satan. They persecuted Wyckliffe, have forgotten the precepts of Christ—nay, not a single one of the Beatitudes do they exemplify. The monks are but little better.' 'Pierce,' I begged, 'tell me thy Creed.' 'Believe on God, his Son, the Holy Ghost, the Church'—and so he taught me."

In *Pierce the Plowman's Crede,* the satire is exclusively religious and the attack is against the friars alone. The simple irony of the tone is not ineffective, though towards its close the poem grows seriously didactic. The extreme realism of its descriptions, which would seem to preclude much exaggeration, indicate a minimum of the "satirical commonplace." Such an attack on the four mendicant orders is all the more bitter in that the friars, having begun as actual beggars, appealing to the people at large, and living entirely on alms, had now achieved wealth and vast influence. Yet still they maintained the fiction of mendicancy—an arrant kind of fraud that provoked the indignation of the moralist and invited the attack of the satirist of the period.

The plowman of Langland, the honest, hard-working peasant, is here again—in *Pierce the Plowman's Crede*—the type of the truly spiritual man. In this conception there is something strangely incongruous at this time of the Peasant Revolt. The latter was a political rebellion, aroused by long oppression on the part of the nobility and of certain monasteries, and precipitated by intolerable taxation. It was far from being a religious crusade, and could not have afforded a very favorable idea of the spirituality of men who brutally murdered the Prior of St. Edmundsbury, the Archbishop of Canterbury, and the Lord Chief Justice of England. But it should have impressed upon the upper classes some conception of the spiritual needs of the people. However sympathetic and ideally true this exaltation of the peasant from the religious standpoint, at this era it must have seemed to the aristocrat peculiarly ironical.

During the early years of Richard the Second's unhappy reign, there were growing two quite distinct, but somewhat analogous, movements; one political, which finally led to the Peasants' Revolt; the other ecclesiastical, which resulted in the religious agitation of the Lollards. Since the early part of the century, that spirit which broke out in the violent attack made by the villeins on the Abbey of St. Edmundsbury in 1327 had been fed by continued oppression on the part of the upper classes and by the heavy tax burdens resulting from the unfortunate foreign ventures following the Peace of Bretigny in 1360; and had been encouraged by the unjust and totally unreasonable Statute of Laborers, which flew in the face of every economic law. All these causes, together with the peasants' increased realization of power after the depopulation caused by successive ravages of the plague, operated in producing that terrible uprising among the Kent and Essex people in 1381 known as "Wat Tyler's Rebellion."

If the peasant class was led by these events of the summer of 1381 to produce any political verse beyond John Ball's doggerel rhymes, such verse has not been preserved any more than the songs of the French *Jacquerie* in the same century.[3] The

[3] See Lenient, Ch. XIII. The rise of the French peasants about 1100 A. D. survives in the song of the peasants in Wace's *Roman de Rou:*

"Nos sumes homes cum il sunt,
Tels membres avum cum il unt,
Et altresi granz cors avum,
Et altretant sofrir poum." (See Lenient, pp. 11 and 12.)

conservative side, however, is represented by two surviving poems, which ring with indignation against the presumption of the peasantry. Both writers, though utterly opposed to the rebellion and out of sympathy with the lower classes, yet admit that the kingdom is in a deplorable condition. The first poem, in a kind of doggerel verse of alternate English and Latin lines, asserts that the poll-tax was at the bottom of the trouble.[4] The second poem is a mere lamentation over the state of the kingdom and the death of the good prelate Sudbury, who lost his life in the struggle.

Probably belonging to this period, and connected with the rebellion, is a *Satire on the Men of Stockton*,[5] written by some monk addressing himself in leonine verse against the serfs of his monastery at Stockton. They have risen against their masters, but have lost their case in the law-courts. The writer naturally rejoices over their defeat, but his Satire clearly shows the terrific and widespread struggle between the peasantry and the land owners of the fourteenth century. Its various allusions to " Allan " and " Robert " and " William " perhaps refer to quite imaginary persons. The burlesque of the Council held by the leaders, and their subsequent defeat, reminds us somewhat of the Lollard poem on the famous Council of London.[6]

It was soon after the Peasants' Revolt, and inspired by that event, that Gower produced his sombre and elaborate Latin poem, *Vox Clamantis*.[7] Gower is thoroughly a didactic poet, and the present poem, though mainly destructive in its criticism, is often didactic too. Absolutely devoid of humor, it employs argument rather than invective to enforce its moral, and though occasioned by specific circumstances, is but very general in its criticism. The *Vox Clamantis*, in short, all through its ten thousand morally admirable—and fatiguing—verses manifests the same spirit that shows itself in English

[4] *Political Poems*, I, 224.

[5] Wright's title; see *Anecdota Literaria*, pp. 49–51.

[6] See *infra*, p. 87.

[7] For this and other of Gower's poems treated here, see *The Works of John Gower*, ed. Macaulay, 4 vol., Oxford, 1899–1902.

didactic poetry throughout its history—in that of Wither, for instance, in a later age. Gower, with country seats in both Kent and Essex, is in the very midst of the rebellion. But his sympathies are far from being with the rebels. Quite the contrary. He is something of a courtier, much more of a moralist; stands aside from the course of events, reflects, and finally delivers himself of this treatise on the condition of the State. Very much of the English character is in the poem. The tendency to analyze, to draw a moral, to instruct, as well as the interest in public affairs and the daring utterance, are characteristic of the race as well as of the man.

Gower sees in the recent rebellion the effect of certain causes into which he purposes to inquire. A description of the revolt under an allegorical guise, in which the peasants are likened to wild beasts, is but an occasion for an elaborate inquiry into its sources. The poet reaches the conclusion that the whole calamity is a visitation from God for the sins of the country. The subject-matter for criticism is now shifted to the immoralities of the various classes of society. The idea that chance rules the destinies of men is argued out of existence, to the poet's satisfaction, and replaced by the demonstration that man's free-will alone orders his destiny. At great length, Gower inveighs against the vices of the clergy. The complaints are conventional, but strongly urged. They are the charges that began in the twelfth century and have since furnished inexhaustible food for satire. Gower is implacably stern, and holds the clergy, as the supposed spiritual guides and examplars of the people, accountable for the nation's immorality. If the shepherd be false, he cries, how can the sheep be true? "The hungry sheep look up and are not fed." He deals at length with the cloistered clergy, the monks, and also the friars; ending with a reference to Wireker's "Novus Ordo Burnelli"; and a contention that the "Order of the Ass" is now the dominant one. After the clergy have been sufficiently reproved, the soldier, the serf, the merchant, the lawyer, and the officers of the law, are treated in turn, according to the methods of the now conventional "class satire." Each class is weighed and found wanting; but Gower is not without hope that the country may be redeemed by a moral purgation. The *Vox Clamantis* is so largely a compilation from Ovid, Alexander Neckham, and Nigellus Wireker,[8] that one wonders how far it may be trusted as a picture and criticism of contemporary life.

Gower's *Tripartite Chronicle,* a supplement to the *Vox Clamantis,* written after the accession of Henry IV, is in leonine hexameters, and divided into three parts. Part I.—*Human Work*—is a narrative of the events of 1387–1388, in which Richard II figures as the villain; Gloucester (the Swan), Arundel (the horse), and Warwick (the bear), as the heroes. Part II.—*Hellish Work*—details the eight following years of Richard's miserable reign and the tragic fate of the three great dukes; while Part III.—*Work in Christ*—narrates the coming of Henry Bolinbroke and the downfall and wretched end of Richard. Although sixteen years intervened between the composition of *Vox Clamantis* and of its sequel, the two are written in an identical spirit. But the later poem, though largely and fearlessly personal, loses in dignity as a polemic in that it was written after the conditions it arraigns had ceased to exist.

But apart from this more or less direct expression in verse, the Peasants' Revolt holds another interest for us depending on its connection, so the opponents of Lollardry asserted, with the ecclesiastical movement led by Wycliffe. For the time being this movement was equally unsuccessful, but in the end it contributed to the religious emancipation of the kingdom.

The growing national sense in England, intensified by Edward the Third's foreign victories, further increased that resentment against papal domination which had been accumulating for at least two centuries. Wycliffe voiced this common feeling and also the old complaint of the State against the wealth of the Church, which he deprecated not as a political but as a religious evil. At first John of Gaunt, for reasons of his own, lent his active support to Wyckliffe personally, until the great schoolman, advancing far beyond his original

[8] See *The Works of John Gower,* ed. Macaulay, Vol. 4, Introduction.

position, uttered his heresy against transubstantiation, and stood heroically alone. Wycliffe's itinerant preachers, later very generally distributed over the country, vigorously preached greater purity of life among the clergy and the spiritual benefits arising from clerical poverty; and thus gained for the new movement a large and rapidly increasing following among the people. Alarmed by the vigor of the heretical sect, the Church began those active measures for its suppression which took shape at first in the attempted trial of Wyckliffe by the Archbishop of Canterbury and that energetic bigot, Courtenay, Bishop of London, at Westminster, in 1377. The riot that followed the attempt postponed the affair, and meanwhile occurred the Peasants' Revolt, which afforded an excellent opportunity for clergy of the anti-Wycliffite party to cast additional slurs upon the Reformer and his followers, by asserting that Lollardry had been at the bottom of the recent uprising; that John Ball was a Lollard; and Wycliffe a promoter of sedition, privy conspiracy, and rebellion.

It was in 1381 that the first protest in verse appeared, in some six hundred lines of academic Latin, the work of a conservative friar.[9] Heretofore religious satire had come from the advocates of reform against the dominant ecclesiastical bodies. Now it comes from a member of one of those bodies against a religious sect, a species of the satire that is to continue for three centuries and over—the strife between Catholic and Protestant, High Churchman and Puritan, Episcopalian and Dissenter, from the fourteenth through the eighteenth century.

"Lord, root out from Thy garden these noxious tares, the Lollards!" prays the orthodox friar. "These Lollards, outwardly meek, within are ravening wolves, arousing strife among the clergy, destroying the peace of the kingdom—":

"Johannes Balle hoc docuit,
Quando morti succubuit
Propter suam nequitiam.
Quod quidem nidus tenuit
Pullos pravos, et aluit

[9] *Political Poems*, I, 231.

In regni ignominiam.
Monstrans Wycleffe familiam,
  Causam brigae primariam,
Quae totum regnum terruit.
  Praebens experientiam
Quam gravidam stultitiam
  Haec secta vulgus inbuit."[10]

The various heresies of the Lollards are enumerated, and it incidentally appears that our satirist's ire is chiefly aroused by the bitterness, as he alleges, of their slanderous attacks upon the friars! This union of personal and religious invective gains its vitality and interest from its source of inspiration in burning contemporary issues. It represents the orthodox party, but has its counterpart in favor of the Lollards in a Latin poem on the Council of London, written probably in the year following that event.[11]

In May, 1382, an ecclesiastical council, presided over by Courtenay, now Archbishop of Canterbury, met in London to pronounce judgment on the various heresies of the Wycliffites. A terrible earthquake that occurred on the day of assembly was said by the Lollards to announce the wrath of God on the Prelates and persecutors; but Courtenay interpreted it with an opposite signification, and coolly pursued his course amid the terror of his colleagues. At this time one of the now chronic recurrences of the plague was thinning the population, and floods in the previous December had wrought widespread havoc. All these circumstances are utilized by our Lollard poem, which begins with a lugubrious wail over the condition of England. "Pestilence, earthquake, wind, and flood, have lately attested the anger of God at the wickedness of the people. The nation is desperately depraved, for the impiety of prelates, monks, and friars, has vitiated the whole kingdom. That all this is true of the Benedictines, also, I know by ex-

[10] "This fact John Ball taught us before he died for his iniquity; because that nest held bad chickens and nourished them for the degradation of the country, showing that the brood of Wycliffe was the first cause of the rebellion that terrified the whole kingdom, giving evidence with what miserable folly this sect hath imbued the vulgar."

[11] *Monumenta Franciscana,* Vol. 1, p. 591 f; *Political Poems,* 1, 253.

perience; for I spent my novitiate among them, but escaped in time. Wycliffe has attacked these iniquities, and is therefore persecuted." The writer now passes into a burlesque account of the London council[12] assembled to try the heretics. Wycliffe, being ill, was represented by his chief lieutenant, Nicholas of Hereford.

"John Welles opened fire upon the Lollards in a pompous, senseless speech, which Nicholas of Hereford confuted with ease," says the poem. "But the attack was continued by Goydoun, a layman clothed like a monk, and by Crophorne, with his worthless jargon. After the monks, began the friars. A Franciscan named Merton chattered like a raven, and Whoppelode, a famous liar, talked to no purpose"—and so on, through the remainder of the controversy, in which the Lollards are, of course, finally triumphant. The charges so elaborately urged against the clergy are in substance those brought by previous satire of this type, but the remarkable feature of the poem is the change of tone from invective to burlesque when the writer describes the ecclesiastical council.

This burlesque is interesting as the satirical picture of an actual event, and as, in a measure, a personal Satire on the various anti-Wycliffite clergy. There is a distinct gain, too, in the humor of the latter part, though the whole is inferior in this respect to a contemporary English song against the friars. The latter was written probably by some Lollard; for at this time the friars were the especial objects of Lollard attack.[13] The tone of this song is at first ironical, finally *directly* satirical, yet throughout of considerable humor. "Friars are given to heavy penance," cries the ironical Lollard; "one may see as much in their appearance. I have lived forty years, and ne'er saw I fatter men. Shameful it is that they should be compelled to seek their bread from house to house—these poor mendicants! With them they carry articles to please the women; let the goodman beware! Clever traders they are and drive a hard bargain, but they know not virtue.

[12] Cf. p. 83, *supra*.

[13] *Monumenta Franciscana*, 1, 601 f.; *Political Poems*, 1, 263.

Verily, for a pair of shoes, they will absolve a man for the murder of all his kindred. Hell is so filled with friars that soon no room will be left for other people":

> "Ful wysely can thai preche and say;
> But as thai preche no thing do thai.
> I was a frere ful many a day,
> Therefor the sothe I wate.
> Bot when I sawe that thair lyvyng
> Acordyd not to thair prechyng,
> Of I cast my frer clothing,
> And wyghtly went my gate.
> Other leve ne toke I none,
> fro ham when I went,
> Bot toke ham to the devel ychone,
> the priour and the covent."

Both in form and in tone this *Song against the Friars* is perhaps the most popular piece of satirical poetry we have yet considered. But we find no such humor in that far more elaborate religious poem, *The Complaint of the Plowman,* which followed perhaps in 1394, and is entirely argumentative and didactic.[14] This earnest religious poem was written possibly by the author of *Pierce the Plowman's Crede.* Though its sober allegory is in no wise satirical, its contemporary significance is great.

The writer professes neutrality towards the two religious parties. He overhears in a wood a dispute between two birds, a griffon[15] and a pelican; the first, the advocate of the Romish church, the second, its opponent. The pelican brings the conventional charges against the clergy, and contrasts with these conditions the humility and poverty of Christ. Saint Peter held the key of heaven and hell, but—

> "Peter was never so great a fole
> To leave his key with such a lorell,
> Or take such cursed soch a tole,
> He was advised no thing well.
> I trowe they have the key of hell;
> Their master is of that place marshall;

[14] *Political Poems,* I, 304–46.

[15] Not the mythical creature, but the vulture.

For there they dressen hem to dwel,
And with false Lucifer there to fall."

Yet such men are permitted to preach. The griffon inquires the pelican's opinion of the secular clergy. "They are haughty, sensual, selfish, extortionate," replies the pelican. "What of their works?" asks the griffon; and he is told they have wandered far from the pathway trod by their Master. "As for the friars, they are exposed in *Pierce the Plowman's Crede,*" says the pelican. The griffon now retorts with an angry argument in defense of the clergy, and becomes more and more infuriated at the pelican's replies. This exchange of argument continues through almost a thousand lines, and is anything but exhilarating reading. Finally the griffon flies away, to return soon with an army of birds of prey, and the pelican retreats to seek the aid of the phoenix, who appears after a season and utterly routs the griffon and his allies.

Both in use of the vernacular and in sober argumentative tone, the tradition of *The Complaint of the Plowman* is continued in the long Lollard poetical tract, *Jack Upland,* which, with the reply thereto by an author styling himself Daw Topias, stretches out through almost four thousand short alliterative lines.[16] Henry the Fourth's accession to the throne in 1399 brought increased danger of persecution to the Lollards; and this danger expressed itself in the terrible Statute "De Haeretico Comburendo," of 1401, which ordained the burning of any convicted of heresy by the ecclesiastical courts. Such extreme measures, though not preventing the growth of the new sect, rendered the Lollards more secret and circumspect in circulating their propaganda. In this very year was indited, it may be by one of Wycliffe's itinerant preachers, this violent diatribe against the friars, *Jack Upland.* The author begins:

"I, Jacke Upland, make my mone to very God,
and to all true in Christ,
that antichrist and his disciples,
by colour of holines,
walking and deceiving Christs church
by many false figures—

[16] *Political Poems,* 2, 16–114.

do infest this land with abominable vices. The church of Rome is antichrist, and the worst of its sects is that of the *friars*!" Then follows a long series of charges, accusing the friars of every imaginable impiety. Jack Upland has departed very far from his master Wycliffe's abstruse scholastic method of reasoning, but he applies the foundation of his master's doctrine, common-sense. His argument is one to appeal to the most illiterate:

> "Go now forth, and fraine your clerks,
> and ground ye you in God's law,
> and when he han assoiled me
> that I have said sadly,
> in Truth I shall soile thee
> of thine orders,
> and save thee to heaven."

To this lengthy arraignment a friar, calling himself Daw Topias, replies with far more vindictiveness and far less reason, but, most significantly, meets the reformers on their own ground: he uses English and simple speech, and appeals to the people. Charges are brought against Wycliffe and his followers, the Lollard's various accusations are met in some fashion; and to all of this Jack Upland again replies in the same uncouth strain.

Though wholly an argumentative poem, quite devoid of humor, this long religious tract is interesting for its use of the vernacular, its popular tone, and its treatment of contemporary subject-matter. But it is in every respect less interesting than the two last echoes of the Lollard heresy in verse, which were evoked, one by the first defection, the other by the execution, in 1417, of Sir John Oldcastle—the latter an event that marked the culmination of Lollard persecution under Henry V.

The first of these two poems, by the poet Occleve,[17] was written probably in 1415, and reads like an expostulation, addressed

[17] It seems best to conclude just here the treatment of the satire on Oldcastle, though we are thereby carried perhaps thirty years beyond our present period. This explains the introduction of Occleve's poem before the last mention of Gower.

to Oldcastle by an apparently friendly person, concerning the knight's heretical opinions.[18] Oldcastle is besought to repent, renounce these devil's doctrines, and return to the bosom of the church. Let him not argue about matters of faith. That is not our business. The poet passes on to an enumeration of the Lollard doctrines and an attempted refutation of them, with incidental invective against the heretics, continuing through many stanzas; ending in a final appeal to this arch heretic to turn and repent him of his damnable heresy.

But Oldcastle was deaf to Occleve's friendly warning. He persisted in his bold but fruitless resistance, and finally met the martyr's death in 1417. It is perhaps in the following year that some ardent opponent of heresy takes this tragedy as a text for a bitter diatribe against Lollardry, and so writes the sequel to Occleve's more kindly poem of three years before.[19] The author makes frequent allusions to Oldcastle, on whose name he puns through several stanzas with more labor than wit:

> "Hit is unkyndly for a knight,
> That shuld a kynges castel kepe,
> To bable the bibel day and night,
> In restyng tyme when he shuld slepe,
> And carfoly awey to crepe,
> For alle the chief of chivalrie,
> Wel aught hym to waile and wepe,
> That suyche lust hath in lollardie."—

and so on, through nineteen stanzas, in the characteristically bitter tone of religious controversy in all ages.

III

Richard's reign was productive of still another species of pseudo-satirical verse: that general lament which has become conventional and which may safely be supposed to embody the largest amount of "satirical commonplace." We have now one of these jeremiads over the melancholy times

[18] *Hoccleve's Minor Poems,* ed. Furnivall, E. E. T. S., Ex. Ser., 61, p. 8.

[19] *Ancient Songs and Ballads,* ed. Ritson, Vol. I, p. 121; *Political Poems,* 2, 243.

written in the same peculiar English-Latin verse used in the ballad on the Peasants' Revolt:[20]

"Syngyn y wolde, but, alas!
descendunt prospera grata;
Englond sum tyme was
regnorum gemma vocata;
Of manhood the flowre
ibi quondam floruit omnis;
Now gon ys that honowr,
traduntur talia somnis."[21]

Somewhat more vital than this trite lament, in so far as they were inspired by specific events, are two short poems, one in English, on the earthquake of 1382;[22] the other in Latin, on the pestilence of 1391.[23] Both are equally didactic, looking upon these calamities as the vengeance of God. The rising of the "Commons," pestilence, earthquake, the degradation of the Church are not themes that readily lend themselves to a humorous treatment; hence it is not surprising to find both the Latin and the English poem heavy and severe.

But allowing for inevitable exaggeration and customary lament, there was ample excuse for the clerics' wail over the condition of the Church, which was as bad as it had ever been, and the corruption of society, whose follies were encouraged by a luxurious court. The king had now freed himself from all restraint, and was making enemies of both commons and nobility alike. Toward the close of the reign, when these conditions had grown worse, we are presented with another diatribe against popular vices. This is a Latin poem of three hundred elegiac lines—a form well chosen, for an elegy it is—by the learned and pessimistic poet of the *Vox Clamantis,* "the moral Gower." The poem has for name and for subject-matter "the manifold pestilence of vices, by which our land was especially visited during the reign of Richard II"; and declares it the poet's duty to speak out in times of national

[20] See *supra,* p. 83.
[21] *Political Poems,* I, 270.
[22] *Ibid.,* I, 250; *Archæologia,* Vol. 18, p. 26.
[23] *Political Poems,* I, 279.

danger. Gower divides his poem into several sections and devotes each of them to the reprehension of a particular vice. Such a method is ominous of deadly dullness at the outset. The brilliant illustrative method of the classical satirists,[24] and the less interesting but still far from ineffective method of personification employed by Langland,[25] are both disdained. Gower prefers the orderly, dry, generalized attack on utter abstractions.

It is difficult to imagine anything more dreary, more remote from actual life, or less calculated to affect in the slightest degree the society which it arraigns. The same criticism applies without modification to a second Latin poem, in hexameter verse, written by Gower at about the same period—*The Search for Light.* Here the moralist uses a different method, and instead of inveighing against abstractions, attacks, in equally characteristic medieval fashion, the various social classes, from the Court of Rome to the public plunderer. The poet seeks in vain for light at Rome or in the Church at large, which is ruled by simony. Monks and secular clergy alike are dwelling in utter darkness. Kings and nobles, who trust only the arm of flesh, cannot furnish light; or merchants, whom usury has corrupted; or lawyers, who are ruled by bribery.

So also in the prologue to his *Confessio Amantis* Gower does not fail to moralize over and lament the deplorable condition of the country, the loss of the old virtues, and the universal prevalence of vices that have caused

> "This newé sect of Lollardie,
> And also many an heresie."

And the poet proceeds in the body of his voluminous treatise to "satirize" the deadly sins by the somewhat novel fashion of telling a story to illustrate each one of the seven.

Apart from its prologue, however, the subject-matter of the *Confessio Amantis* has no direct relation to its times. It remained for the author of *The Vision of Piers the Plowman*

[24] See *supra*, p. 15 f.; and cf. p. 162 f., *infra*.
[25] See *supra*, p. 73.

to review the social and political conditions of Richard's reign and sum them all up in that terrible indictment against royal maladministration which Professor Skeat calls *Richard the Redeless.*[26] In the same alliterative measure of his earlier poem, in somewhat the same allegorical style, Langland,[27] the genuine censor of society, voices the protest of the people against the corruptions of the king's court and reign, welcomes the popular favorite, Bolingbroke, and directly rebukes the redeless Richard for his misdeeds:

While King Richard is warring in Ireland, strange tidings have reached the poet in Bristol. They say that Henry of Bolingbroke has entered England by the east. The poet is troubled, for he has hitherto been loyal to the redeless king, and has hoped that he would amend his youthful faults. He now writes this treatise to teach men the lesson of Richard's reign, the sad results of wilfulness. The poet passes into an exhaustive, sober, and straightforward account of the untoward measures of Richard's whole administration. The loyalty of his subjects has been estranged. The king has despoiled the nation in order to enrich a few favorites. Richard came to the crown under most auspicious conditions, but by his own misconduct he has deliberately destroyed himself. His counsellors were foolish and selfish young men, and through favoritism he lost the heart of his people. The Eagle, Henry of Bolingbroke, spreads his wings to shelter the nation. The Eagle will destroy the King's evil favorites, such as Bushey, Scrope, and Greene, who are thus alluded to:

> "Thus baterid this bred on *busshes* abouȝte,
> And gaderid gomes on *grene* ther as they walkyed,
> That all the schroff and *schroup* sondrid ffrom other."

We have next a parable of the Hart and the Adder, bringing in the Horse (Arundel), the Bear (Warwick), and the Swan (Gloucester). The inference seems to be that in the ruin of

[26] *Piers the Plowman and Richard the Redeless, ed. Skeat,* 2 vols., 1886; under the name of *Alliterative Poem on the Deposition of King Richard II,* ed. Wright, Cam. Soc. Pub., Vol. 3; *Political Poems,* 1, 368.

[27] I here follow Professor Skeat's attribution of the authorship to "William Langland." The question is unsettled.

these three noblemen Richard has destroyed his best friends. Another parable tells us how, when the partridge leaves her eggs, another sits on them; but the young birds, if ill-nourished, remember the voice of their mother. So the nestlings know the voice of the Eagle, Bolingbroke, though he has been long absent from them, and they tell him of the woes of Richard's two and twenty years. Then the other fowls, heavy for hurt of the Horse (Arundel), look to the eagle for leadership. Now the poet leaves this allegorical strain, to dwell severely on the luxury of the court, foolish fashions in dress, and Richard's extravagance with money gained from oppression of the poor. The parliament has been degraded into the instrument of the king's will, he cries, and the voice of the people has been silenced.

Richard the Redeless, the protest of one speaking for the people, forms a link between such criticism as Gower's, which is the meditation of a thoughtful scholar, and that thoroughly popular satire on these same circumstances and events which sprang directly from the people themselves. As an illustration of the last-named type, the remarkable ballad on King Richard's ministers is as truly popular a production as could be desired, and would seem to indicate that a large body of such verse was once in existence. As we have seen from *Richard the Redeless,* the king, by his headstrong violence, extravagance, and even cruelty, had been rapidly alienating the sympathy of Nobility and of Commons, and finally of the people at large. The Earl of Warwick (the Bear), his former Councillor, had been exiled; the Earl of Arundel (the Horse), condemned and executed in a single day; the Duke of Gloucester (the Swan), Richard's uncle, imprisoned in Calais, where he suddenly died,—made away with, it was openly asserted, through the connivance of the king. Moreover, Richard surrounded himself with a set of unscrupulous favorites, who managed the court to suit themselves and were very justly the objects of deep and widespread popular hatred. In 1399, just before Richard's reign came to an end, when Henry of Bolingbroke had already landed in England and was soon to execute summary vengeance on the royal favorites, there sprang from some anonymous source this very popular ballad, to do good work, doubtless, for the Lancastrian cause:[28]

> "There is a *busch* that is forgrowe;
> Crop hit welle, and hold hit lowe,
> or elles hit wolle be wilde.
> The long gras that is so *grene,*
> Hit must be mowe, and raked clene;
> forgrowen hit hath the fellde."

The fates of Gloucester, Arundel, and Warwick, the Swan, the Horse, and the Bear, respectively, are referred to regretfully. The Eagle, Lancaster, is welcomed: he will destroy the *bush,* the *bag,* the *green* rank grass.

In this we have a union of personal and political satire quite new to English literature. Though in a crude way, the people are at last learning to express themselves about political affairs. That this feeling against the favorites is not, however, confined to one class, is manifest in a Latin poem written on the expected arrival of the new ruler.[29] Some general complaints against the tyranny of the nobles, the arrogance of the court, and the oppression of the people, end in a stanza that singles out Scrope, Earl of Wiltshire, Bagot, and Vere, for especial condemnation. These men are obnoxious not only to the body of the people but to the clerical classes also:

> "Fraus latet illorum propter thesaurum,
> *Scrope, Bagge, Ver, Dumus,* tormentorum parat humus
> Damnarunt forti justorum corpora morti,
> Sanguis qui quorum vindicta clamat eorum."[30]

This poem closes the formally satirical poetry of Richard's reign—satire more extensive by far both in quantity and in

[28] *Political Poems,* I, 363 f.

[29] *Ibid.,* I, 366 f.

[30] This Latin is so execrable that it may be well to attempt some sort of translation: "Their fraud for the sake of money lies hidden, but the grave of the tormentors is being prepared (?). They have condemned the bodies of the just to a terrible death, and the blood of these cries out for vengeance."

range than that of any other period previous to the English Renaissance. The great Peasant Revolt, pestilence, earthquake, heresy, royal follies, in addition to the persistent immorality of the clergy, furnished such a variety of subject-matter for satirical treatment as perhaps no other reign before or since has ever known.

IV

Leaving far behind the moral platitudes of Gower, the stern diatribes of Langland, the lamentations of clerks, and the ballads of the people, we pass for a time into the more genial atmosphere of Chaucer's astonishing pictures of life.[31] The satire of the *Canterbury Tales* is chiefly incidental, and the subject-matter utilized is mainly conventional, but the method is something astoundingly new and effective. There is no trace of the moral indignation of Langland, nothing of the didactic tendency of Gower; no voice of the people speaks here, no clerk laments in platitudes the decadence of the age. The satire of Chaucer is not that of a reformer; hence no polemic note is sounded. He has no cause to gain, no lesson to teach, no prophesy to cry aloud in the streets; hence the utter absence of the qualities that color and universally characterize the satirical productions of his contemporaries. Chaucer's satire is, with the chief exception of *Sir Thopas,* mainly social;[32] and so far from excluding and concealing the personality of its author, as has heretofore been the case in English satirical poetry, it depends as much on the satirist's individuality as does the satire of Horace and of Pope.[33] The gulf separating Chaucer from Langland and the popular satire of his period is that between the reformer, who is but incidentally a man of letters, and the man of letters who is but incidentally, and even then unconsciously, a reformer. The gulf separating Chaucer from such a moralizer as Gower is that between the true satirist and the merely didactic poet. Those social, political, and religious phenomena, that moved

[31] *The Complete Works of Chaucer,* ed. Skeat, 6 vols., Oxford, 1894.
[32] See *supra,* p. 32 f.
[33] *Ibid.,* p. 15 f.

some of his contemporaries to scorn or to tears, affected Chaucer in a very different way. As a literary man, he looks upon the world from a point of view far removed from that of these ardent souls who felt inspired to reform the universe. He selects his material with care, and uses it for purely literary purposes. He perceives the evils that move others to protest, but, feel these inconsistencies keenly as he may, in the main he is moved not to tears and indignation, but to jest and laughter; for, if not a moral reformer, he possesses an inestimable gift almost unknown to his contemporaries—a bountiful sense of humor. His object, then, is to mirror the life of his time, to show men and women as they are, not to make them better. Society has its faults, but the world is a fairly good world for all reasonable people; it is comfortable; it is certainly amusing.

In the incidental satire of the General Prologue, the interludes, and here and there through the *Tales,* Chaucer largely utilizes subject-matter rendered quite conventional by long use. The life of the clergy, the impositions of pardoners, the avarice and licentiousness of friars, the rascality of summoners—in all this there is nothing new. But the method is new —a method and a lightness of touch that certainly were not an English inheritance, but that might possibly be learned abroad in France and Italy; a humor and wit quite unsurpassable, which could not be learned anywhere and were just as certainly no more an English inheritance than the method, but were innate in Chaucer himself. This satirist brings no general abstract charges against the religious orders,[34] but uses the descriptive and dramatic method of Horace, whereby the type, and not merely the type, but the individual monk, friar, pardoner, summoner, Wife of Bath, and others of the wonderful motley crew, actually live before the reader. With the highest art of the satirist, Chaucer either makes his characters reveal themselves, or, where he merely describes them, describes them with humor and wit inimitable.

In his satire, Chaucer employs two different methods: one,

[34] Such as had been the stock in trade of preceding satire.

the direct,[35] the descriptive, illustrated chiefly by the General Prologue, occasionally by the minor prologues; the other, the indirect or dramatic,[36] illustrated by the *Tales.* In the minor prologues and interludes, while both methods are combined, the indirect predominates. Hence, if we here distinguish between the satire of the General Prologue and that of the minor prologues and the *Tales,* it is not because the two differ materially in subject-matter, but because the satirical method of the former is merely descriptive, while that of the latter is mainly dramatic.

Almost three hundred and fifty of the eight hundred and fifty-eight lines of the General Prologue are more or less satirical. The pictures of the ecclesiastical types—the Monk, the Friar, the Pardoner, and the Summoner; and of the lay types,—the Reve, the Manciple, the Doctor, the Miller, and the Wife of Bath, are portrayed by the descriptive method; yet the satire is so insidious, so permeated with laughter, that the result has the effect of a dramatic rather than of a personal expression. Perhaps no man of the time was more alive to ecclesiastical abuses, more sensible of the degradation of the clergy, than was Chaucer. But his method of criticism was a world removed from that of a Langland or of a Gower. Centuries before, Nigellus Wireker, as may be remembered, had laid it down as his theory of satire that "more diseases may be cured by unguents than by caustic." [37] And Chaucer being perhaps a satirist of like spirit to that of the humorous precentor of Canterbury, implicitly voices the same theory.

Chaucer's monk, an admirable picture, we may take as the contemporary monastic type. He follows the hounds, for

> "What sholde he studie, and make him-selven wood,
> Upon a book in cloistre alwey to poure?"

He enjoyed the good things in life, as was evidenced by the fact that

> "He was a lord ful fat and in good point"—
> "He was nat pale as a for-pyned goost."

[35] See *supra,* p. 14 f.
[36] *Ibid.,* p. 18 f.
[37] *Ibid.,* p. 43.

The friar, too, as here portrayed, justifies the bitter reproaches heaped upon him by other satirists of the period; the character is just the same. But how different the method of attack! When the severe arraignments of Chaucer's contemporaries shall have been forgotten, Chaucer's own most exquisite irony, his apparent sympathy with the friar's point of view, will still hold the type up to an undying contempt. It had originally been the duty of the various orders of friars to minister to the needy and nurse the sick; but, with growing wealth and prestige, the old ideal had given place to an ideal of worldly ease and position:

> " For un-to swich a worthy man as he
> Acorded nat, as by his facultee,
> To have with seke lazars aqueyntaunce.
> It is nat honest, it may not avaunce
> For to delen with no swich poraille."

The Pardoner is he of the olden time, but described with a richness of humor that makes him a new personage. Here the satire is more obvious:

> " He hadde a croys of latoun, ful of stones,
> And in a glas he hadde pigges bones."—

> " And thus, with feyned flaterye and Iapes,
> He made the person and the peple his apes."

This is one of the four great pictures of the Pardoner in English satire. Over a century later, *Cock Lorell*[38] is to portray the type with unctuous humor, Heywood is to present the pardoner in dramatic form in his two interludes *The Four P's* and *The Pardoner and the Friar,*[39] and Lyndsay is to equal this portrait in his wonderful dramatic picture of *The Satire of the Three Estates.*[40]

Perhaps quite equal to Chaucer's Pardoner is his Summoner, who is represented by the same method and with the same half

[38] See *infra,* p. 178 f.
[39] *Ibid.,* p. 213.
[40] *Ibid.,* p. 207; cf. also the Pardoner in Bale's *Kyng Johan,* p. 216, *infra.*

sympathetic, half contemptuous humor. He is sensual, ignorant, repulsively ugly; but, says Chaucer,

> "He was a gentil harlot and a kinde."

That is sufficient; the Summoner has his good points: though Chaucer laughs, he does not utterly despise. It is no part of his satirical method to make his types—or rather characters—absolutely loathsome. The Summoner grows learned in his cups:

> "And whan that he wel dronken hadde the wyn,
> Than wolde he speke no word but Latyn.
> A fewe termes hadde he, two or three,
> That he had lerned out of som decree"—

In Chaucer's pictures of his lay characters, we find something new in material as well as in method. Langland had inveighed here and there against millers and reves, but nowhere in previous or contemporary English satire do we discover anything comparable to these elaborate pieces of characterization in the Prologue. The reve, or steward, is a sly knave, a thrifty thief, who, having gained his master's confidence, fleeces him *ad libitum:*

> "His lord wel coude he plesen subtilly,
> To yeve and lene him of his owne good"—

The Manciple is a knave of the same stripe. By his thrifty cunning he has fleeced "an heep of learned men." Even while laying bare the rascality of his rogues, Chaucer has to give a sly chuckle over their shrewdness and their deception of their over-trustful superiors. The Miller, too, is a calculating knave with a keen eye for business:

> "Wel coude he stelen corn, and tollen thryes;
> And yet he hadde a thombe of gold, pardee."

The doctor is a new character in English satire. While paying a certain tribute to his learning and gravity, the poet has to laugh at his avarice:

> "He kepte that he wan in pestilence.
> For gold in phisik is a cordial,
> Therefore he lovede gold in special,"

and remarks that "His studie was but little on the bibel"; which perhaps means that the doctor's whole thought was of his own material comfort and worldly gain. In a later age LaFontaine satirized the physician of his time under the guise of the wolf—deceitful and servile, a charlatan and a knave. Chaucer's physician is a personage of much greater dignity, and is far from being contemptible.

But the "Wife of Bath"! What picture in all medieval satire can stand beside this incomparable portraiture of a thrifty, industrious, calculating, vulgar, sensual woman of the lower middle class of Chaucer's England? This characterization is no mere conventional satire on woman,[41] but only on a certain type of woman. After detailing the industry and skill and churchly devotion of his Wife of Bath, the satirist ironically adds:

> "She was a worthy womman al hir lyve,
> Housbondes at chirch-dore she hadde fyve,
> Withouten other companye in youthe;
> But thereof nedeth nat to speke as nouthe."

So much for the satirical characterization in the Prologue. Here and there in the portraits of the Prioress and others are scattered satirical lines, but it does not appear that Chaucer was holding these characters up to ridicule. Apart from the General Prologue, we must search chiefly in the interludes, the *Tales,* and finally in *The House of Fame* for the poet's further contribution of satire.

The Pardoner appears again as a satirical type in the prologue and the conclusion of his own Tale. The prologue consists of sixty-seven, and the epilogue of about sixty, pentameter couplets. Together they form a Satire against cupidity—the pardoner's confession of his own frauds, his avarice, his hypocrisy. While the satire is in the dramatic method, the method

[41] Such as was to follow in such copiousness a century later; see "The Satire on Woman," *infra,* p. 175 f.

is here hardly natural: the Pardoner, one cannot help feeling, would scarcely so confess himself to a motley company some of whose members he must have looked upon as fair game for his tricks. The satirist here speaks really in *propria persona:*

"'Lordlings,' quod he, 'in chirches whan I preche,
I peyne me to han an hauteyn speche,
And ring it out as round as gooth a belle,
For I can al by rote that I telle.
My theme is alwey oon, and ever was—
"*Radix malorum est cupiditas.*"'"

"'And after that than telle I forth my tales,
Bulles of popes and of cardinales,
Of patriarkes, and bishoppes I shewe;
And in Latyn I speke a wordes fewe,
To saffron with my predicacioun,
And for to stire men to devocioun.
Than shewe I forth my longe cristal stones,
Y-crammed ful of cloutes and of bones;
Reliks been they, as wenen they echoon.'"

The elaborate prologue to the Wife of Bath's Tale, eight hundred and twenty-eight lines, is a Satire on a certain feminine type whose original suggestion lay in the old duenna who watches over Bel Acueil in the *Roman de la Rose.*[42] It is spoken by the wife herself, the same fleshly creature of the General Prologue, amorous, loud and crude, domineering, yet capable, domestic withal, and apparently quite above marital infidelity and treachery. By the highest satirical art, she is made, while detailing her conjugal experiences and giving her views —rather startling in their freedom—on love and matrimony, to exemplify in her own person, and unconsciously to satirize, feminine lechery, selfishness, and tyranny. No other such portrait exists in English satire; and other mere "satires against women" compared with this immortal picture become colorless and feeble.

And yet, after studying the wife's character as given in the

[42] See Lounsbury, *Studies in Chaucer,* Vol. 2, p. 526; Mead, *The Prologue of the Wife of Bath's Tale,* Pub. Mod. Lang. Ass. Am., Vol. 16, new ser., Vol. 9.

General Prologue, the prologue to her own tale, and, by implication, at least, in the *Tale* itself, one begins to wonder if, after all, Chaucer's picture is purely satirical. A suggestion of pathos, an undercurrent of sympathy on the part of the poet, in this marvelous piece of characterization, render the Wife a more complete personality than any merely satirical picture could ever be. It may be, too, that the Wife's prologue is, as has been suggested, a Satire against celibacy; for the poet puts into her mouth arguments irrefutable though often frankly animal. There is good sense in her talk. Throughout the whole picture, in short, Chaucer shows his sympathy with the Wife's point of view: he seems to see every side of her character, the ignoble as well as the admirable, the silly as well as the sensible.[43]

This satire, if satire it be, on a particular type of woman takes a more general range in the envoy to the Clerk's Tale. The Clerk has been discoursing on the patience of Griselda, and in his playful yet really satirical envoy, advises the wives of his time to make no attempt to emulate the admirable yet fatiguing patience of his heroine.

Chaucer, probably unconsciously, continues the Goliardic tradition when he attacks celibacy. An eminent Chaucerian critic sees in the prologue to the Wife of Bath's Tale simply a satire on celibacy.[44] However this may be, satire on celibacy frank and undisguised is certainly to be found in the interlude before the Monk's Tale. In "The Meerye wordes of the Hoost to the Monk," ll. 36–76, the host, with a mingling of humor, vulgarity, and common sense, expresses his opinion of the celibate state, and asserts that the monk is too fine a specimen of manhood to be celibate. The best-formed men, those very ones who should be fathers, the Church claims as her own.

> "Not only thou, but every mighty man,
> Thogh he were shorn ful hye upon his pan,
> Sholde have a wyf —."

[43] See the admirable analysis of the Wife's character given in Mr. R. K. Root's *The Poetry of Chaucer,* p. 231 f.

[44] See Lounsbury, 2, 522.

While treating the interludes and the minor prologues, it may be well to enter a *caveat* against the supposedly satirical character of the interlude following the Monk's Tale and of the *Tale* itself, a lengthy and often tedious, but occasionally beautiful and tender, narrative *de Casibus Virorum Illustrium.* The genre, of course, derives from Boccaccio. In the tale itself, wearisome as it often becomes, the serious and often elevated tone would tell heavily against Professor Lounsbury's assumption that the nature of the tale is parodic.[45] Furthermore, any genre has to reach its climax and enter its decline before the parody appears. Now the *de Casibus* genre was still very young,—Boccaccio's *De Casibus* was written between 1363 and 1373—and Chaucer's Tale is its first exemplar in England, while its long-continued and widespread popularity was not reached until the fifteenth century.[46] For these two reasons, stylistic and chronological, the *Tale* must be taken seriously, as it was by Chaucer's successors; and we are compelled, in order to sustain the parodic theory, to fall back upon the *Interlude.*

The Interlude, indeed, on the face of it—at least the speech of the Host—certainly seems satirical. The Monk is abruptly "stinted of his tale" by the protests of the Knight and the Host. The Knight wants no sad stories, but only those of "joie and great solas." The host approves the protest of the Knight. This "tragedy" cannot be amended by crying:

> "Sir Monk, na-more of this, so god yow blesse!
> Your tale anoyeth al this companye;
> Swich talking is nat worth a boterflye —."

Had it not been for the clinking of the monk's bugle-bells, the host would long since have slumbered through the "Tragedy"!

It looks difficult to dispose of this interlude. If supported by the *Tale* itself, we should instantly agree on its satirical intent. Yet it is possible that the poet adopted this informal close to what threatened to be a tedious narrative; the Knight

[45] See Lounsbury, 3, 332–4.

[46] For valuable suggestions concerning the intent of the Monk's Tale, I am indebted to Professor K. C. M. Sills, of Bowdoin College, who agrees with the view here given.

and the Host not representing two orders of society,[47] but merely the two individuals best fitted to protest against so dignified a personage as the monk. Chaucer himself was not opposed to "tragedy," as certain of his own works testify. It may be, as has been suggested, that Chaucer wrote these "tragedies" constituting the Monk's Tale long before he designed *The Canterbury Tales,* and now utilizes this old material in his new scheme,—voicing, in the comments of the Knight and of the Host, his own mature opinion of the literary badness of his early work.[48] According to this, the Monk's Tale itself is in no sense a burlesque, but entirely serious, and represents the serious side of the poet's nature. Chaucer's dramatic instinct asserts itself in the prologue. The poet here appears in two characters: his serious side is represented by the Knight, while his humorous side seeks outlet in the comments of the Host, who finds the Monk's tale both ridiculous and dull.[49]

When we look for a manifestation of the satirical spirit in the *Tales* themselves, we find that, while Chaucer may have been independent of satirical traditions in England, he was deeply indebted to the Continental *fabliau.* He did not create his plots, and, moreover, gained from his foreign sources much of his indirect satirical method. The satire of the General Prologue, the interludes, and minor prologues, is entirely Chaucer's own; but the subject-matter as well as much of the method and spirit of his *Tales* he owes to others, despite the local coloring and the Chaucerian touch.

It is customary to speak of the *fabliau* as a satirical genre, with the easy incorrectness with which the words "satire" and "satirical" are commonly applied. The *fabliau,* or "conte à rire," a narrative poem picturing, in the main, contemporary life, frequently with humor and power, is a French form that perhaps takes its remarkable rise with the fabliau *Richert* about the middle of the twelfth century. For about a century and a half (1156–1300) it expanded and flourished,

[47] But cf. Lounsbury, 3, 332–4.

[48] Root, p. 206.

[49] For this suggestion I am indebted to Miss M. P. Conant, author of *The Oriental Tale in England.*

its subject-matter often being common property.[50] Its pictures of *bourgeois* life, graphic, humorous, often coarse, even extremely licentious, set in the foreground three typical figures—the husband, the wife, and the clerk. These are the chief favorites, but the picture gallery includes every contemporary type.[51] While the *fabliau* often entertains a profound contempt for women, and sometimes, though but incidentally, attacks the ecclesiastical orders—chiefly the monks and the friars—it is yet, as a genre, not truly satirical. Its object is not to reform, nor even, primarily, to ridicule, but largely to amuse—perhaps, though incidentally, to instruct.[52] Neither the writer nor the reader feels himself above the characters and manners portrayed. A clerk is chosen as the hero of an episode of marital infidelity less because the typical clerk is worse than the typical soldier or merchant than because the contrast between the clerk's preaching and his practice is the most glaring, therefore the most humorous. The whole society concerned in the writing, the reading, and the subject-matter of the *fabliau* is morally homogeneous. Vice, if shrewd enough, often triumphs; the villain may lose, but through his stupidity, not through his moral obliquity. Such would seem to be the typical *fabliau*—not a satire, but a humorous portrayal of manners. How easily and how effectively it could become really satirical, Chaucer himself shows us in more than one of his *Canterbury Tales.*

Of the three English *fabliaux* in England before Chaucer, that of *Dame Sirith* or *Siriz,*[53] in the time of Henry III, tells a story that goes far back to Hindoo sources, with the real *fabliau* spirit and indecency. At least one critic sees in it satire on the clergy and on women, from the fact that the English writer has substituted a clerk instead of a young layman as the lover.[54] But probably we have in *Dame Siriz* merely

[50] See G. Paris, *La Littérature française au Moyen Age,* p. 118 f.

[51] The material, however, is not always contemporary; it is sometimes drawn from antiquity; nor is it always humorous, but sometimes moral and religious. See Lenient, Ch. V.

[52] See Bédier, *Les Fabliaux, passim.*

[53] Maetzner, I, 103 f.

[54] Haessner, pp. 67–8.

the ordinary spirit of the *fabliau,* lacking in real satirical characteristics.

A second so-called *fabliau, The Fox and the Wolf,*[55] is merely a humorous beast-fable, without a superficial trace of that "symbolic satire on the clergy" which has been claimed for it; while the third, *The Land of Cockaygne,* is undoubtedly satirical, whether it be taken as a parody of the *Vision* genre or merely as a terrible gibe at the sensuality of the clergy. The last named, however, either derived from, or thoroughly analogous to, a French original, has been elsewhere treated.[56]

Either *fabliaux,* or in the *fabliau* spirit, are Chaucer's *Tales* of the Miller, the Reeve, the Shipman, and the Merchant. None of these is truly satirical, and the last named, the *Merchant's Tale,* on the famous "January and May" theme, perhaps derived from Boccaccio, may be taken as representative of the unsatirical *fabliau.* This is a story of marital infidelity, in which the young lover, with the consent and assistance of the young wife, outwits and befools the old and credulous husband. The merchant, in his prologue, asserts that his own wife is a shrew fit to overmatch the devil, and his *Tale,* of course, illustrates the sly infidelity of that feminine type. Perhaps it might be said that the tale ridicules the absurd credulity of the typical old husband. But the motive—simply to amuse—is too plainly evident. Narrator, actors, and audience, move on the same level. The audience may place its sympathies anywhere it pleases—with the old husband or with the unfaithful wife.

The Nonne Preestes Tale is a delightfully humorous beast-fable founded on an incident taken from the *Roman de Renart.*[57] That the tale is allegorical—that the beasts are to stand for human beings—Chaucer gravely assures us in the "moral." Chanticleer falls through vanity; Dan Russel the Fox, through pride and imprudence. The moral is as grave as that of a fable by Æsop. From this point of view, the *Tale* is simply didactic; certainly it could, as a whole, form

[55] *Early Popular Poetry,* ed. Hazlitt, Vol. I, p. 58 f. See *supra,* p. 27.
[56] See *supra,* p. 58.
[57] See Miss K. O. Petersen, *On the Sources of the Nonne Preestes Tale.*

but a very general and rather ineffective satire on human folly. Furthermore, the moral—which mars the tale—reads like an afterthought—a concession by the poet to the taste for didacticism characteristic of his period. But the humor and the elaborate realism that run through *The Nonne Preestes Tale,* while they do not transform it into a Satire, yet render it something quite unique in its charm. The eternal masculine and the eternal feminine are embodied in the relations between Chanticleer and Pertelote. Her well-meant medical advice, his rejection of it—how characteristic of each sex! Yet this picture is humorous, not satirical. Again, while Chanticleer's deliberate mistranslation of the Latin proverb may be intended as a satirical reference to marital deception, the passage is too brief to color the whole poem. It is true that the poet himself speaks some eleven ironical lines against woman—lines undoubtedly satirical and stinging as a lash. But these, too, are incidental—a digression. Furthermore, it is remarkable how many lines in the *Tale,* so far from being satirical, are not even humorous. The lengthy dream-tales, while of course incongruous in the mouth of a cock, are in themselves quite serious.

Surely, it is only as a Satire on human folly that *The Nonne Preestes Tale* as a whole can be termed satirical. Granting that its humor lifts the *Tale* from sheer didacticism into satire, how little of the story is really given to the incident of the Cock and the Fox! The general setting, the conversations between Chanticleer and Pertelote, the mock-heroics after the capture of the Cock, predominate not only in bulk but in interest over all other elements. But, after all, the chief argument against the formally satirical nature of *The Nonne Preestes Tale* lies in nothing of the foregoing, but simply in this: one feels, when he reads the *Tale,* that Chaucer is laughing, that a *sympathetic* humor permeates the piece, that both didacticism and satire are here subordinated to a most delicate and delightful *fun!*

From such *Tales* as these, humorous, witty, not satirical, we turn to those three—the *Tales* of the *Friar,* of the *Sum-*

moner, and of the *Canon's Yeoman*—in which the satirist is clearly at work. With their sources we are not here concerned, but we may find in them, as Chaucer made them over for us, excellent examples of that satirical method which we have termed dramatic or indirect, as distinct from the descriptive and direct method of the General Prologue.

The Freres Tale, in three hundred and sixty-six lines in pentameter couplets, is a narrative Satire on summoners. The story tells of a lecherous, avaricious summoner, and how he falls by his own tricks into the hands of the devil, who carries him off to hell, where, intimates the Friar, all summoners ought to be. While humor is abundant, the satire, though altogether implied, is scathing. The friar, at the beginning of the story, paints a picture of his summoner so unflattering and rude that one cannot wonder at the strenuous protests made by Chaucer's Summoner, who is listening to the story:

> "And right as Iudas hadde purses smale,
> And was a theef, right swich a theef was he;
> His maister had but half his duëtee.
> He was, if I shal yeven him his laude,
> A theef, and eek a Somnour, and a baude."

However, the Summoner, in his own tale, more than repays his obligations to the Friar. This story, five hundred and eighty-six lines in length, is a thoroughly humorous, and rather indecorous, exposure of the avarice, deceit, sensuality, and gluttony of the typical friar. It is a rare satiric art that sets these two abominable types of the period to exposing each other's rascality.

According to the Summoner, his friar, under pretense of begging for his friary, lines his own pockets and sack:

> "In every hous he gan to poure and prye,
> And beggeth mele, and chese, or elles corn."

On his tablets he writes the names of those who give, that, as he assures the givers, he may pray for their salvation—

> "And whan that he was out at dore anon,
> He planed awey the names everichon."

From Thomas, a dying man who has given liberally in the past, the friar begs further alms. But Thomas has learned his lesson: though he has given freely, he has gotten no good:

> " 'As help me Crist, as I, in fewe yeres,
> Han spended, up-on dyvers maner freres,
> Ful many a pound; yet fare I never the bet.
> Certeyn, my gold have I almost biset.
> Farwel, my gold! for it is al ago!' "

The friar, meanwhile, has, through the good-will of Thomas' wife, enjoyed a good dinner at the rich man's expense. Finally, Thomas, indignant at the pertinacity and hypocrisy of the Friar, plays him a rough trick, and sends him away wrathful and disappointed. The story ends with a contemptuous burlesque in which the friar is altogether discomfited. Owing to the indecorous nature of the theme, quotation from the story is largely forbidden. Yet the burlesque moves along rapidly and lightly, replete with humor and vigor. The satire is of course dramatic and indirect, and is at least as effective as that of *The Freres Tale.*

Yet in all this, however new and fascinating in method, we find nothing distinctly new in subject-matter. But when we consider the *Tale* told by the Canon's Yeoman, we enter a new field. For this tale is the first English Satire against alchemy. It is to be followed in time by divers attacks, finally culminating in Ben Jonson's immortal *Alchemist* over two centuries later.

Up to Chaucer's time English satire had not been startlingly original in its subject-matter. It preferred rather to follow the old lines of moral diatribe, to attack political follies, or to ridicule fashions. In other words, its material was largely external and superficial. One might ask why no attacks were made against the pseudo-sciences, astrology, alchemy?—against the medical science of the age?—against its philosophy?—its social economy? The answer is not far to seek. False sciences as they were, astrology and alchemy were grounded in the belief and upheld by the good-will of all classes of the people. The same was true of the medical science, the scholastic philosophy, the medieval social economy. Only the Renaissance was to break the bonds, to let in the light. Even as it was, the belief in alchemy persisted for centuries after Chaucer, and astrology still finds its devotees at the present day. The scholastic philosophy alone was satirized—and that briefly, though effectively, in a Goliardic poem in the reign of Edward I.[58] So *The Canon's Yeoman's Tale* is a pioneer and as such deserves full credit.

The Canon's Yeoman's Tale, seven hundred and sixty-one lines, is divided into two parts: the first, a direct attack on alchemy; the second, a humorous illustrative story. In Part I. the yeoman relates his experiences as the servant of a canon who practiced the art of the alchemist, giving his life, time, means, to the search for an impossibility. The yeoman is a grave personage; he comments on the art feelingly as one acquainted with it to his own cost, but he is not mirthful:

> " This cursed craft who-so wol exercyse,
> He shall no good han that him may suffyse;
> For al the good he spendeth ther-aboute,
> He lese shal, ther-of have I no doute
> Who-so that listeth outen his folye,
> Lat him come forth, and lerne multiplye;
> And every man that oght hath in his cofre,
> Lat him appere, and wexe a philosofre."

The story, however, is humorous enough. A canon-alchemist, shrewd and tricky, finds a credulous priest whom he resolves to dupe. From this priest he borrows one mark a day for three days, repays promptly, and so gains the priest's confidence. Then, by an amusing and clever trick, he shows the priest, to the latter's satisfaction, how to make silver. For the recipe the Canon receives forty pounds—and is never seen again. In this there is great humor of situation, and the satire, not merely by its originality but by its vigor, must rank among the best in the *Canterbury Tales.*

Chaucer's one formal piece of literary satire is *Sir Thopas.* There can be little doubt that this is a deliberate attempt to burlesque a certain exaggerated type of the contemporary

[58] See *supra,* p. 62.

metrical romance. The tale, told by the poet himself, is in some thirty-three stanzas, which vary in form, the prevailing type having six lines, rhyming *a a b c c b;* the *b* lines of three accents; the others, four. The whole is merely a caricature of the tedious and senseless details of the less admirable examples of the metrical romance, dull, vapid, never-ending. The tale is abruptly broken off by the significant statement, "Here the Host stinteth Chaucer of his Tale of Sir Thopas."

> "'No more of this, for goddes dignitee,'
> Quod oure hoste, 'for thou makest me
> So wery of thy verray lewednesse
> That, also wisely god my soule blesse,
> Myn eres aken of thy drasty speche—.'"

But Chaucer's satire does not end with the *Tales. The House of Fame,* that strange but powerful mixture of satire and pure allegory, while not a formal Satire, is yet, in effect, largely satirical.

This important poem, two thousand one hundred and fifty-eight lines in length, is written in tetrameter couplets and is allegorical in form. While it owes much to Dante both in general resemblances and in particular details, it is in no sense a parody of *The Divine Comedy.* Chaucer does not ridicule Dante's work, nor, though *The House of Fame* is largely satirical, does he use a dignified form as a vehicle for inferior or ludicrous subject-matter.[59]

In the first of the three books into which the poem is divided the poet dreams. He finds himself in a glass temple dedicated to Venus. This stands for the realm of love-poetry in which Chaucer has been idly wandering. He steps out of this temple into the world of reality—and finds it a desert: he has been living a life too remote from the actual.[60] From the desert, the poet is carried aloft by an eagle to the Temple of Fame, betwixt heaven, earth, and sea. Book second is filled with a description of the journey in the eagle's claws. The third book

[59] See *supra,* p. 20; Ten Brink, *Chaucer: Studien,* etc., p. 88 f.; Rambeau, *Chaucer's "House of Fame,"* Eng. Stud., Vol. 3, p. 209.

[60] See Root, *passim.*

describes the House, built on a rock of ice, slippery, impermanent, engraved with multitudinous names, many fast fading, some, on the northern side—the side of toil and effort—standing eternal. Within, upon a throne of carbuncle, sits the goddess Fame, many-eyed, many-eared, many-tongued, changing in form incessantly,—for earthly fame ever waxes and wanes,—while the Muses sing eternally her praise. Countless are the strange personages the poet finds collected together in this mighty fane:

> "Ther saugh I pleyen Iogelours,
> Magiciens and tregetours,
> And phitonesses, charmeresses,
> Old wicches, sorceresses,
> That use exorsisaciouns
> And eek thise fumigaciouns;
> And clerkes eek, which conne wel
> Al this magyke naturel,
> That craftely don hir ententes,
> To make, in certyn ascendentes,
> Images, lo, through which magyk
> To make a man ben hool or syk."

Now are made manifest the inexplicable caprices of Fame. Before her kneel nine successive companies. The first ask fame for their good works, but are denied report either good or ill. Still others obtain the renown they merit for their goodness. Some who have done good wish only oblivion—and receive it. Others desire the same, but obtain fame unwillingly. One company who have done nothing ask and gain fame undeserved; others who ask for unmerited fame, gain but slander. Wicked men pray for good report and obtain it. Still others who have done evil are denounced by Æolus through his trump of ill-report. Finally, as a crowning caprice of Fame, a company of those who really merit well are rewarded only with eternal obloquy.

Now the poet is carried by the eagle to the House of Rumor, a cage built of twigs, sixty miles long. Here, under Rumor's sway, men are constantly seeking news, circulating reports, distorting, exaggerating:

"And every wight that I saugh there
Rouned ech in otheres ere
A news tyding prevely,
Or elles tolde al openly
Right thus, and seyde: 'Nost not thou
That is betid, lo, late or now?'
'No,' quod [the other], 'tel me what;'—
And than he tolde him this and that
And swore there-to that hit was sooth —"

. . . .

"But al the wonder-most was this:—
When oon had herd a thing, y-wis,
He com forth to another wight,
And gan him tellen, anoon-right,
The same that to him was told,
Or hit furlong-way was old,
But gan somewhat for to eche
To this tyding in this speche
More than hit ever was."

In one corner of the vast exchange, where love-tidings are received, the poet hears a great noise. With this, the unfinished poem abruptly ends.

What is satirized in *The House of Fame?* The caprices of fortune and reputation, the dissemination of slander, the exaggerations of rumor. Thus far, the satire is general. But we seem to hear a personal note also. The great poet is perhaps here voicing his own sovereign contempt for slander, rumor, the vicissitudes of fortune, and most of all, for the insensate caprices of Fame. All this satire, incidental, informal, is narrative and descriptive. It is entirely social, but far more severe than Chaucer's wonted tone. The dramatic method is maintained, however, though the allegorical form necessarily precludes the lambent humor and the sparkling wit of the *Tales.*

The minor poems of Chaucer, while not entirely free from occasional satirical touches, offer little that is new or significant. The balade *Against Women Unconstant,* is not genuinely satirical, nor is the *Lenvoy de Chaucer a Scogan.* But the *Lenvoy a Bukton,* against marriage, in its irony, half playful, half bitter, is true satire. This envoy is in four eight-line stanzas, rhyming *a b a b b c b c;* and the best of it is the following:

> "I wol nat seyn, how that hit is the cheyne
> Of Sathanas, on which he gnaweth ever,
> But I dar seyn, were he out of his peyne,
> As by his wille, he wolde be bounde never.
> But thilke doted fool that eft hath lever
> Y-cheyned be than out of prisoun crepe,
> God lete him never fro his wo dissever
> Ne no man him bewayle, though he wepe."

Since his satire is almost wholly social, Chaucer disregards as unfitted to his purpose the political events and the public disasters of the stormy time in which he lived. All this subject-matter is left for others to treat, and finds scarcely an echo in his verse. He seems to be as little affected by these passing conditions as he is by the other satirical productions of his time. He stands apart, amused, critical, uninfluenced by his contemporaries. It seems impossible to establish any connection between his methods of satire and those of his English predecessors, or indeed with the methods of those who follow him. No work comparable with this had been produced in England or on the Continent; and nothing equal to it as verse-satire was to appear again in England for almost three centuries. Indeed, even in the evolution of English satirical poetry, Chaucer stands apart, and can hardly be said to form a real link. Yet, in his careful observation of inconsistences in conduct, his method of selection, his power to draw the portraits of social types, his pervading humor and wit, Chaucer anticipates the finished satire of Dryden and of Pope.

CHAPTER IV

FROM LYDGATE TO THE RENAISSANCE

Decline of satire after the time of Chaucer.—Lydgate.—*London Lick-penny.*—*Ragman Roll.*—Political Satire.—Absence of satire under Henry IV and Henry V.—Satire against Burgundy.—Allegorical satire: cognizances of the nobles.—Personal satire.—Suffolk.—Political satire.—Lancaster and York.—Religious satire.—The friars.—Social satire.—*How Myschaunce regneth in Ingeland.*—Contribution made by this age to the Satire.

Chaucer's immediate successors, while they did not perpetuate his methods of satire, at least endeavored to imitate his style, and traces of his influence are to be found in many anonymous productions within the fifty years following his death. The rhymed couplet that enabled Chaucer to anticipate the rounded apothegm and epigrammatic point of a much later satirical school, was unfortunately abandoned, however; and, in satiric poetry, only the stanzaic forms were utilized. With this reversion, came again the looseness of structure, the repetition, the lack of progress and climax, that had previously characterized English satirical poetry. Chaucer, student of society and close observer as he was, could not teach others his art. Hence satire continued its prosy way uninterrupted, on the old lines of general and ineffective diatribe and moral disquisition, with their modicum of humor and their remoteness from actual life. The exceeding humanity of Chaucer's poetry had merely preluded the Renaissance, not commenced it. His dawn soon faded away, as the ecclesiastical influence again prevailed. Again the individual was lost in the generalization. Again at every step was intruded the conventional moral, and again platitudes were substituted for acute criticism founded on observation of life. Wit and humor as the supremely effective weapons of satirical attack[1] could not be utilized under these conditions. Such is, in general, the character of the satirical poetry produced within the

[1] See *supra*, p. 8.

thirty years after Chaucer ceased to portray actual life; when Lydgate and Occleve were the great names in contemporary literature. Their productions are extremely literary, self-conscious, and reflective; far removed from that stream of popular satire which continually flows unheeded, and which, had Occleve and Lydgate drunk of it, might have given vitality to their dull and barren diatribes.

The inconsistency of men's actions is one of Lydgate's themes, in a poem of which every stanza ends with "It may wele ryme, but it accordith nought." [2] There is here certainly no lack of perception of general inconsistencies, but the perception arouses no sense of humor in the poet; quite the contrary. The poem is not without clearness and point, fair metrical form, and unimpeachable morality; but at best how vague and futile it seems after the vital satire of Chaucer or even the merely popular political ballad! "Flesh and spirit," says the worthy monk of Bury, "are incompatible as fire and water. No man can serve two masters":

> "A mighti kyng, a poore regioun,
> An hasty hede, a comunalté nat wise,
> Mikel almes-dede, and false extorcioun,
> Knyghtly manhode, and shameful cowardise;
> An hevenly hevene, a peneful paradise,
> A chast doctryne withe a false thought,
> First don on heede, and sithen witte to wise,
> It may wele ryme, but it accordith nought."

—and so on through eleven stanzas of admirable platitudes.

And in its abstract subject-matter, didactic tone, lack of humor, and general ineffectiveness, the same poet's *A Tale of Thescore Folys and Thre* is a worthy companion piece.[3] This is a contribution to that mass of medieval "fool-satire" which is to culminate in Sebastian Brandt's *Narrenschiff*[4] at the end of the century. The old classical idea of the essential foolishness of any deviation from the moral norm, is utilized by Lydgate in a fashion that might have evoked a smile from

[2] *Lydgate's Minor Poems,* ed. Halliwell, Percy Soc. Pub., No. 2, p. 55 f.
[3] *Ibid.,* p. 164 f.
[4] See *infra,* p. 155 f.

Juvenal himself. Just as the medieval cyclopædia embodied all human knowledge, so here the precise moralizer distinctly defines every possible species of folly. There are precisely sixty-three—no more, no less—in the moral universe. From these types there can be no variation. This is the *ne plus ultra,* with limits set and classes catalogued. One stanza alone may illustrate the beautiful rigidity and finality of this medieval system of character analysis:

> "The chief of foolis, as men in bokis redithe,
> And able in his folly to hold residence,
> Is he that nowther lovithe God ne dredithe,
> Nor to his chirche hathe none advertence,
> Ne to his seyntes dothe no reverence,
> To fader and moder dothe no benyvolence,
> And also hathe disdayn to folke in poverte,
> Enrolle up his patent, for he shal never the."

In Lydgate's two satirical poems on the times, *So as the Crabbe gothe forwarde,*[5] and *As Straight as a Ram's Horn,*[6] we might expect perchance a little gain in human interest, a closer observation of men. We are disappointed. The subject-matter is as general, the intent as didactic, as ever. But the ironical tone marks a real gain. A cruder form of irony could scarcely be possible, for, lest we think the good monk serious, he closes each stanza with the assurance that this ideal state of affairs is no more actual than the fact that a crab travels forwards or that a ram's horn follows a right line. But irony it is, rather bitter than humorous, yet a cause for thanksgiving amid a dreary waste:

> "This world is ful of stabilnesse,
> There is therein no variance,
> But trowthe, feythe, and gentilnesse,
> Secretnesse and assurance,
> Plente, joye, and plesaunce,
> By example who can have rewarde,
> Verraily be resemblance,
> So as the crabbe gothe forwarde."

[5] *Ibid.,* p. 58 f.
[6] *Ibid.,* p. 171 f.

A Satyrical Ballad,[7] said to have been written by Lydgate, as given by Wright, is, though perhaps no ballad, certainly satirical. On the face of it, it looks personal, but its chief figure, "Maymond,"—a lazy, idle, dissipated young knave, whose chief accomplishment is to "pluk out the lyneng of a bolle,"—is probably a type rather than an individual.

London Lickpenny, formerly attributed to Lydgate, but now acknowledged to be of unknown authorship,[8] gives an interesting and fairly vivid picture of London life, somewhat after the method of Langland. The poet makes a journey to London, but is disappointed in obtaining anything, even justice, without money. "But, for lack of money, I cold not spede," he cries cynically and not without humor, as he describes his visit to lawyers for justice; to cooks and hucksters for food; to merchants, for clothing; to tavern-keepers for shelter; to barge-men for a boat—all in vain; not charity, but universal avarice sways the hearts and purses of the metropolis. Not only does the seeker for justice fail in his mission, but he has his hood stolen soon after beginning his search. Finally, he is returning home in despair, when he espies the said hood already, with commendable mercantile despatch, displayed for sale:

> Into Cornhyll anon I yode
> where is moche stolne gere amonge
> I saw wher henge myne owne hode
> that I had lost in westminster amonge þe throng
> then I beheld it with lokes full longe
> I kenned it as well as I dyd my crede
> to by myne hode agayne, me thought it wrong
> but for lack of money I might not spede

In its realistic and fairly humorous description of actual life, *London Lickpenny* more nearly attains the truly satirical than

[7] *Reliquiæ Antiquæ,* ed. Wright, vol. 1, p. 13.

[8] There seems to be no evidence either external or internal that *London Lickpenny* is the work of Lydgate. There are two existing MSS. of the poem, Harley 542 and Harley 367. The latter, until recently considered the authentic text, is merely a sixteenth century recension. See the work of Miss Eleanor P. Hammond, *Anglia,* vol. 20, whose text is used here.

any other production of its time. For Occleve, apart from the poem addressed to Sir John Oldcastle, never remotely approaches a satirical tone. A blood-thirsty appeal to Henry V, beseeching that orthodox monarch to root out heresy, forbid religious disputation, and slay the foes of Christ;[9] and a Ballade,[10] occasioned by Richard the Second's interment in Westminster, containing a similar appeal, are his sole contributions to destructive criticism. And Occleve was as innocent of humor as he was of poetical talent.

Produced at this same period, the anonymous tract known as *Ragman Roll*[11] is one of the earliest of those conventional attacks on women which later became so common.[12] We have had the type exemplified two centuries earlier in the Goliardic poem, *De Conjuge non Ducenda,* and shall meet it again and again for two centuries to come. The verse of *Ragman Roll* is in Chaucerian style, but the poem as a whole is an odd mixture of eulogy and vulgar abuse. Women of all types are represented, and each stanza contains a separate portrait, some very noble tributes to womanly character alternating with others very gross and abusive. From among these, says the writer, the reader may select as best pleases her. Bits of irony abound, such as

"O constant womane, stabill as the mone."

A poem contemporary with *Ragman Roll, Syr Peny,*[13] also recalls Goliardic times, and is an imitation of *De Nummo,* above mentioned.[14] It is one of the conventional ballads on money that are to become more common a century later.

Apart from these unimportant productions, and certain others of like tenor, we find through the greater part of the

[9] *Hoccleve's Minor Poems,* ed. Furnivall, E. E. T. S., Ex. ser., No. 61, p. 39.

[10] *Ibid.,* p. 47.

[11] *Early Popular Poetry,* vol. 1, p. 68 f; *Anecdota Literaria,* ed. Wright, pp. 83–8.

[12] See *infra,* p. 175 f.

[13] *Early Popular Poetry,* I, 159; for *A Song in Praise of Sir Penny,* see *Ancient Songs and Ballads* (1829), I, 134.

[14] See *supra,* p. 42.

fifteenth century little but political satire. Far removed from literary tradition, such satire has the advantage of live subject-matter and popular appeal.[15]

The absence of any satirical attack against Henry IV would seem to indicate that he was welcomed by all classes of the people. The unsuccessful conspiracy against his life and throne made by Rutland, Kent, Salisbury, and other disaffected nobles, was too personal an affair to find any echo in verse. But it is rather remarkable that the great revolt of the Welsh under Owen Glendower, in 1402; and the rebellion of the Percies, which was quelled at Shrewsbury, furnish us with no extant political poems either popular or academic. It is not until 1405 that these revolts against the house of Lancaster are recorded in any partisan verse. In favor of the young Earl of March, whom Henry was keeping in confinement, Northumberland had formed a second conspiracy. Among his associates were young Thomas Mowbray, Duke of Norfolk, son of Henry's old enemy; and Richard Scrope, Archbishop of York, brother of that Earl of Wiltshire whom Henry, on his arrival in England, had so summarily beheaded. The plot was frustrated, and both Duke and Archbishop were executed at York. The Archbishop was a favorite with the populace, who straightway, to the king's disgust, began to venerate him as a saint and make pilgrimages to his tomb. The prelate's fate is lamented in a long Latin elegy which becomes something of an attack on the reigning house of Lancaster.[16] This, though premature, is the beginning of that satire produced by the Wars of the Roses which is to follow half a century later.

The writer complains of the haste and injustice of the Archbishop's trial, which disregarded his rank as a peer and his exemption from lay jurisdiction. His sentence is described and the manner of his conveyance to the place of execution. We are told how the Archbishop encouraged his young com-

[15] The well-known *Turnament of Totenham* (see *Early Pop. Poetry*, 3, 82 f.; *Ancient Songs and Ballads*, 1, 85) is a humorous burlesque, but scarcely satirical. It is full of fun, but hardly seems a true parody of the romance of chivalry.

[16] *Political Poems*, 2, 114.

panion Mowbray to meet death serenely. The prelate's fate, and that of others who perished through the conspiracy, is lamented. The whole kingdom has suffered in the death of these leaders, says the eulogist.

Apart from the Lollard poem of *Jack Upland*,[17] nothing else of a satirical character has come down to us from the fourteen years of Henry IV's reign, though they were troubled with internal conspiracy, with wars against the Scotch, and with Welsh rebellion. Indeed, it is not such periods as this that give us a great variety or quantity of satire; but rather the reigns of weak or unpopular kings, such as Edward II, Richard II, and Henry VI, when internal disorders were rife, and disasters abroad inflamed the discord at home.

As with the reign of his father, so it was with that of Henry V, who succeeded to the throne of 1413. Except the two poems connected with Oldcastle, nothing approaching the satirical has survived to us from the brilliant reign of the Victor of Agincourt. Ballads on Agincourt and the siege of Rouen we have, paeans of triumph, but no echo of internal strife at a time when it would seem that all classes of society were united by one spirit of national enthusiasm. During a period of successful foreign wars, such as that of the early years of Edward III and of Henry V, what satire we find is directed against the foe, and notes of domestic discord are drowned in the great shout of national victory.

This tide of foreign conquest continued to rise for years after the death of Henry V in 1422. Yet the position of the English abroad was rendered precarious by the defection of the Duke of Burgundy, their old and powerful continental ally. Dissatisfied with the attitude of the English, Burgundy broke the alliance, and to the grief and rage of his former allies made, in 1435, a separate treaty with France. In the following year he attacked that darling of the English heart, Calais. The siege was unsuccessful, but the Duke's bad faith seems to have aroused all classes of the English people, for the event is recorded in a number of political poems that are at once a per-

[17] See *supra,* p. 90 f.

sonal attack on the Duke and on all Burgundians, and a mingling of invective and genuine ridicule that marks a striking advance beyond any previous political satire. The first dart is hurled in a short, imperfect English poem in which Philip of Burgundy is upbraided for having forgotten the succor afforded him by Henry V—to whom he vowed faithful allegiance. On the holy sacrament was this vow made, and Philip is now false both to God and man![18] Burgundy evidently made an overture also to the Scottish King, James I, for some clerk, in a short poem in Latin hexameters, declares that both rulers are treacherous, and that alliance between Scotland and Burgundy is natural, for—

> "Est et semper erit similis, similem sibi quaerit;
> Ambo perjuri, sunt ambo simul perituri."[19]

The siege of Calais itself is celebrated in two excellent ballads, largely burlesque in tone, which are quite the best political satire yet produced in England. The first minstrel begins in romantic style, and tells how the Duke of Burgundy assembled his chivalry from Flanders, Picardy, Burgundy, Brabant, Hainault, and Holland. The gay appearance of the troops is described, and their extensive preparations for the siege.[20] The second and much superior ballad[21] also contains a burlesque account of the action, but is couched in the form of a direct address to the Flemings, who are taken as the representatives of the entire Burgundian realm. It is rather remarkable for its burlesque tone and genuine satire, as well as for its unusually melodious verse, and connects itself with the songs of Lawrence Minot and the popular ballads of the reign of Edward III:

> "Remembres now ye Flemyng, upon your owne shame
> When ye laid seege to Caleis ye wer right full to blame
> For more of reputacion ben Englisshmen þen ye,
> And comen of more gentill bloode, of olde antiquiteè
> For Flemyng com of flemed men, ye shall well understand,
> For flamed men & banished men enhabit first youre land!"

[18] *Political Poems*, 2, 148.
[19] *Political Poems*, 2, 150.
[20] *Ibid.*, 2, 151.
[21] *Archæologia*, 33, 130.

Shortly after this series of events, and fifty years after the ballad on King Richard's ministers in 1399,[22] we meet again the interesting and thoroughly popular form of satire exemplified in that ballad—viz., the satire in which great noblemen are allegorically represented by their cognizances. This peculiar style is confined mainly to the political poetry of the Wars of the Roses. During that miserable epoch, no dweller outside the towns was safe unless enrolled under the banner of some feudal lord and wearing his livery. Knights, squires, yeomen flocked to the standards of Warwick, of Salisbury, of Somerset; and, although the whole system was actually tottering to its fall, undermined by new conditions, the army of retainers possessed by a great noble of this period was greater than ever before in English history. Hundreds or thousands of retainers of many a great noble ravaged the country, marched through city and village up to parliament at Westminster, or met on the field of battle; and it was inevitable that such standards as Warwick's *Bear and Ragged Staff,* Gloucester's *Swan,* and Exeter's *Cresset,* should be recognized by all classes of the people. Thus, until Edward IV was firmly seated on the throne, and the feudal system fallen with Warwick at Barnet, this peculiar and characteristic method was employed by all the political satire of that period of civil conflict.

In 1447, Humphrey, Duke of Gloucester, and his great rival, Cardinal Beaufort, both passed away; leaving William de la Pole, first Earl, then Marquis, and finally Duke, of Suffolk, who had arranged King Henry's marriage with Margaret of Anjou, the only minister whose counsel was much regarded by the king. Three very unpopular courtiers, Daniell, the "Lily"; Norris, the "Conduit"; and Trevilian, the "Cornish Chough," stood high in the king's favor, and were hated by the people as the promoters of unjust taxation, the proceeds of which they were accused of appropriating largely to their own use. The Duke of York, a great fighter and actual heir to the throne, was being forced out of his neutral atttiude, and had been practically banished to Ireland.

[22] See *supra,* p. 97.

All these conditions, the disasters abroad, the dissensions at home, the death of public favorites, and the supremacy of hated royal advisors—best known to-day, if known at all, through Shakespeare's King Henry VI—are mirrored in a ballad produced about the year 1449.[23] Bedford, *the Rote,* Gloucester, *the Swan,* Exeter, *the Cresset,* Norfolk, *the White Lion,* Warwick, *the Bear,* Arundel, *the White Hart,* Devon, *the Boar,* York, *the Falcon,* are all mentioned:

> "The *Rote* is ded, the *Swanne* is goone,
> The firy *Cressett* hath lost his lyght;
> Therefore Inglond may make gret mone,
> Were not the helpe of Godde almyght."

The unpopularity of Daniel, and also of Lord Say, the Treasurer, is further attested by another poem in English written about the same time. The house of Lancaster had long been proverbial for its poverty. The expensive foreign wars had drained the royal treasury, and, since the days of Henry IV, the expenditure of the government had greatly exceeded its revenue. The deficit resulted in heavy and unjust taxation, for which the ministers of finance, and not the king, were blamed. The popular indignation that resulted a few months later in "Jack Cade's Rebellion" (1450), finds expression in this poem. Suffolk's unpopularity is growing. He has been hated ever since he effected the King's marriage, which involved a cession of English territory in France, and, as the people claimed, a loss of national honor. Continued disasters abroad, culminating in the loss of Normandy, are all laid to his charge; the unfortunate and almost innocent duke is made a scapegoat for the entire maladministration of Henry's reign.

In his warning to King Henry,[24] the writer very characteristically has no blame for the weakness of his King, but rebukes those whom he considers responsible for the domestic dissensions. "Ye that have extorted grants from the king, restore them or else fly for your lives. Ye have so impoverished the king that perforce he begs from door to door.

[23] *Excerpta Historica,* ed. Bentley, p. 159; *Political Poems,* 2, 221 f.
[24] *Excerpta Historica,* p. 360; *Political Poems,* 2, 229.

Lord Say, and Daniel, begin to make reparation, or you perish! Throughout all England are poverty and truth oppressed, and the King knoweth it not."

Belonging to this same period and in English, though far less popular in character, is the piece of invective that some enemy,—possibly a jealous ecclesiastic, though he seems to voice a popular sentiment,—has directed against William Boothe—Bishop of Coventry and Lichfield in 1447, and Archbishop of York in 1453.[25] Between these two dates the poem was written. Bishop Boothe was scarcely a sufficiently prominent figure in the political life of his time to be coupled with Suffolk or held responsible for the general state of affairs. But the writer seems to see in him a type of the worldly, simoniacal prelate, in every way unworthy of his exalted position, and an ill-adviser of the King. "Boothe, thy wealth bought thee preferment, and Chester [Coventry and Lichfield] cries out against the indignity. By simony thou hast feathered thy nest, and all the world knows it!"

> "Prese not to practise on the privité
> Of princes powere, but pluk at the ploughe;
> Clayme thou a Carter crafty to be;
> Medille the no ferthere, for that is ynoughe.
> Thow hast getyne gret goode, thou wost welle how.
> By symoni and usure bilde is thy bothe;
> Alle the worlde wote welle this sawys be sothe."

"But may God save the king from Suffolk and all his other foes, who lead him to destroy such men as Gloucester, Bedford, and Beaufort! As for Boothe, all men know he labors but for lucre."

That Suffolk was in any way responsible for the deaths of Bedford, Beaufort, or Gloucester, was, of course, totally false. But the accusation, and the frequent mention of the Duke's name, show how the clouds are gathering around his head. Some one must die for all this general maladministration, and Suffolk is to be the victim.

Our next ballad[26] rejoices over the arrest of the unpopular

[25] *Excerpta Historica*, p. 357 f.; *Political Poems*, 2, 225 f.

[26] *Political Poems*, 2, 224 f.; for the *satirical ballad* in general, see *supra*, p. 7.

minister. This was in 1450, when the loss of Normandy and other disasters in France led to Suffolk's impeachment in Parliament under various preposterous charges. He was accused, among other things, of betraying England to France, and of desiring to elevate his son to the throne. Suffolk was popularly referred to as the "*Fox*," and "*Jack Napes*," the vulgar name for a monkey. The present ballad expresses the joy of the people at his arrest, and reiterates the charges of his having "tied Talbot,[27] our dog," and brought "good" Duke Humphrey of Gloucester to his death.

"The fox hath been driven to his hole; yet some of you are his friends, and with him hunt the hares. He hath tied Talbot, our dog: evil may he fare for it!"

Only a short time elapsed before Suffolk's enemies were enabled to celebrate in verse an event still more final and satisfactory than his arrest. King Henry was compelled to yield to the popular clamor against his minister, and bade him absent himself from England for five years. The issue was disastrous, for it saved neither Suffolk's life nor Henry's reputation. After embarking hastily for Flanders, the Duke was overtaken in the Channel by a ship called "Nicholas of the Tower," of uncertain commission, but of very certain purpose, by whose master he was saluted with the ominous greeting "Welcome, traitor," and was told that he must die. After a day for confession, he was beheaded, and his body flung on the Dover Sands.

In a hideous parody of the Mass, some popular writer celebrates the unmitigated joy that this tragic event brought to the great majority of the English people.[28] It is a personal attack on a dead man, but also on the man whom the people regarded as the representative of treachery and national dishonor. The absence of invective only renders the ironical personalities more terrible. The ballad assembles together at the death of the hated minister every unpopular ecclesiastic of the realm, among them Booth, Bishop of "Chester."

[27] Lord Constable of England.

[28] *Political, Religious, and Love Poems,* ed. Furnivall, E. E. T. S., vol. 15, p. 6 f. *Ancient Songs and Ballads,* 1, 117; *Archæologia,* p. 29, vol. 320; Turner, *Hist. Eng.* (1830), vol. 3, p. 74; *Political Poems,* 2, 232 f.

However unjust, the hatred of a nation is a terrible thing; and this personal attack upon Suffolk was the sharpest of its kind up to that time known to English literature. Parliament had learned its power; the impeachment of royal ministers was now its right; and the people, too, were learning to express their opinion in "good set terms." And this is true despite the fact that Jack Cade's Rebellion in 1450 found no echo in verse that has survived to the present day. It won its cause, for the sympathy of a nation was with it; and hence no clerks attacked it in vituperative Latin or English rhymes, as they did the "upstart peasantry" in 1381. It is true, too, that during the Wars of the Roses, from the first battle at St. Albans in 1455 until 1471, when Edward IV was firmly seated upon the throne, very little really satirical poetry was produced in England. But political ballads there are in plenty, pæans of victory, eulogies on the leaders of both parties, abuse, invective. Many of the ballads, which show a distinct gain in form over those of any preceding period, are allegorical. The great nobles are referred to by their cognizances, as in the more satirical poetry of the earlier part of the century. March is the *Rose,* Salisbury, the *Eagle,* Warwick, the *Bear;* and these, together with other great leaders, figure as the object either of eulogy or of vituperation.

It was probably within the few months of truce before the battle of Wakefield, December 30, 1460, that some Yorkist partisan uttered his warning to the *Rose,* the *Eagle,* and the *Bear* against the wiles of the Lancastrians.[29] "Beware, lords of York, of the false dealings of the Lancastrians. They are arrant hypocrites, who profess to admire the Rose and have stilled their barking at the Bear; yet both would they gladly destroy."

Very different from these popular and enthusiastic ballads is that Latin poem on the civil war, written shortly after Towton, by John de Wethamstede, monk of St. Albans.[30] It is a chronicle of events of which St. Albans was the center, but

[29] *Archæologia,* 29, 340.
[30] *Political Poems,* 2, 258.

the reflections upon the Lancastrians are frequent and bitter. The civil war is detailed so far as concerns St. Albans, with severe protest against the outrages committed by the northern troops of the Lancastrians. The battles of St. Albans and Wakefield and the sack of the abbey are described, with renewed and indignant reproach of the northern troops for their gross outrages. The poem ends with a defense of Edward's rights to the throne and an argument of Henry's disability.

The popular English ballad and this academic Latin chronicle are at opposite poles, yet both go to show the well-nigh universal feeling that placed Edward of York upon the throne. In English, and in very tolerable metre, yet more like the monkish chronicle than like the ballad, is the strangely Chaucerian political tract in favor of the Yorkist party.[31] The poet must have written between the time of Edward's coronation in 1461 and Warwick's defection some three years later; for he represents the great earl as still loyal to York. The history of the house of Lancaster is traced; the evils of the time ascribed to Queen Margaret, who was, indeed, partly responsible for them; and Warwick and Edward are extravagantly eulogized.

It is inevitable, during such a period of strife as existed in England through the greater part of the fifteenth century, that such satire as was produced should be mainly political. The Wars of the Roses, with all the evils of their tempestuous period, seemingly pushed into the background the perennial sources of complaint. Amid the strife of factions and the terrible uncertainty of life itself, a strife and an uncertainty in which every class of society participated, very little literature of any kind was produced, and the satirical part of this product was inevitably colored by the stormy temper of the times.[32]

Yet a few examples of religious and of social satire appear even in this period of political upheaval. Those ecclesiastical

[31] *Political Poems*, 2, 267.

[32] A number of popular ballads, celebrating Yorkist victories and Yorkist heroes, belong to this period, and in spirit and style show a considerable gain over any predecessors. Interesting in themselves, they are yet eulogistic rather than satirical; *Archæologia*, 29, 343; 2, 267; 29, 130; *Political Poems*, 2, 271; etc.

conditions that have so long furnished food for satire have not been materially mitigated. Lollardry, to be sure, has learned discretion, and after 1418 suffers no further poetical attack. That the friars, however, are still a source of disquietude, appears from a little poem in alternate English and Latin lines produced probably in the early part of Henry the Sixth's reign.[33] In form and tone so similar, it is perhaps a direct imitation of two poems written in the latter part of the previous century. "Friars are false, immoral, lascivious," says the accuser; "it is dangerous for a householder to admit them into the same house with his wife and daughters."

It is not until the beginning of the civil strife in 1456 that we find the next conventional complaint of the kind,—in this instance, a lugubrious wail over the evils of the times, chiefly the prevalence of deceit in the State. Each one of the ten stanzas ends "For now the bysom leads the blind," or with a slight variation of this refrain.[34] Probably by this same sombre critic, certainly employing similar material and treated in a like tone, though more elaborate, is the complaint entitled *How myschannce regneth in Ingeland.* Each of its nineteen stanzas ends with the refrain "Of al oure synnys, God, make a delyveraunce."[35] The writer, very pardonably rendered pessimistic by the deplorable conditions surrounding him, sums up the immoralities of his time in Church, State, and Society—vice after vice being taken up and directly inveighed against in stanza after stanza, without either the personification or the attack on social classes which marked the period before the Wars of the Roses.

The extravagances of Edward the Fourth's court were perhaps responsible for a short diatribe against the corruption of public manners, in which gallants and priests are the special objects of censure:[36]

> "Ye prowd gelonttes hertlesse,
> With your hyghe cappis wittlesse,

[33] *Political Poems,* 2, 249.
[34] *Ibid.,* 2, 235; *Reliquiæ Antiquæ,* 2, 238.
[35] *Political Poems,* 2, 238.
[36] *Political Poems,* 2, 251.

> And your schort gownys thriftlesse,
> Have brought this londe in gret hevynesse."

In these several pieces, we have a great deal of conventional complaint; satirical commonplace, moral, sombre, wholly destitute of humor, however inspired, perchance, by genuine feeling. Such trite lament may be sincere: it is certainly ineffective. The real contribution that this age—from Chaucer to the Renaissance—makes to the Satire, is the marked advance in the public capacity for satirical expression, accompanied by a certain amount of genuine humor.

CHAPTER V

Henryson, Dunbar, Skelton, and Barclay

The Renaissance.—Robert Henryson.—His Fables.—*The Dog, the Scheip, and the Wolf.*—*The Wolf and the Lamb.*—Their significance.—Dunbar.—His range of subject-matter and tone.—His humor.—His power in the grotesque.—His satirical poems.—Dunbar as a satirical poet.—Skelton.—The New Learning.—Skelton's life.—His peculiar verse.—His heritage from the past.—*The Bouge of Court.*—*Elynour Rummyng.*—*Speke Parrot.*—Wolsey.—*Colyn Cloute.*—Skelton's attitude toward reform.—*Why Come Ye not to Courte?*—Its attack on Wolsey.—Its place as a Satire.—Skelton as a satirist.—Barclay.—Brandt.—*The Narrenschiff.*—*The Ship of Fools.*—Its general character.—Its popularity.—Its form.—Its motley company.—Its satiric methods.—Its social satire.—Its lack of poetry.—Its medievalism.—Its glimpses of characterization.—Its Renaissance elements.—Barclay *vs.* Skelton.—Influence of *The Ship of Fools.*—Barclay's Eclogues.—Change from chronological to topical treatment in the following chapters.

With the reign of Henry VII came the Renaissance. It was an era of great names. The stream of anonymous and desultory satire seems to disappear between the years of 1480 and 1520; from the reign of Richard III, of Henry VII, and the early years of Henry VIII, nothing of the popular product survives. Instead, we find the same subject-matter, the same tone, exemplified in the more formal and elaborate productions of Barclay and of Skelton in England; of Dunbar and of Lyndsay in Scotland. Together with these, though a far lesser light as a satirical poet, stands Robert Henryson, the Scotchman, who deserves mention if only on account of the unique character of his contribution to the English Satire. Henryson, Dunbar, Skelton, and Barclay, may well be treated together in the present chapter, but Lyndsay will find more fitting treatment in connection with the Satire of the Reformation.

I

Robert Henryson, the poet of *Robene and Makyne* and *The Testament of Cresseid,* wrote also, between 1470 and 1480, thirteen "fables."[1] These are largely imitated from Æsop, but, rather incongruously, are couched in Chaucer's favorite *rime royal.* From several points of view these fables are of interest. They are the only representatives of their kind in English literature before the time of Elizabeth, at least. Again, while all are thoroughly didactic, two of the thirteen are, in a certain sense, satirical. These two are *The Taill of the Dog, the Scheip, and the Wolf,* and *The Taill of the Wolf and the Lamb.*

In the former, the Dog, needy and poor with a poverty that is not honest, determines to get a living by falsely accusing the innocent sheep. Judge Wolf, who is in the plot, summons the sheep to court. The Raven is apparitor; the Kite and the Vulture appear as advocates for the Dog; and the Fox is clerk. The Dog asserts that he has paid money to the Sheep for bread which the latter has never delivered. The Bear and the Badger, appointed by the Court as arbitrators, of course decide the case against the Sheep, after lengthy perusal of Digests and of Codes. The Sheep, pleading vainly for justice, is forced to travel to town and sell the wool off his back to buy bread for the rascally Dog. In the *Moral* appears the satire. The Sheep is the poor "Commons"; the Wolf is the cruel and oppressive Sheriff,—and so on. The whole is a stern arraignment of the Consistory Courts—a complaint to be echoed, a generation later, by Lyndsay, with increased power.

In *The Wolf and the Lamb,* the familiar apologue of Æsop is adorned with a *Moral* almost as long as the fable. The Lamb is the tenant, the merchant, or the laborer; the Wolf is the lawyer, the rich man, or the lord. The poor man suffers the same lot described so often in the satire south of the Border; and Henryson utters his complaint with the homely earnestness and deep feeling that Lyndsay was to give to the same theme in his *Satire of the Three Estates:*

[1] *The Poems of Robert Henryson,* ed. Laing, Edinburgh, 1865. A later edition is edited by G. Gregory Smith, Scot. Text. Soc., 1906. To this I have not had access.

"His hors, his meir he mon lend to the laird
To dring, and draw in court or in cariage;
His servand, or his self, may not be spaird
To swink and sweit, withouttin meit or wage.
Thus how he standis in laubour and bondage,
That scantlie may he purches by his maill,
To leve upon dry breid and watter-caill."

In these two examples we find the didactic fable applied to contemporary themes. They are neither the purely moral apologues of Æsop nor the fables of Marie de France or of LaFontaine.[2] This fact, together with their isolated position in the history of English literature, render at least these two of Henryson's fables significant. Furthermore, their direct vigor and moral earnestness point the way to Lyndsay.

II

William Dunbar's satirical verse, though without appreciable influence on later satire south of the Border, yet displays many English characteristics. As Dunbar, during an almost complete dearth of satirical poetry in both England and Scotland, continued something of the Chaucerian traditions, and, in the vigor and wit of his satirical verse, far surpassed the other productions of his time, it may be well to consider briefly his contribution to the Satire.

At last, through the crafty policy of Henry VII, England and Scotland were at peace. Under this benign and unusual condition of affairs, Scottish literature again flourished, and Dunbar —wit, scholar, court-poet, and priest—was the consummate flower of his time. Though possessing many popular Scottish characteristics, Dunbar was yet an even more typical product of the court of James IV. It was a dissolute court; and Dunbar's poetry, for all its undercurrent of earnestness, bears the stamp of the poet's environment. He was not primarily a satirist. Indeed, his purely satirical poems form but a small part of his productions, and, with one or two exceptions, that part is also unimportant. The poet of those elaborate Chaucerian allegories, *The Thistle and the Rose* and *The Golden Targe,* made

[2] See *supra*, pp. 27, 28.

of his short and formless satirical poems mere *jeux d'esprit,* outlets for an occasional satirical mood. But these short poems are still replete with vigor. They are a real literary product, far removed from popular satire, representing, in the main, no popular idea, but merely the poet's personal predilections. They spring from no great moral conviction, and are calculated to effect no great moral reform. Dunbar was no protestant by nature, but a close observer and a wit who wrote either to amuse himself, to espouse the cause of his patrons, or, perhaps, to voice the discontent arising from hope of preferment long deferred. It naturally resulted that he dissipated whatever satirical force he possessed in a number of little efforts, informal and occasional. Consequently, these short satirical poems are difficult to analyze and classify. They represent a side current, though a highly refreshing one, in the dreary stream of fifteenth century satire. Something of their spirit may have passed into Lyndsay's poems, but what Lyndsay may have in common with Dunbar is probably rather the native Scottish character than any personal inheritance. Yet, despite their insignificant length, their apparently purposeless, and certainly informal, character, Dunbar's short satirical poems possess some unique characteristics which upon close reading grow more and more apparent.

In something less than a dozen poems[3], varying from forty to five hundred and thirty lines in length, the poet ranges through political, personal, social, and religious satire,[4] with an ease and felicity amazing to one who has followed the course of previous satire in English. *How Dunbar was desyrd to be ane Freir* ridicules the Franciscans; *The Turnament* hits at the galvanized chivalry of James's Court; *Tidings from the Session*[4a] touches both politics and society; *Ballat of the Fenȝeit Freir* is wholly personal; *The Tua Mariit Wemen and the Wedo* is wholly social. All these are perhaps equally felicitous in expression.

[3] *The Poems of William Dunbar,* ed. Small, S. T. S., vol. 2, vol. 4. Edinburgh and London, 1893.

[4] See *supra,* p. 30 f.

[4a] This is the editor's title, as are all titles given in modern English.

Apart from this versatility in the choice of subject-matter, the quality and range of Dunbar's humor are also noticeable. Chaucerian as he was in his more elaborate poems, his satirical poetry shows little of Chaucer's sane, consistent, observation of life and knowledge of human nature. Dunbar is Chaucerian now and then in a happy hit, but his humor has nothing of the subtlety, his observation nothing of the realism, of Chaucer. On the other hand, this humor of Dunbar's, though not acute, has an extensive field of activity. It is moralistic and rather bitter in *Tidings from the Session;* entirely bitter in the attack on Donald Owre; burlesque in the Franciscan ballad; and merely grotesque in the *Turnament.* We pass from the savage invective of one or two personal Satires to the good-humored raillery of *The Telȝouris and Sowtaris.* At one time we are listening to a personal diatribe, of which one would have fancied Dunbar incapable; straightway we hear some homely news from the " Session "; again we are spirited away to hell to witness a grotesque tournament between tailors and cobblers. The grotesque is Dunbar's forte. It is here that his finer qualities of sincerity, originality, and force appear. These traits go far to redeem the slenderness of the product, its lack of great purpose and of consistent form; and even to atone for a less pardonable coarseness that is likely to creep in and defile Dunbar's best work—a coarseness due, however, rather to the poet's period than to his personality. Indeed, Dunbar's remarkable force in grotesque caricature renders his best work quite unique in English satire.

The form of these various satirical poems, with one notable exception, is stanzaic; stanzas of five, six, seven, eight, ten, and even twelve lines. The metres are equally various; but the verse-form invariably fits the subject-matter—whether the former be the slow rhythm of the *Tidings from the Session* or the rapid, fierce verse of the invective against Donald Owre.

Tidings from the Session is written in eight seven-line stanzas. The " Session " is the Supreme Court recently established. Two countrymen meet. One has just returned from

Edinburgh, and gives the news: "People do not trust one another there. The criminal gets the best of honest people. Many are the hypocrites. Some win their suits through their army of retainers—others by bribery. Some perjure themselves; some bless, and others curse, the saints. There are wolves in sheep's clothing, and all manner of criminals."

> "Sum with his fallow rownis him to pleiss
> That wald for invy byt of his neiss;
> His fa sum by the oxstar leidis;
> Sum patteris with his mowth on beidis,
> That hes his mynd all on oppressioun;
> Sum beckis full law and schawis bair heidis,
> Wald luke full heich war not the Sessioun."

This stanzaic form of course precludes the point, the antithesis, and the epigram of the couplet; and while it perhaps affords lightness of touch and rapidity of movement, it also makes against any steady sequence of thought.

In material for satirical treatment Dunbar was rich: of this the Court of James IV afforded an unlimited quantity. The short *jeu d'esprit* in twenty-six lines of rhymed couplets, *Aganis the Solistaris in Court,* attacking hangers-on at Court and their way of obtaining favor, seems to be the first example in English of what may be termed "Court-satire." Chivalry had decayed, and modern courts, replete with characteristic court vices, were now established in both Scotland and England. Dunbar's little poem is a pioneer, and its species is to be prolific through succeeding centuries.

Less novel and original is the social Satire beginning *Devorit with Dreme, devysing in my Slummer,* in which Dunbar, reverting to the old English type of general diatribe, attacks in turn various social classes. Despite its conventional material, the poem has in it more life and sincerity than ordinarily characterize its species, as it seems to have been inspired by immediate conditions. This conventional satire again appears in the dull diatribe, *Against Evil Women.* Such poems represent not the satirical poet Dunbar, but the priest.

That Dunbar, however, is capable of much less conventional,

and much more original and effective, satire against women appears in his famous but highly indecorous *The Twa Mariit Wemen and the Wedo.* This scathing burlesque, so bitter in its implications, is written in five hundred and thirty lines of the old alliterative verse to which, strangely enough, this master of stanzaic form now reverts. The form here employed is indirect and dramatic—that of a conversation between the two married women and the widow, who exchange confidences and divulge their conjugal experiences in terms indecorous, unquotable, but, satirically, not ineffective. This poem of course connects itself with the perennial Satires on women,[5] though its dramatic method makes it akin to Chaucer's work rather than to the typical poem of its class, and its bitter gibes and horrible insinuations fortunately render it a thing apart.

Scarcely less severe than *Against Evil Women,* but far more vital and effective, in the *Satire on Edinburgh,*[6] which describes the condition of the city streets, and rebukes the citizens in no measured terms for allowing in their capital so horrible a state of affairs.

In complete contrast to this moralistic tone, is the burlesque—almost grotesque—flavor of the best of these social Satires, *The Turnament.* This piece includes a two-fold object of ridicule—the antiquated and perfunctory chivalry of a Renaissance Court, which struck Dunbar as absurd, and the trades of the tailor and the cobbler, which seem to have been prominent in Dunbar's Edinburgh, and to have been warmly disliked by the poet. The form of the burlesque ballad suits the gross satirical humor of the theme.

Social and political satire are combined in *We lordis hes chosin a chiftane mervellus,* addressed to Albany (1520?). There was certainly ample material for satire in the surprising political conditions that developed in Scotland after Flodden Field. The regent Albany, whose presence seemed essential to the political welfare of the nation, continually absented

[5] See *infra,* p. 175 f.

[6] Cf. Fergusson's *The King's Birth-Day* in Edinburgh; *Auld Reike; The Town and Country Contrasted,* etc. For these references I am indebted to Mr. S. L. Wolff.

himself in France and left his country, rent by domestic discord, to care for itself.

In vice most vicius he excellis (1506)—a bitter attack on Donald Owre—adds a personal element to the political. This unrelieved invective, in eight six-line stanzas, directed against the rebel and political pretender, illegitimate son of Angus of the Isles, perhaps represents the height of Dunbar's talent for invective:

> "In vice most vicius he excellis,
> That with the vice of tressone mellis;
> Thocht he remissioun
> Haif for prodissioun,
> Schame and susspissioun
> Ay with him dwellis."

Wholly personal, without admixture of either social or political elements, is the famous ballad in sixteen eight-line stanzas entitled *The Fenȝeit Freir of Tungland.* This is a thoroughly justified attack on an impostor named Damian, one of the king's favorites, who worked upon his master's credulity. The poem gives a burlesque account of Damian's attempt to fly into France. Its tone represents the mean between Dunbar's soberer attempts and the wild *grotesquerie* of such ballads as *The Turnament.*

Wholly personal, too, is *The Flyting of Dunbar and Kennedie,* which must be mentioned here if only to say that this remarkable piece of mock-invective is in no way satirical.[7] Walter Kennedy, the poet, was Dunbar's contemporary and friend. The "flyting" of the two embodies merely an interchange of ridicule, good-natured, so far as we can judge, without any satirical motive whatever.

The Dance of the Sevin Deidly Synnis is perhaps Dunbar's most remarkable poem. Though grotesque, it also is free from

[7] "Flyting" comes from "flit" (contention); and the "flyting," a metrical scolding match, is analogous to the *jeu parti* of early Provençal poetry (see Morley, *Eng. Writers,* VII, 140). In Italy, Luigi Pulci and Matteo Franco had indulged, without any ill-will, in just such interchange of vituperation. In England, we have the "flyting" of Skelton and Garnesche.

satire except in its last stanza, which shows the old hatred of the Lowland for the Highland Scotch. The scene is in hell. After a dance by the Seven Deadly Sins, described with a perfect genius for weird and grotesque effect, the devil calls for a Highland pageant to crown the saturnalia. He is, however, so deafened by the outlandish noise made by the Highlanders that he smothers them with smoke in the "deepest pot of Hell."

Again, Dunbar's *Dergy,* though a parody, is not a Satire. The form, that of a parody of the solemn services of the church, was not uncommon; we have seen it in the horrible parody of the Mass celebrating the death of the Duke of Suffolk.[8] In Dunbar's poem, the Trinity, the Virgin, the Patriarchs and Apostles, are petitioned with parts of the Lord's Prayer, and other sacred forms of the liturgy, to persuade the king to leave the poor cheer of the monastery at Stirling for the delights of Edinburgh. There is in this no hint of satire; though the form is parodic, the object is merely to amuse.[9]

When we consider, however, one of Dunbar's most successful efforts—the short religious Satire directed against the Franciscans, *How Dumbar was desyrd to be ane Freir,*—we find a tone at once highly humorous and thoroughly satirical. Here we reach the extreme of the poet's satirical range,—a range culminating in masterly burlesque. The satirist is visited during the night by one whom he supposes to be Saint Francis, who tries to persuade him to become a monk. Dunbar flies in terror from the habit which is offered, and, when asked the reason for his refusal, says that he has known of few holy friars; and, furthermore, the offer comes too late, for

"Gif evir my fortoun wes to be a freir,
The dait thairof is past full mony a ȝeir;
For into every lusty toun and place
Off all Yngland, frome Berwick to Kalice,
I haif in to thy habeit maid gud cheir."

He has travelled as a friar from Canterbury, over the ferry at

[8] See *supra,* p. 129.
[9] *Ibid.,* p. 20.

Dover, through Picardy, and knows the order. At this rebuff, the supposed saint vanishes away in fiery smoke: he was not St. Francis at all, but a fiend in holy shape. The poet awakes wondering if the devil has become the patron of the Franciscans.

In summing up the characteristics of these various sporadic attempts, we may note first of all their brevity and their wide range of material and tone; and secondly, their directness, vigor, and sincerity. Dunbar stands alone in the peculiar quality of his humor, and though not a satirist in any formal sense, he is still entitled to consideration for his admirable qualities. His work embodies less of the purely conventional, and shows greater originality, than that of any other satirical writer of his time.

III

From the Scottish poet whose brilliant sporadic attempts in a satirical vein scarcely entitle him to serious consideration as a Satirist, we turn to his English contemporary, John Skelton, who perhaps may be called the first dominating figure in the line of English satirical poets. Skelton's poetry gathers into itself much of the conventional material of previous English satire, but also includes a great deal that is strictly contemporary and individual. In range of tone and form, few satirists are more restricted than Skelton; in range of material, few are so broad and inclusive.

Since Lydgate's time, England had known no great voice crying in the wilderness. Ineffective as were Lydgate's lugubrious cries, they were still an echo from the past and continued a time-honored English tradition. For over half a century, through civil war and a deluge of domestic evils, England, south of the Border, had no genuine poetry of any kind; and, as has been seen, the satirical spirit found expression only in popular ballads and occasional wails from the monasteries. Still, the voice of the people speaks in these attempts and gives them significance. At times these half-inarticulate cries merge into one, which comes from the lips of the man who speaks with the authority born of strong purpose and deep conviction. This man we call a satirist—whether, like Dryden, he employs a consummate literary form; or, like John Skelton, he speaks in a voice unequal and harsh.

Henry VII once seated on the throne of England, peace came again. Conditions grew favorable to literature. Colleges and schools were founded; the New Learning came over the Alps and found a home in the universities. Grocyn, Linacre, and Colet; Erasmus, Thomas More, and a host of other scholars, thronged the church, the court, the schools. Gross evils still afflicted the nation. The clergy were corrupt; the people poor and miserable; the State was threatened with a despotism which the Tudors were rapidly making an accomplished fact. Yet, the Court favored the New Thought, and gave the new education a decisive impetus.

One of the products of these newer and more favorable conditions was Skelton. Yet, in respect to literary form, Skelton, court-poet and defender of the New Learning though he was, was *in* the Renaissance but not *of* it. His point of view, his poetical forms, show no trace of the new order. He is thoroughly English, and medieval at that; using his classics as Gower used them. He reads Juvenal's Satires, yet writes with no pretense to classical form,[10] and is no herald of Wyatt and the Elizabethan satirists, save perhaps in his vigorous Anglicism. Furthermore, the Satire to Skelton—as it was to his predecessors—is but an instrument, a means. It is not a cultivated literary form, remote from actual life, but is an expression of national discontent. And the rough verse-form, fitting the still more rugged subject-matter, has much of the Anglo-Saxon in its short irregular cadences, and was suited to the untuned ear of the contemporary public.

Skelton's life, roughly contemporary with that of Dunbar, stretches through the reigns of Edward IV, Richard III, and Henry VII, to the middle of the reign of Henry VIII. He saw a feudal chivalry replaced by a modern court, replete with those traditional follies that from his time on furnish so fruitful a source of satire; and these court follies he satirized in *The Bouge of Court*. He saw a totally corrupt clergy, tainted

[10] For the classical Satire, see *supra*, p. 15 f.

with the vices that had aroused the ire of all satirical writers since the time of the Goliards; and these vices he attacked especially in *Colyn Cloute.* He saw all power secular and religious gathered into the hands of one arrogant minister of state, and this minister, Wolsey, he assailed in his *Why Come Ye not to Court.* These three elaborate Satires embody almost all that Skelton has to say about Court, Church, Society, and State, and contain the elements of all his minor poems save *The Tunning of Elynour Rummynge.*[11]

Excepting *The Bouge of Court,* which is an example of fairly good form, all of Skelton's elaborate satirical poems are couched in an outlandish verse which he made so peculiarly his own that it has gained the epithet *Skeltonical.* The irregularity of meter that distinguishes this Skeltonical verse, renders it an admirable vehicle for the torrents of invective in which Skelton loves to indulge. The normal measure is iambic; the syllables average six; the number of accents averages three; the rhymes are double, triple, and sometimes quadruple. From the standpoint of invective, some of its cadences are wonderfully telling. It flows in an irregular current—at times comparatively smooth, but only for a few lines; again, moving as roughly as human ingenuity could well effect. It babbles, it roars, it storms, and jerks its way along. Its waters are muddy, but its current is irresistible. This verse with its short irregular alliterative lines, perhaps long existing among the people, was now for the first time used as a literary vehicle. It served its purpose, and was employed for a few years by some of Skelton's worthless and anonymous imitators, who aped their master's faults and lacked his virtues; then happily it disappeared forever before the more polished forms of the new poetry.

Skelton's heritage from the past, however, does not consist merely in a tremendous breadth of material and a popular verse that he perhaps adapted to his own purposes. His rude strength and vigor, his intolerance of wrong and oppression, his calls for reform in Church and society, his power of invective and lack of sympathetic humor, were native to the man, it is true, but were also an English inheritance from a long

[11] *The Poetical Works of John Skelton,* ed. Dyce, 2 vols., 1843.

line of satirical predecessors. He embodies all the ideals of previous English satire; his work is the consummation of all that preceded it; he is the last of the medieval satirists, as he is the greatest. This is what he gained from the past. What his own times gave Skelton we shall see as we consider his greatest Satires more in detail.

Skelton's career of satirist seems to have begun after he had reached middle age. It is reasonable to suppose that his Court-Satire, *The Bouge of Court,*[12] at once the most formal and poetical of his satirical productions, was written after 1500, when he was at least forty years old. The poet as University man had written various minor poems before this period, but now his true temper began to find expression. We have seen how the old chivalric court had passed away and the new social court had come into existence in both Scotland and England. Dunbar had written perhaps the first true Court-Satire, and now in England Skelton was to inaugurate a species destined to endure for centuries. Himself at the court, the poet found material about him in abundance. The subject-matter of the *Bouge of Court* has perfect unity; its form remarkable regularity; and in both subject-matter and form it contrasts strangely with Skelton's later Satires. Wolsey's career had not yet begun; the poet's eyes were perhaps not yet awake to the flagrant evils he was later to attack so bitterly; at any rate, political, religious and personal satire are entirely wanting in this his first satirical poem.

The Bouge of Court, written in regular and fairly musical *rime royal* stanzas, is in the form of an allegory.[13] The alle-

[12] "Bouge" is the French *bouche* (the mouth); and "bouge of court" is an old term signifying the right to feed at the king's table. "Court rations" is the definition given in the *New Eng. Dict.* As Skelton uses it, the term means "court favor."

[13] Cf. the *Roman de la Rose;* the two are similar in that in each the narrator tries to gain access to the Lady, and is helped or encouraged by one set of allegorical personages, and hindered or discouraged by another set; and, more particularly, in that Danger is in each case one of the discouragers. In the *Roman de la Rose,* Bel-Acueil allows the Lover to approach the Rose (11, 2886–2918); Dangier expels the Lover (11, 3013–3053). In *The Bouge of Courte,* Danger taunts the author: Desire encourages him. (For these suggestions and references, I am indebted to Mr. S. L. Wolff.)

gorical personages, Dissimulation, Favor, Flattery, Debauchery, and others, the vices that rule the Court, are enemies of the young aspirant to Court favor, and attempt to injure him. The would-be courtier has to struggle against these evil persons, and finally loses the fight.

The poet sleeps in the port of Harwich, and dreams that he sees sailing into harbor a goodly ship[14] laden with costly merchandise. The ship is boarded by traders, also by the poet. There is much confusion until it is learned that the ship is the "Bouge of Court," and the owner Dame Sauncepere; the merchandise is called "Favor," and costs dear. The poet presses forward to behold the fair owner, but is stopped and taunted by Danger, her chief attendant. But Desire encourages him to persevere, and gives him a jewel called "bonne aventure," telling him to make friends with Fortune, who steers the ship. Every one is now suing for the friendship of Fortune, who distributes favor to them all. Thus ends the prologue.

The ship now puts to sea:

"The sayle is vp, Fortune ruleth our helme,
We wante no wynde to passe now ouer all;
Fauore we haue tougher than ony elme,
That wyll abyde and neuer from vs fall:
But vnder hony ofte tyme lyeth bytter gall;
For, as me thoughte, in our shyppe I dyde see
Full subtyll persones, in nombre foure and thre."

These four and three disagreeable passengers are hangers on and friends of Fortune, named Flattery, Suspicion, Disdain, Riot, Dissimulation, Harvey Hafter, and Deceit—the seven sins of the Court. They are inimical to the new courtier, who thus far has fared so well, and whisper about him and conspire against him. Each draws him into conversation with sinister intent. At last, to avoid being killed, the poet is about to leap into the sea, when he awakes.

[14] This ship shows the influence of Brandt's *Narrenschiff*. But Skelton includes in his ship only one class of Brandt's fools—that of the false, flattering courtiers. See Herford, *Studies in the Literary Relations of England and Germany in the Sixteenth Century*, pp. 355–6.

This allegorical form,[15] conventional as it is, Skelton adapts to strictly contemporary conditions and so breathes into it a certain amount of vitality. The story lacks progress, and is too abrupt in its close, but it is powerful in its way and remarkable for certain features new to English satire—features characteristic of the age of individualism that was just in the dawn. One of these features is the beginning of character study. It is description rather than genuine characterization, and the figures are not individuals, but types. Yet even this is an advance beyond what has preceded it. Favell (Flattery), Suspecte, Harvey Hafter, and Subtylte, are indistinct, though their speeches are somewhat individual; but Dysdayne and Ryotte are on the borderland of characterization. We see in these vividly pictured types, which are foreshadowed by those in *Piers Plowman,* how allegory is at last passing into characterization. Here we have a description of Disdayne:

"Wyth that, as he departed soo fro me,
Anone ther mette with him, as me thoughte,
A man, but wonderly besene was he;
He loked hawte, he sette eche man at noughte;
His gawdy garment with scornnys was all wrought;
With indygnacyon lyned was his hode;
He frowned, as he wolde swere by Cocke's blode;
He bote the lyppe, he loked passynge coye;
His face was belymmed, as byes had him stounge;
It was no tyme with him to jape nor toye;
Enuye hath wasted his lyuer and his lounge,
Hatred by the herte so had hym wrounge,
That he loked pale as asshes to my syghte:
Dysdayne, I wene, this comerous crabes hyghte."

Also foreshadowed by Langland[16] was the description of low life, introduced in Riot's speech—disgusting, but real and, in its way, effective. Comparatively new to English satire as is this kind of description, it shows that at last men are opening their eyes to see vividly the world about them. The Renaissance has come, and with it have come realism and characterization.

But Skelton's power of description finds yet more effective

[15] See the "Allegorical Satire," *supra,* p. 26 f.

[16] See *supra,* p. 76 f.

scope in his satire on drunken women, *The Tunning of Elynour Rummynge.* "Tunning" means brewing. Elynour Rummynge was the notorious keeper of an ale-house favorably known to the courtiers of Henry VIII. In this picture of the degradation of the women of the lower classes, Skelton describes an evening in the ale-house, with all the scurrility and vulgar talk, the low morals and manners typical of such a place in such an epoch. Its contrast to *The Bouge of Court* is complete. From the court we descend to the hovel; from the vices of the upper classes we turn to those of the lower; in place of allegory we meet intense realism; instead of form, we find six hundred and twenty-three lines of Skeltonical formlessness. Despite its thoroughly disgusting subject-matter, *Elynour Rummynge* presents a picture of low life unapproached in previous English satire. Its form is entirely objective; the picture is drawn to speak for itself, without comment from the satirist.

From these purely social Satires, which are of general application and are free from contemporary allusions, we turn to that strange medley of moral, social, personal, and political satire, which Skelton calls *Speke Parrot.* The form of this unspeakable production is somewhat conventional. Parrots had recently, since the discovery of America, become household pets, and were supposed to possess wisdom as well as the power of speech. The comment on current affairs is put into the mouth of the wise bird, and the speech of the parrot contains a certain amount of character. It speaks a confused medley of languages and dwells on a confused medley of themes. The form is stanzaic, *rime royal,* and the Satire is a reflective diatribe against the times in general. The poem does not progress; its stanzas might be indefinitely shifted without either adding to or detracting from its unity of form. The subject-matter is divisible into three classes: first, many of those vague and general censures that seem to be of universal application; again, more specific accusations which especially apply to this particular period, such as,

"So myche translacion in to Englyshe confused";
"So myche decay of monesteries and of relygious places";

and, finally, references that could apply only to Cardinal Wolsey:

> "So bolde a braggyng bocher, and flesshe sold so dere";
> "So mangye a mastyfe curre, the grete grey houndes pere."

In the main, the theme is a very extraordinary mingling of general moralizing and sharp personalities. Of the latter Wolsey is the target, and this fact shows a change in the poet's attitude toward his former friend. Wolsey's public career began in 1514; his rapid rise to power was equalled by his rapid growth of arrogance and personal ostentation. This accession of pride and pomp must have alienated many who were once his friends—certainly it alienated Skelton, for his allusions in *Speke Parrot* can point only to Wolsey, and he refers repeatedly to the arrogance of the "bragging butcher," the "mastiff cur," who fancies himself the peer of the great greyhounds; the "Proud prelate" who makes such an assumption of grace, with so little grace within. These scattered references to Wolsey in *Speke Parrot* show Skelton's change of attitude toward the great minister. He makes no allusions to Wolsey's political moves; and this would seem to indicate the later date of *Colyn Cloute,* the second of Skelton's three most elaborate Satires, which alludes to Wolsey unmistakably and at greater length.

Colyn Cloute is twelve hundred and seventy lines in length. Its verse is the characteristic Skeltonical form already described. The method is that of direct attack, sometimes addressed to the objects of the satire. The figure of Colyn Cloute represents the laborer—both rustic and urban—the hard-headed, not over acute, observer, whose righteous wrath has at last been excited by the abuses he sees about him:

> "My name is Colyn Cloute,
> I purpose to shake oute
> All my connyng bagge,
> Lyke a clerkely hagge;
> For though my ryme be ragged,
> Tattered and iagged,
> Rudely rayne beaten,
> Rusty and moughte eaten,
> If ye take well therwith,
> It hath in it some pyth."

He reports what he hears against the Church—the common complaints in all men's mouths, and occasionally calls upon the ecclesiastics to disprove these slanderous charges. But this ironical tone is forgotten, as the satirist lays aside his thin disguise and pursues his quarry more eagerly. The subject-matter shows no unity of treatment, the form no progress and no organism. The whole is a thoroughly Skeltonical medley; constantly digressing, yet actually making every utterance contribute something to its central theme.

The subject-matter of *Colyn Cloute* is purely ecclesiastical, and includes an attack on every order of the clergy. The prelates, their pride, selfishness, lack of spirituality, form the principal theme; but the friars, too, are bitterly arraigned. All Skelton's charges are in substance those of preceding centuries, but presented in far more earnest and effective fashion. There is nothing remote or academic in the work of this scholar who can write for the common man. Here is a satirist who studies the people and voices their complaints; a satirist of strong moral convictions, yet not without his own peculiar humor. However general the complaint, it is very much alive; though without personalities, except in certain passages which point unmistakably to Wolsey as a type of prelatical wickedness. The partly ironical tone of *Colyn Cloute;* its humor, arising from the perception of inconsistency, rather bitter, grim, indignant; its moral earnestness, speaking in every line; its rebuke that almost becomes sheer invective—all these are the expression not of the man who merely contemplates, but of the active reformer.

It is evident that Skelton is of the long and honorable line of satirist-reformers that began with Walter Map. He would change corrupt practices, but he is no heretic; for, while a reformer in his moral creed, he yet despises Wycliffe, Luther, and all their following. Skelton's subject-matter, also, while so similar to that of his predecessors, is no literary inheritance. Its whole interest and value lies in its immediate origin in actual life. In its strong statement and popular expression we see a need and a prophecy of that Reformation now at last about to come—a reformation extending, however, far beyond what Skelton either expected or desired.

But this spirit of reform carried Skelton himself far beyond the generalities of *Colyn Cloute.* It was not only ecclesiastical reform the satirist desired, but also political. Wolsey in *Colyn Cloute* is an incident; Wolsey in the later and more virulent Satire, *Why Come Ye Not to Courte*, is the prime object of attack. In the years intervening between the composition of the earlier and that of the later Satire, Skelton seems to have been dividing his time between his rectory at Diss and the Court of Henry VIII. During these years he saw the astonishing rise of Wolsey to greater and greater power. In 1519, the man whom Skelton regarded as the archetype of ecclesiastical pride and debauchery, was made the Pope's sole legate *a latere;* in 1522, he was maintaining war against France without the sanction of Parliament, and was levying a loan of a tenth on lay subjects and of a fourth on the clergy. In 1523, when Convocation and Parliament met, the minister demanded from the clergy one half their annual revenue, from the laity, four shillings on the pound, and actually got half the latter amount. Such exactions were intolerable. Both clergy and laity were groaning under these burdens, while the great minister was luxuriously domiciled in his palace of Hampton Court. Wolsey's influence over the king seemed unlimited. Parliament did his bidding; war was levied at his command. His Court outshone that of the King: gentleman were his servants, and great nobles waited on his summons. The mighty Earl of Northumberland himself seemed afraid of the "butcher's dog." Moving among these conditions, watching this extraordinary career, Skelton finally saw in Wolsey not merely the type of ecclesiastical wickedness depicted in *Colyn Cloute,* but also the type of political tyranny satirized in *Why Come Ye Not to Courte.*

The form of this virulent personal invective of over twelve hundred lines, is that of a direct address to those who shun the Court on account of Wolsey's arrogance. Wolsey is the unifying theme to which, after numberless digressions, Skelton always returns with some bitter gibe, each one more stinging than the last. In the object of his satire Skelton naturally sees nothing good. Wolsey's great traits, his public services, are forgotten or ignored. He is represented as utterly depraved, and thoroughly incompetent for his exalted offices; yet master of both king and Court. *Why Come Ye Not to Courte* is perhaps the bitterest personal Satire in literature. Through its historical significance, it evokes profound interest. Whatever may have been Skelton's private quarrel with Wolsey—we know little of their personal relations—this Satire must have been largely inspired by a grievance not private, but public. Skelton is again the voice of the people, lifted against what they deemed intolerable tyranny. Such a protest, uttered in the days of Wolsey's supreme power, indicated superb moral courage. As it was, Skelton had to fly for his life to sanctuary in Westminster, and there he died, probably in 1529.

Humor in *Why Come Ye Not to Courte* there is none; nor is there any moralizing; but invective against Wolsey, inspired by bitter indignation, violent, even terrible at times, always thoroughly alive, there is in plenty. Indeed, Wolsey, as has been said, is the unifying theme. As Skelton reviews the foreign and domestic affairs of the kingdom,—dishonor abroad and discord at home, religious, political, and social dissension,—he sees in Wolsey the author of it all.

The Scots need not fear us; we are not sufficiently united among ourselves to give them trouble. We are bought and sold by the foreigners, while our proud and pompous Cardinal riots at Hampton Court. What news of Lancashire? of Cheshire? of the Scotch? of Lord Dacres?

"The Erle of Northumberlande
Dare take nothynge on hande:
Our barons be so bolde,
Into a mouse hole they wolde
Rynne away and crepe,
Lyke a mayny of shepe;
Dare not loke out at dur
For drede of the mastyue cur,
For drede of the bochers dogge
Wold wyrry them lyke an hogge."

Where are the great nobles of the realm? Why come they not to court? To the king's court, or to Hampton Court? Why, to the Cardinal's Court which overshadows that of the king! This shameless, ambitious, profligate butcher's dog has forgotten his humble origin. His royal master raised him from obscurity to power, and yet he repays the king with base ingratitude:

"How be it the primordyall
Of his wretched originall,
And his base progeny,
And his gresy genealogy,
He came of the sank royall,
That was cast out of a bochers stall."

After reiterated charges against Wolsey,—blackening his character as man, statesman, and ecclesiastic, branding him as the false adviser of the king and the scourge of the people,—Skelton ends his terrible arraignment with an apology. Why write satire?

"For trewly and vnfayned,
I am forcebly constrayned,
At Iuuynals request,
To wryght of this glorious gest,
Of this vayne gloryous best,
His fame to be encrest
At euery solempne feest;
Quia difficile est
Satiram non scribere."

Replete with contemporary allusions to men and things, this remarkable piece of invective shows nothing of classical influence in style or form. English of the English it is—rugged, violent, frequently coarse, even repulsive in its details, and yet at the same time courageous, original, and effective.

And these qualities characterize Skelton as a satirist. There is nothing beautiful in his satire, but there is something strong. After every possible detraction, he yet remains, with his English love of right, hatred of abuses, and splendid courage, the great figure of the pre-Elizabethan Satire. The power to speak plainly, to hit hard, he had both by tradition and inheritance and by nature. His material came straight from the world about him in ample measure.

On succeeding satire, Skelton's form had happily little influence. But it is not from this point of view that this satirist interests us: he is the protestant voice crying aloud in the wilderness against the evils of his time; the herald of reformation and a new order. It was many a year before the line of English satirists could boast so effective and imposing a figure as that of John Skelton.

IV

Contemporary with Dunbar and Skelton lived the learned and pious clergyman Alexander Barclay—a humanist who, despite his mastery of the New Learning of the Renaissance, used in his satire a tradition distinctly medieval. Translation though it was, Barclay's *The Ship of Fools* was so well adapted to English conditions and became so thoroughly identified with English literature, that it may well be considered a link in the chain of the English Satire.

Sebastian Brandt, German scholar and moralist, produced in 1494 that voluminous compendium of medieval ethics which he called the *Narrenschiff*. This poem takes its name from a ship carrying all the fools of earth, of every manner and order, and forms a vast panorama of society, picturing all sorts and conditions of men and drawing from their foolish lives grave lessons of wholesome counsel. The *Narrenschiff* met with universal popularity, and brought to Brandt enduring fame.

This great work made a powerful appeal to a nature very similar to Brandt's—that of Alexander Barclay, probably Scotch by birth but English by adoption. Barclay, scholar and moralist, afterwards rector of St. Mary Ottery, was twenty years old when the *Narrenschiff* appeared. The young scholar assimilated the German work, perhaps largely through a Latin translation, found it wholesome for doctrine, universal in its application and therefore as well adapted to the English as to the Germans; and in 1508 gave it forth to his own people in his famous translation *The Ship of Fools.*[17]

On first opening *The Ship of Fools* we are impressed with its enormous length of fourteen thousand lines; then with its multitude of emblematic pictures. What is this quaint ponderous work that has given both author and translator literary immortality, and what is its position in the history of the English Satire?[18]

First of all, Barclay's variations from his original are not of great importance. He omits practically nothing, while his additions are, for our present purpose, insignificant. A few personalities, relating either to himself or to those whom he wished to censure; a few patriotic passages; an attack on French fashions; a diatribe against false religions—these are additions of small bulk and importance, and in no whit vitally alter the character of the original. Yet, as concerns the history of English satire, Barclay is an original satirist, and his *Ship of Fools* native to the English soil. This book continued many of the traditions of previous satire in England; in it English society at large found itself mirrored; subsequent English satire indirectly owed something to its influence. Hence, through this discussion, Barclay's name will be used to represent the author, whether the touch be that of the German or of the English writer.

So much for the relation of the *Ship of Fools* to the *Narrenschiff.* Barclay's purpose in writing is stated in his prose argument, where he tells us that "the present book might well have been called the Satyr—that is 'the reprehension of foolishness,'" and goes on to say that, as the old satirical poets in divers poesies reproved the sins and the ills of the people at that time living, so he essays to follow in their illustrious footsteps and do his duty by the present age. This is well; and, furthermore, according to the prologue furnished by Locher,

"Sothely he hathe taken vpon hym the translacion of this

[17] *The Ship of Fools,* ed. Jamieson, 2 vols., Edinburgh, 1874.

[18] See Alden, pp. 15–21, for a brief but scholarly treatment of the relation of *The Ship of Fools* to the Classical Satire.

present Boke neyther for hope of rewarde nor laude of man: but onely for the holsome instruccion commodyte and Doctryne of wysdome, and to clense the vanyte and madnes of folysshe people of whom ouer great nombre is in the Royalme of Englonde."

A fitting introduction to *The Ship of Fools*! Permeated with "wholesome instruction" and "doctrine of wisdom" as it is, tedious, often intolerable though it be, never does it swerve from its moral purpose either for "hope of reward or laud of man." It is a moral treatise, a system of ethics, a vast didactic poem written on a characteristic medieval plan. Humor plays no part in such a scheme; neither does acute observation, nor profound knowledge of human nature. These latter qualities are not compatible with that utter lack of moral perspective shown in placing on the same moral plane, side by side, as equal sinners, the comparatively innocent geographer whose only fault is an untoward disposition to visit foreign lands, and the criminal who has been guilty of arson or murder. In fact, Barclay's disposition is to rebuke the fool more sharply than the criminal.

Such is the moral character of the book. Its literary character is marked by an utter absence of poetic or imaginative qualities. A sermon in verse, with illustrations; a twice-told tale; a vast compilation of ancient commonplaces, now brought together into something approaching unity; it is, withal, a *book*. Some of its qualities are even transitional and prophetic: not wholly of the old time, they dimly foreshadow the Renaissance of newer and more vital things in literature.

Yet this great sermon mightily pleased the readers of its day, became the popular work of its period, and bred a host of little imitations. To a modern mind its popularity amply demonstrates the contemporary lack of good reading matter. Maybe its precise arrangement and orderly classification pleased the early sixteenth century reader, accustomed to scholastic tradition; perhaps its clear commonplaces made it easy reading; possibly, its realistic, illustrative types gave it a novel character; but most probably its instant and prodigious popularity was won by its long series of really remarkable emblematic wood-cuts, which constitute the chief interest of the book for the latter-day reader, and which are still striking and extremely effective. For the sake of the interesting pictures, the reader of that day perhaps endured the sermonic comment—entirely reversing the good Barclay's intention, but probably effecting his purpose quite as well.

In form, the *Ship of Fools* is a didactic poem of about two thousand *rime royal* stanzas, the whole divided into one hundred and twenty-three sections. All the follies of human society are passed in review—for folly in this system of ethics includes both vice and crime. The criminal is the fool gone mad. A great ship is about to sail to some distant port and into this ship are to be gathered all the fools of the world, from the fool who fills his shelves with books he cannot read to the fool who does violence to his neighbor. Every trade, every profession, every order of society, furnishes its quota. Folly is of one hundred and ten distinct varieties—an advance beyond Lydgate, who found only "three-score and three," as we may recall. Each folly receives its share of attention, is catalogued, rebuked, and passed on. Brandt and Barclay do not indulge in burlesque, or show character in action. Their method is almost wholly descriptive; their form that of direct address on the part of the satirist.

Aside from its length, perhaps nothing in this vast poem is so striking as its lack of any progress or climax. There is here no idea of structure, no organic whole. Not only may the order of the Follies be indefinitely varied without doing violence to the form, but even the stanzas of any one section may be shifted at random without affecting the sense. Together with this lack of organic unity goes a tedious diffuseness of style. Barclay proses interminably. Ten stanzas might well be boiled down into one with a gain in interest and in solidity of structure. The style is remarkably uniform, rarely varying from an even tenor of mediocrity—though even *The Ship of Fools* has its "purple patches."

Despite the allusions to the ship in Barclay's two prologues

—one verse, the other prose—the poem is in no sense a narrative. Indeed, when we reach the body of the poem, we find the initial idea entirely forgotten, and no further allusion to a ship or a voyage is forthcoming. The ship has presumably long since begun its voyage, and the moralist now confines our attention to a description of the passengers.

What a motley company is this of the Fools of the World! The Fool of Books, The Evil Men of Law and Judgment, The Fool of Prodigality, the Fool of Avarice, Fools of New Fashions in Dress, the Old Fool, the Negligent Father, The Fool of Strife, The Tale-Bearer, The Fool of Broken Friendships, The Improvident Fool, The Fool of Disordered Love, The Drunken Fool, The Unprofitably Rich, The Blasphemous Fool, The Envious Fool, The Fool who marries an old woman for her money, The Impatient Fool, The Sensual Fool, The Clerical Fool, The Fool of Geography, The Fool of Astrology—but the list is endless and the range well-nigh universal. The great range and complexity of this material make it difficult to classify. Barclay does not confine himself to the reprehension of abstract follies as did Lydgate; nor does he merely reprimand each class of society in turn as illustrating these follies. His method is almost as varied as his material. Social, religious, even some personal satire, make up this gigantic *pot-pourri.*

Barclay's most distinct gain over the majority of his predecessors consists in his method of illustrating an abstract folly by the life of an individual. This is his characteristic method, and consists in illustrating the folly of envy, say, by a realistic description of an envious man. Here is a step toward characterization, though the result is, of course, at best a type, and often a very wooden type. Still, this method renders the satire on abstract follies a hundred fold more effective than was the method of the medieval satirist, who, like Barclay, took up folly after folly, but inveighed against them in a fashion entirely abstract.

This, however, while perhaps Barclay's most characteristic, is not his only method. Here and there in *The Ship of Fools,* we find the old medieval satire on social classes; as in the attack on "Evil Counsellors, Judges and Men of Law" (vol. 1, p. 24); and a modification of this method in "The Extortion of Knights, Great Officers, Men of War, Scribes and Practicers of the Law" (vol. 2, p. 80)—where one particular vice is illustrated not by a single individual, but by a whole class—thus uniting the two methods in one portrayal.

Neither does Barclay altogether abandon the old way of attacking vices entirely in the abstract, for he arraigns Avarice, Covetousness, and Prodigality without illustrative characterization or comment (vol. 1, p. 29). Apart from the medieval Satire on social classes, Barclay indulges in what may be called a classification by moral orders, when he inveighs against "Card-Players and Dicers" (vol. 2, p. 69); though, to be sure, such is but a modification of the method by which the satirist attacks a particular vice as embodied in an individual. Again, in at least two instances, he inveighs against a folly and confines its exhibition not to an individual, but to one class—the clergy. In the "Clattering and Babbling of Clergy in the Choir," he says of the gossiping priest:

> "He rennyth about lyke to a pursuyuant
> With his whyte staffe mouynge from syde to syde
> Where he is lenynge talys ar nat skant
> But in one place nat longe doth he abyde
> So he and other them selfe so lewdly gyde
> Without deuocian, by theyr lewd neglygence
> That no thynge can bynde theyr tunges to sylence."[19]

Such is the social satire of *The Ship of Fools.* Its religious satire is of the same order and bound up with the former variety. Against plurality of church livings and begging Barclay grows stern, but otherwise he handles the clergy gently. Of personal satire we find very little, for Barclay was not the man to single out an individual for chastisement; and this makes his bitter yet humorous reference of his neighbor "Mansell of Ottery"[20] all the more striking.

Barclay's remedy for all these follies which permeate so-

[19] *The Ship of Fools,* vol. 2, p. 155.

[20] And to eight of his neighbors who belong to the class of "fools who will not learn"; see vol. 2, p. 82.

ciety is, like that proposed by Langland, no great iconoclastic reform, no revolution, no violent change in the old order, simply more religion. Let men do right: this will purify society and rid the world of folly, which is another name for madness. This theory is set forth throughout the great length of Barclay's treatise; through all its one hundred and twenty-three sections, each a little "Satire," or rather, if you will, each a little ethical treatise on a particular folly, vice, or crime, in which the worthy philosopher inculcates his moral with threats of hell and hopes of paradise.

Barclay lived in interesting times, but contemporary affairs find little echo in his *Ship of Fools.* The material is mainly an aftermath from the past. It gives one the impression of a bookish origin; it is the work of a man who elaborated a system of ethics in his study, and not from first-hand observation of mankind. Yet with all of this, here and there come flashes of insight into actual contemporary life, an approach toward the picturing of social conditions. Even sketches of low-life are not wanting. The conduct of servants when escaped from their master's authority, is in itself something new, but forms one of the series of the *genre* pictures that are scattered here and there in English satire from the time of Langland:

"Whan mayster and maystres in bed ar to rest
The bordes ar spred, the dores open echone
Than farys the Coke and Butteler of the best
Other both togyther, or eche of theme alone
With wyne and ale tyll all the best be gone
By galons and potels they spende without care
That whiche theyr lorde for his owne mouth dyd spare."

A step towards characterization and observation of life is taken in "The Card Players and Dicers" (Vol. 2, p. 69); and again in the diatribe against Beggars, which is to be imitated in later satire:[21]

"Such yonge laddys as lusty ar of age
Myghty and stronge, and wymen in lyke wyse
Wanton and yonge and lusty of cowrage

[21] See *infra,* p. 117 f.

Gyueth them selfe vtterly to thus gyse
The cause is that they labour do despyse
For theyr mynde is in ydylnes to be styll
Or els in vyce to wander at theyr wyll."

Against Geographers and Astrologers Barclay is especially severe; and this material, comparatively new to English satire, except for the astrological satire in Chaucer, is also largely contemporary. The new mania for exploration, so distasteful to the home-staying Brandt, was at least as much English as German, and this satire against "the foolish description and inquisition of divers countries and regions" comes strangely from the pen of an Englishman!

Barclay's verse, always unimaginative and prosaic, suffering, in the main, from a deadly mediocrity, rises in the stanzas against Astrology and Geographers, into a style at least strong and effective, if not poetical; e. g.,

"Some gaze vpon wandrynge of the mone
Another deuysyth the cours of Phebus clere
Gasynge on the Sonne at mornynge nyght or none
And by other planetis shewyth what doth apere
Howe some of them whan they do gyde the yere
Engendreth plenty pleasour myrth and ioy
And howe some other doth man and beste destroy."

But despite these passages of some beauty and power, Barclay, in his style and material, rather harks back to medievalism. For instance, he is thoroughly medieval in his use of the classics. In this respect he is, like Skelton, in the Renaissance, but not of it. Classical writers furnish him with endless illustrations and quotations, but he knows very little of the breadth of classical humanity, and of classical method and form, nothing at all. Classical satire does indeed show its influence in Barclay's method of picturing a folly illustrated in an individual, thus producing a type. Horace did this, and Juvenal. But their types are more elaborate, have more vitality, are characterizations rather than descriptions. Barclay seems to build his type on one folly: the folly is uppermost, not the individual. This is largely the method of Theophrastus and the English "character" writers of the seventeenth century. The classical satirists did not thus work from without inward, but seemed to select an individual as an illustration of a folly, rather than to construct a type upon a folly as its foundation.

Glimpses of characterization had for centuries existed in English satire, but they were never uppermost, and had been at length obscured, perhaps by the ecclesiastical influence that created the earlier and typical Morality play, which embodied a system of abstractions in itself antipodal to the picturing of actual life. From this deadening medievalism English satire at the beginning of the sixteenth century was just emerging. The emancipation was greatly hastened by the influence of Barclay's German importation. Brandt, a classical scholar, was influenced by classical method to the extent already mentioned—a half-way achievement, but a triumph in its way, an advance beyond the medieval. The change was needed in England. Barclay felt the thrill imparted by the Renaissance, attempted the closer observation, applied himself to the picturing of contemporary life. But the old order imposes itself upon the classicist, and the result is a queer and interesting medley of tones and methods. Barclay's psychology and ethics are medieval, showing that exact classification, that perfect system, which takes no thought of the individual;—apart from life, remote, cold, dead. All this was upon him, and he could not throw off the cumbersome garment; hence the one hundred and ten varieties of follies in *The Ship of Fools.* But just here comes an advance in method, gained by Brandt from the classics, doubtless, but still, in a small desultory way, something of an inheritance in English Satire. This new method—that of presenting a vice or folly as illustrated by an individual—has been referred to. In this consists the chief interest of *The Ship of Fools* to the student of English literature.

This method is to have its influence. A host of minor imitations, such as *Cocke Lorell* and his brethren, for a generation or more, are to adapt and elaborate each his own peculiar feature of the great work. *The Ship of Fools* is too large in scope to be effective. It is universal in its way, but this universality is not of a high creative type; what it gains in universality it loses in strength and virility. But its imitators did not so err. They elaborated one feature of their original, lost in universality, but gained in force.

Glancing for a moment, in conclusion, from Barclay's influence to his sources, we observe again that the "fool satire" goes back to Nigellus Wireker; more directly, however, to Lydgate, and that Barclay's gain over Lydgate is tremendous. Yet Barclay's work is, of course, of German origin. It is doubtful if an Englishman would ever have originated this ponderous ethical treatise. For *The Ship of Fools* is in fact no ideal Satire, lacking in humor as it is and with so large a constructive element. However, German though it may be, it fits into the history of English satire in a very remarkable fashion.

From previous English satire, Barclay, like Skelton, received much:—but, as we have seen, Barclay and Skelton, though contemporaries, had little in common in their literary methods. Skelton is the voice of the people militant; Barclay is the student, contemplative. Yet each possesses a certain English heritage. Skelton's we have already considered. Barclay's is an unswerving and permeating—even obstrusive—moral purpose, a serious, didactic tone, a manner capable of forceful thrusts.

Apart from its direct imitations, the influence of *The Ship of Fools* over subsequent satirical literature is not so apparent. Although this influence can be traced in other literary genres, neither the renascence of the classical Satire, which Wyatt inaugurated, nor any subsequent satire of the classical type, owed anything to Barclay. It is safe to say, however, that *The Ship of Fools* at least indirectly fostered the manifestation of the satirist's personality, realistic method, contemporary portraiture; however remote, tedious, ineffective, academic, Barclay's style and method may seem in comparison with those of his successors.

V

But Barclay's literary activity did not cease with the publication of *The Ship of Fools*. Mantuan, the Italian humanist and Latin poet, had imitated the eclogues of Virgil in a series of moralizing, didactic poems, pseudo-pastoral, which he termed "satirical." In turn, Barclay wrote, perhaps about 1514, five eclogues,[22] two of which were imitated, in form and subject-matter, from those of Mantuan; while three were paraphrases of the work of Aeneas Silvius. These five "eclogues" are pastoral dialogues, which vary in length from eight hundred and fifty to over thirteen hundred lines, and are written in pentameter couplets of fair regularity. They have in truth very little that is bucolic about them, and not much local color. Innocent of humor, destructive in tone, often vituperative in style, each has far more right to the designation of "Satire" than has *The Ship of Fools,* though all are in fact rather didactic than satirical.

Barclay's first three eclogues are adaptations—with large additions—from the *Miseriae Curialium* of Æneas Silvius, Pope Pius II. At great length, with wonderful and tedious minuteness, they describe the life of the courtier; and, allowing for exaggeration, present some interesting pictures of contemporary life at court. This court-satire connects itself, in its distinctive tone, with other court satire of this new period. Such criticism of court-life could have had no significance for the English reader of a former generation; and even now, its foreign source and its obvious imitation—almost translation—of Italian models, rather vitiate any attempt to connect it with previous or contemporary English satire.

In his Fourth Eclogue, Barclay, with somewhat greater originality, indulges in literary satire, and bewails the neglect of poetry. Minalcas, the shepherd-poet, in appealing for aid to Codrus, the rich shepherd, declares that his desires are moderate and his wants but few:

> "I aske no palace, nor lodging curious,
> No bed of state, of rayment sumptuous.
> . . . .
> Grant me a living sufficient and small,
> And voyd of troubles, I aske no more at all;
> But with that little I hold myself content,

[22] Spenser Soc. Pub., 1885; for fifth eclogue and parts of four others, see also Percy Soc. Pub., vol. 22, ed. Fairholt.

If sauce of sorowe my minde not torment;
Of the court of Rome, forsooth, I have heard tell,
With forked cappes it folly is to mell."

The Fifth Eclogue, *The Cytezen and Uplondyshman,* or *Amintas and Faustus,* is an imitation from Mantuan. Two shepherds debate concerning the relative desirability of town and country life. Faustus utters a lengthy and detailed indictment against the traditional sins of the city, in a tone severe enough, but in a style general, commonplace, totally without allusion of any kind, without humor, severe, didactic, and thoroughly medieval. In its attack on hucksters and costermongers, presumptuous fools who essay theological argument, flattering friars, apothecaries, whose craft "—is all frauds and gylefull policy,"— in all this the eclogue continues the medieval tradition of the class-satire. Of this class-satire, the attack on Alchemists and Magicians is by far the best, and reminds us forcibly of the Astronomer section in the *Ship of Fools:*

"As alkemystys, wenynge by polecy
Nature to alter, and coyne to multyply;
Some wasshe rude metall with lycours manyfolde
Of herbes, weynge to turn it into golde;
All pale and smoky by suche contynuall,
And after labour they lose theyr lyfe and all!
Another sorte is to this not moche unlyke,
Whiche spende theyr tymes in wretched art magyke,
Therby supposynge some treasore to have founde,
Whiche many yeres is hydde within the grounde!"

After their publication in 1540, these satirical eclogues of Barclay's, though foreign in their origin and without precedent in English literature, had yet a perceptible influence over Elizabethan pastoral poets. In their satirical tone, often approaching invective, they bear fruit in the eclogues of Googe, in the *Shepherd's Calendar* of Spenser, and in the sporadic attempts of other Elizabethans.

So far it has seemed advisable, owing to the comparative scarcity of any one variety of satire in any one period, to adopt for our material the chronological rather than the topical treatment. Between 1520 and 1550, however, the bulk of the social satire, its largely anonymous character, together with the fact that it was all produced within a short period, render the topical treatment indispensable. The same is true of the religious satire of this era—the satire of the Reformation; though in this variety we meet with some celebrated names, notably that of Sir David Lyndsay.

CHAPTER VI

SOCIAL SATIRE, 1520–1550; SATIRE OF THE REFORMATION

Social changes under Henry VIII.—Social satire.—*Nowadays.*—*Manner of the World Nowadays.*—*Treatise of this Gallant.*—*The Ruin of a Realm.*—Dissolution of the monasteries.—"The Pilgrimage of Grace."—*An Exhortation to the Nobles and Commons of the North.*—Social satire under Edward VI.—*Vox Populi, Vox Dei.*—The Satire on Woman.—*The Proud Wives Pater Noster.*—The Satire on Rogues.—*Cocke Lorells Bote.*—*The Hye Way to the Spyttell Hous.*—Other Satires on Fools and on Rogues.—Relation of such satire to that of the later Moralities.—The Satire of the Reformation.—Its varieties.—Its general lack of literary merit.—Tyndale's New Testament.—The *Replycacion.*—*Rede Me and Be Not Wrothe.*—Its form, tone, and subject-matter.—Its value as a Satire.—*A Proper Dialogue.*—*Doctor Double Ale.*—*The Image of Hypocrisy.*—*John Bon and Mast Person.*—The Conservative side.—Its Satires.—*A Poor Help.*—Growth of the Reformation under Edward VI.—*A Ballad of Luther, the Pope, etc.*—*Little John Nobody.*—General character of the Reformation Satire.

I

There was ample material for social satire during the reign of Henry VIII and of his son and successor, Edward VI. It was a period of social, political, and religious change, a period crowded with momentous events.

The Reformation; the decay of the old nobility; political follies and crimes, such as the systematic debasement of the currency; the dissolution of the monasteries, casting eighty thousand people adrift without means of subsistence—all this and more furnished material for the social satirists, and it is not strange that the social satire of the period echoes with complaints and with calls for reform.

The old Norman nobility were decaying, their castles falling into neglect. The King's extravagance, which they were forced to emulate, was to them a source of ruin. This degradation of the old nobility was the very object at which King Henry aimed. He filled their places with new men—"upstarts" the old nobility called them. Many of the clergy, carried away by the commercial spirit of the time, became merchants, and used even the very holy places of the church, so it was claimed, for markets of barter and sale. It was also said that in London itself, aliens were outdoing English merchants at their own business, and French wares were outselling English products. Upon the dissolution of the monasteries, vast tracts of land passed into the hands of a new commercial class, the sheep-farmers, and rents enormously increased. The monks had, in the main, been easy landlords, but the new owners, bent only upon money-making, were avaricious and unfeeling. Small farms were united into large inclosures for sheep-raising; whole villages and even churches were razed to the ground; tenants were summarily evicted and turned adrift; the country was overrun with thieves and beggars as never before. From the debasement of the currency, which began in the reign of Edward IV, it resulted that the shilling of 1551 contained less than one-seventh of the fine silver of the shilling of 1527. Between 1495 and 1533, wheat rose from four shillings to over eight shillings per quarter; but the increase in wages during the same period was far from being proportionate—the pay of an agricultural laborer rising only from two shillings to two shillings three-pence per week. All these conditions united to produce deep and widespread misery, which is mirrored in the satirical verse of the period.

Such conditions as these are pictured in the ballad *Nowadays.*[1] Its thirty-five eight-line stanzas are strongly reminiscent in their tone, form and subject-matter, of the poem on the evils of Edward II's reign.[2] Its subject-matter is widely inclusive, for the writer reviews the whole state of the country from the point of view of a moralist and a public sympathizer. While in several stanzas we find general complaints that may or may not spring from specific circumstances, yet there is after all very little of the "satirical commonplace," for *Nowadays* derives its significance and vitality largely from its contemporary references. The absence of any allusion to monastic disestablishment or to the intolerable taxation that marked the last years of Wolsey's régime, would seem to place the

[1] *Ballads from Manuscripts,* ed. Furnivall, vol. 1, p. 93.

[2] See *supra,* p. 64 f.

date of the poem somewhere about 1520. The church and the laity, the lords and the Commons, the city and the country, are alike arraigned with considerable effectiveness, and in an earnest, popular style. Here is the voice of the poor, but also the complaint of the moralist. The old charges against clerical corruption and the sale of benefices are reinforced by a criticism of the commercial spirit among the clergy:

> " Men say that priors & abbottes be
> Grate grosyers in this countre;
> They vse bying & sellyng openlye;
> the church hath the name.
> Thei are nott content with ther possession,
> But gapyng ever for promotion,
> & thus withdrawyng mens Devotion,
> vnto the landes grete shame."

Nowadays is not, on the one hand, the literary Satire of Skelton, popular in form as that is, nor, on the other hand, is it the mere popular political ballad. It seems rather a cross between the two; for, though somewhat self-conscious, it is lacking in literary form, and seems to spring from the people. It shows little personality, for it is both anonymous and without personal allusions, yet it illustrates the English tendency to pass in review public events, and, when necessary, to express freely and fearlessly an adverse opinion.

The extravagant fashions of this period are attacked in *The Manner of the World Nowadays,* a ballad that may have been written by Skelton.[3] While it embodies a mixture of charges, such as might apply to any age, it contains a number of specific references to its own time. It is reminiscent of Lydgate, as it inveighs with a certain amount of humor against pointed caps, pranked coats and sleeves, guarded hose, new-fashioned daggers, and other French importations dear to the courtier and gallant of the period.

Something of this same material is embodied in Wynkyn de Worde's rather more elaborate and far more celebrated *Treatise of this Gallant,* written about 1520, in thirty-two *rime royal*

[3] *The Works of John Skelton,* I, 148 f; *Old Ballads,* ed Collier, Percy Soc. Pub., vol. I, p. I.

stanzas.[4] In this mixture of moral and social satire, we find material that is at times general and again strictly contemporary. The writer begins with a lament on England's present condition, and describes the dress of the gallant of the period—"Warrocked hoode," "parrocked pouche," daggers, "purpled garments," "rolled hodes, stuffed with flockes," doublets open at the breast, slashed gown and coats, tippets like a chain in which they go haltered like a horse to the stable, "the new bulwarks that they wear at the knee." Women are rebuked for infidelity to their husbands, for dressing like men, and for giving themselves to wantonness; and prelates, lords, and merchants are bitterly arraigned. The people, however, are pitied, for they are bare-footed, hungry, and miserable:

> "So moche rychesse and araye and so moche nede
> So many bedes borne and so lytell deuocyon
> So moche fastynge for hungre and so lytell nede
> So moche paynted worshyp and so lytell reason
> I trowe no man hath sene in this regyon
> Our synne asketh vengeaunce I am in grete fere.
> In shorte tyme we shall wayle that euer it came here."

The *Treatise of this Gallant* is interesting in its union of the medieval and the transitional and its very obvious imitation of Skelton's *Speke Parrot.* In the serious, even bitter tone; in the discussion of the seven deadly sins; in the arraignment of various social classes, it is thoroughly medieval; but in the somewhat satirical description of the gallant's dress, and the reference to the follies of the court, it is more characteristic of its own period. Still, as a whole, it is largely a survival of the old moral rebuke in which the satirist was moved to indignation, not laughter, and, being chiefly an imitation, it is not especially significant or interesting, except as giving variety to the social satire of its time.

The *Ruin of a Realm,* also composed about 1520, and written in *rime royal* stanzas, is preserved in manuscript only. It is characterized by very much the same tone as Wynkyn de Worde's lugubrious Satire.[5] No great interest attaches to its

[4] *Ballads from Manuscripts,* 1, 445; *Early Popular Poetry,* 3, 149.
[5] *Ballads from Manuscripts,* I, 158.

academic tone and its general lament. It is a serious, even vituperative, attack in the medieval manner on the vices of the prelates. In its animadversions upon the degeneration of the old nobility and upon the evils of the new court life, it is far more interesting. Feudalism has passed away.

The dissolution of the monasteries consummated in 1536 by King Henry through the agency of his great minister Thomas Cromwell was by no means acceptable to the whole of the English people. Though the monks had degenerated into mere land-owners and the friars into mere beggars; and though monks and friars both were without religious enthusiasm, and the monasteries had outlived their usefulness, still neither monks, friars, nor monasteries were generally unpopular. Indeed, in the north, where the abbeys had long been the refuge of the poor and the dispensers of a generous charity, the disestablishment was bitterly resented, as is witnessed by the famous "Pilgrimage of Grace" in 1536. This strange social uprising in Yorkshire and Lincolnshire, which was at once both "aristocratic and popular, clerical and lay," sprang from a strange mixture of complex motives. The lords of the old nobility rose against the "upstart" Cromwell, who, from a time shortly after the fall of Wolsey, had, under the king, been the supreme power in the state, and was cordially hated by every class of people except the extreme Protestants. The people rose against the enclosures of land and the grasping avarice of the new land-owners, against heavy taxes, and widespread social wretchedness. Both clergy and people together protested against the dissolution of the monasteries. Finally, all classes, the lords, the clergy, and the commons, were up in arms against the religious changes which the king and his iconoclastic minister were forcing upon the nation. The "Pilgrimage of Grace," at first so threatening and formidable, was finally unsuccessful, and accomplished nothing for the alleviation of the conditions that gave it birth. These social evils were not to be remedied even in part until the time of Elizabeth. Disestablishment was to proceed apace until it ended in 1545 in the confiscation of the property of the guilds. The old nobility was to grow weaker and weaker. Religious changes were to proceed until they resulted in the complete protestantism desired by Cranmer and Somerset.

It was just at this period that *An Exhortation to the Nobles and Commons of the North,*[6] in twenty-five six-line stanzas, summed up these conditions. One wonders whether it was written before or after the " Pilgrimage of Grace " and what relation it might have sustained to that famous uprising. Its tone is fanatical, vehement, and wholly polemical. The suppression of the monasteries is the theme, and Cromwell as the author of the mischief is roundly abused. " It is these miserable heretics under Cromwell their chief, who have caused all this trouble:

> This curseide cromwell by hys gret pollicie
> in this Realme haith causid gret exaction,
> then hyly promotyng that settes outte heresie;
> by the aide of the chancellors, vsyng exortacyon.
> Agans them all for to fyght, I think yt conuenient,
> and noit for to seisse tyll ther lyves be spent."

Yet the king, in whose hands Cromwell was but a servile instrument, was alone responsible for disestablishment. It is, however, characteristic of this period of Tudor absolutism that the king's name is never mentioned; first Wolsey and then Cromwell are held responsible for all the evils of Henry's reign.

Ten years pass by before the voice of the people is again heard. Henry VIII is with his fathers, and Somerset is Lord Protector of the realm; but the evils and abuses that had called forth so loud a protest in the former reign have become intolerably aggravated. Enclosures and evictions have grown even more common; the debasement of the currency has continued, with a proportionate rise of prices. At Norwich twenty thousand men have risen, calling for the removal of evil counsellors, prohibition of enclosures and redress for the poor. We should expect such conditions to be mirrored in some popular protest, and so they are. *Vox Populi, Vox Dei,* written about 1547, by some clumsy imitator of Skelton's style, and addressed to Somerset, Lord Protector, is indeed the " voice of the people,"

[6] *Ballads from Manuscripts,* I, 301.

whether or not it be the "voice of God."[7] Through these eight hundred and fifteen Skeltonical lines rings a strong enthusiasm, and a mighty sympathy for the poor. The satire is purely social, with a singular unity of theme and a form well suited to its subject-matter. Replete with allusions to contemporary affairs, the strong and vehement torrent of the verse hurries straight on without any digressions into didacticism or moralizing. The gist is the wrongs of the agricultural laboring classes. Free from any moral protest or satirical commonplace, this strictly contemporary material is treated by some one who has an eye on the objects about which he is writing. In eleven sections of unequal length, the writer refers to the avarice of the great landowners (sheepmasters who had deprived the poor of a livelihood), the debasement of the currency and the misery entailed thereby, the rise in the price of meat, the forced vagabondage of the laboring man:

> "I mene the laboreng man,
> I mene the husbande man,
> I mene the plowghe man,
> I mene the handy-craft man,
> I mene the vy [tal] lyng man,
> and also the gud yoman
> that some tyme in this realme
> hade plente of key and creme,
> butter, egges, and chesse,
> honey, vax, and besse;
> but now, a-lacke! a-lacke!
> al thes men gowe to wrake,
> that are the bodye and staye
> of youre grasis realme alwaye."

Vox Populi, Vox Dei, a genuine popular appeal, purposeful though it be and permeated with a strange sort of power, is too devoid of humor to be satirical. At a time which produced practically no literature of any kind, and perhaps no verse that can be termed in any true sense satirical, the significance and value of the *Vox Populi, Vox Dei,* lies mainly in its direct, fearless, and forcible expression of the hereditary English interest in public affairs.

[7] *The Works of John Skelton,* 2, 400; *Ballads from Manuscripts,* 1, 124.

II

In subject-matter, medieval verse-satire can show nothing more remarkable than its frequent attacks on Woman. These constitute a sort of school of satirical verse, dragging out an existence through centuries. They embody an immense amount of satirical commonplace, set forth in a spirit vituperative rather than critical. The attack is not confined to any one literature or period, but is met with at every turn, often in places the most incongruous. In the Latin poem *Geburt Jesu,* of the thirteenth century, reverence and eulogy of the Virgin Mother are succeeded by gross abuse of contemporary womanhood. From the twelfth century on, innumerable examples occur in both verse and prose, Latin, French, and English. In Goliardic verse we have the *Golias de Conjuge non Ducenda,*[8] and many others. Anglo-French furnishes its full share: *La Jeste des Dames,*[9] of the thirteenth century, in sixteen quatrains, is a lightly satirical attack chiefly on the vanity of women. *Ragman Roll,*[10] and the really satirical but indecent *Song on Woman* of the fifteenth century, perpetuate the tradition in English. In the early sixteenth century it culminates, and, as a formal genre, does not die until Elizabethan times, when satirists find something better to say.

What was the origin of the Satire on Woman? Perhaps the *Roman de la Rose,* with its hundreds of lines of bitter taunts and witty gibes against women, had something to do with the later product. But long before Jean de Meung, the Goliards indulged in it, inspired, perhaps, by the theological doctrine of the Fall of Man through woman, and the teaching of the Church that, to the clergy, Woman was a delusion and a snare, to be shunned and, incidentally, to be vituperated. In the case of the Trouvères, very possibly this Satire on Woman resulted in an attempt to parody and counteract the extravagant love-poetry of the German Minnesängers.[11] Wright thinks it resulted from a corrupt state of society, as did the

[8] See *supra,* p. 41.
[9] *Reliquiæ Antiquæ,* I, 162–3.
[10] See *supra,* p. 122.
[11] Haessner, *Die Goliardendichtung, passim.*

terrific onslaughts of Juvenal. On the whole, however, ecclesiastical influence seems to have predominated, and the Church was probably the main source of this satirical genre. Whatever its origin, the attack became so frequent and so unsparing in the fifteenth century, that replies thereto seemed necessary; and so we find the admirable Occleve in *The Letter of Cupid* taking up the cudgel and defending women against the inconstancy and deceit of men.[11a] These sixty-eight seven-line stanzas should have been sufficient; but none the less the women seem to have attacked Occleve as a defamer of the sex, and he found it necessary in his *Dialogue*—at least through the last eighteen stanzas of the eight hundred and twenty-six lines—to defend himself against the accusation.

The Pain and Sorrow of Evil Marriage,[12] a translation of the Goliardic poem *De Conjuge non Ducenda,* in twenty-two *rime royal* stanzas, appeared early in the sixteenth century. It is a very general but bitter attack on Woman, a warning to youth, didactic in its tone and devoid of merit or of interest. Just as bitter and general, but much more gross, is *The School-House of Women,*[13] written about 1540.[14] It is in one hundred and forty-seven stanzas of seven lines each, with four accents to the line. In this medley of anecdote, of illustrations drawn from Biblical and classical sources, and of direct accusations, every imaginable charge is brought against the sex. It is, indeed, a summary of all satire of its type.

This gross invective and direct abuse changes to a tone at times humorous and really satirical in *The Proud Wives Pater Noster,*[15] written in seventy-two eight-line stanzas. The *Pater Noster* bears little relation to contemporary life; but dialogue and narrative, and freedom from didacticism and

[11a] Cf. Chaucer's *Legend of Good Women.*

[12] Pub. Percy Soc., vol. I, ed. Collier; *Early Pop. Poetry,* ed. Hazlitt, 4, 73.

[13] *Early Pop. Poetry,* 4, 97; *Select Pieces of Early Popular Poetry,* ed. Utterson, vol. 2, p. 51.

[14] Almost a century later, *The School-House* evoked from Edward More a reply entitled *The Defence of Women,*—a late example of the same genre to which belong Occleve's *Letter of Cupid* and *Dialogue.*

[15] *Early Pop. Poetry,* 4, 147; *Select Pieces of Early Pop. Poetry,* 2, 144.

invective, give it an interest superior to that attaching to other satire of the kind. It opens with a visit of a wife to church. She interlards her Pater Noster with frequent expression of most worldly desires. The narrative passes into dialogue as the two wives exchange confidences regarding husbands, and advise together as how best to manage the unreasonable creatures. The first wife returns home to put the advice into practice. Failing to wheedle her husband into foolish expenditures, she steals his money and brings him to ruin. This form has something in common with Dunbar's *The Two Married Women and the Widow,* though here the satire is not so stinging nor the indecorous element so preponderant. Chaucer's Wife of Bath, herself no saint, would have despised such marital conduct.

But this humorous and truly satirical tone fails to manifest itself in a treatise *Showing and Declaring the Pride and Abuse of Women Nowadays,* written by a certain Charles Bansley.[16] This is a sermon of direct rebuke in fifty-nine four-line stanzas, coarse and vituperative in its tone, general in its subject-matter. The author is evidently a Protestant, for we are told

> "From Rome, from Rome, this carkered pryde,
> From Rome it came, doubtless."—

Finally, inane and ineffective as it is, this species—the Satire on Woman—is destined to long life, for it crops out here and there in the informal satire of the Elizabethans. Indeed, has it ever died away?

III

Among the numerous social evils of the times of Henry VIII the most conspicuous was that of vagabondage. This evil had been of slow growth. For centuries it had been increasing—ever since the introduction of sheep raising as a national industry had thrown large numbers of agricultural laborers out of employment. But never had it been so general or so threatening as now. New industrial conditions had arisen, and to these the lower orders had not accommodated

[16] *Early Pop. Poetry,* 4, 227 f.

themselves. The continued and extensive enclosures for sheep raising, which have been referred to, aggravated a condition which Parliament was unable to check by the most stringent laws. These laws not only restricted the landlord in his operations, but imposed severe punishment on beggars and vagabonds. Still the evil grew, and it continued until the economic balance was readjusted in a later reign. England was infested with gangs of mendicants and thieves, some really impotent to gain a living, some able-bodied and "sturdy," seeking honest employment, others professional beggars and cheats, who thus took advantage of the prevailing economic conditions to practice wholesale fraud.

From such transient conditions of this era, sprang a peculiar form of satire. It first appeared in *The Ship of Fools,* flourished for a generation in a number of imitations of the greater work, and gradually died as its source failed with the disappearance of the excesses it essayed to attack. Sporadic satire on beggars and begging there had always been, but it had never developed into a distinct variety until these favorable conditions gave it shape. In form the Satire on rogues and beggars is an elaboration of the old Satire on classes.

Cocke Lorelle's Bote[17] is the best-known and perhaps the most interesting of all the numerous progeny of *The Ship of Fools.* This highly humorous and really satirical burlesque was printed by Wynkyn de Worde some time early in the reign of Henry VIII. Its plan, that of a *ship of rogues,* is of course imitated from the famous and popular work of Barclay. Of the poem, only four hundred and fourteen lines survive, written in a kind of tumbling verse, rhyming *a a b a c b,* usually of three and four accents, but permitting a large variety.

Cock Lorell, a notorious vagabond, has a boat for the reception of all classes of rogues in England. These come together, seeking for passage in the boat, and are described, the first few with some degree of minuteness. The later ones, who come by scores, are merely named. All, of course, are rogues, not only from the class of professional vagabonds, but

[17] Percy Soc. Pub., vol. 6, ed. Rimbault.

also from the trading classes, each of which is represented,—thus we infer that, in the writer's opinion, every class is full of rogues. The abrupt beginning introduces a woman of the lower class, who is followed by a cobbler, a shoemaker, a tanner, a butcher, and so on, and finally by a pardoner. The appearance of this last personage introduces an elaborate piece of burlesque, as the pardoner reads his roll and describes his wares. One is of course reminded of Chaucer's inimitable treatment of this same theme.[18]

Here follows a realistic bit of description, disgusting perhaps, but significant, which fills over one-fourth the extant part of the poem. Best of all the motley throng is the butcher, "gored in reed blode," with his two bull-dogs and his greasy hose. Crowded at last with representatives of every imaginable class of rogues, the ship sails away. The various occupations of the passengers are described. Some merely "whyteled after the wynde." Merry and sportful was the life on the ship as she sailed fair England around, calling at every "vyllage, towne, cyte, and borrowe." As the writer wends homeward, he meets with a company of

> "—ermytes, monkes and freres,
> Chanons, chartores, and inholders;
> And many whyte nonnes with whyte vayles."

They seek passage on the boat, but are too late. The writer advises them to wait another year, until Cock Lorell comes around again.

In this social Satire is a strange mingling of realistic and of burlesque description. In realistic description and in character study, it is a product of the Renaissance, connecting itself in these qualities with other pieces of contemporary satire. Its atmosphere is thoroughly English; and, for verisimilitude, the Pardoner, in his burlesque description, alludes to various London localities,—St. Giles, St. Katherine's, London Bridge. In its Rabelaisian humor and broad burlesque and its absolute freedom from didacticism, *Cocke Lorell's Bote* is utterly dif-

[18] To be followed by the dramatic treatment in the work of Lyndsay and of Heywood, q. v.

ferent from *The Ship of Fools.* In that it is partly a Satire on classes, it connects itself with the past. Yet it is not the product of literary traditions, but of the free, broad, spontaneous impulses of its period. In realism and in power of characterization it perhaps owes something to Barclay; but these qualities, appearing sporadically in satire since the days of Langland, are now in the air. With *Cocke Lorell's Bote* we begin that satire of low life which is hereafter to be perennial in English literature.

Contemporary with *Cocke Lorell* was *The Hye Way to the Spyttel Hous,*[19] ascribed to a certain Robert Copland. This extraordinary production lacks the strong burlesque of *Cocke Lorell,* but is in some respects even more remarkable. Our interest in it arises from its immediate relation to contemporary conditions, its author's clear insight, and his powers of minute description. It is in no sense poetical; nor is it, strictly speaking, a Satire. *The Hye Way* is a versified economic tract, written with a purpose—an unsparing exposure of the frauds perpetrated by the mendicant classes. Its debt to the " Fool satire " is obvious, though its scope is narrower than that of *The Ship of Fools:* its class of fools is that of those beggars who are brought to poverty through their own folly.[20] In its humorous and minute realism, it exemplifies the growing disposition to study and portray low life which appeared first in the work of Langland and intermittently ever after. Now, however, this interest in the lower orders and their habits of life is vastly fed by contemporary conditions—an interest in this case not merely literary but scientific; for our author not only is awake to the life around him, but inquires into its causes. *The Hye Way to the Spyttel Hous* is almost twelve hundred lines in length; written mainly in the pentameter couplet, with an introduction in *rime royal.* The form is narrative and descriptive; the style, simple, direct, realistic, without trace of literary tradition.

The author, taking refuge from a winter storm, stops at a

[19] *Early Popular Poetry,* 4, 17 f.; *Select Pieces of Early Popular Poetry,* 2, 1 f.

[20] See Herford, pp. 359–62.

certain hospital. With the porter he holds a lengthy conversation, which turns on social conditions and reviews the whole range of mendicancy in a series of graphic pictures. These descriptions are not only realistic and humorous, but contemporary. There is in them, however, something universal and permanent as well. One of the most striking of these scenes, selected from a large number almost equally vivid, is that of the porter's description of his experiences at St. Paul's. He tells of dishonest mendicants who simulate indigence, but are in reality more prosperous than the very people who contribute to their support.

Another Satire of this class, *The Twenty-five Orders of Fools,* is so deeply indebted to Barclay as to be a mere epitome —though a lamentably colorless and feeble one—of *The Ship of Fools.* Not only its characters but sometimes its very expressions are drawn from the earlier and greater work. Still another example of this satire on fools and rogues, Awdeley's *Quatern of Knaves,* connects with Barclay through *Cocke Lorell.* It is a class Satire, a genuine study of rogues, and shows a gain in power of realistic character portrayal.[21]

Altogether, this satire on certain phases of low life is closely related, in its realism and its humor, as well as in its didactic purpose, to similar subject-matter found in the more humorous and realistic Moralities of about this same period.[22]

IV

The " Satire of the Reformation " is even more characteristic of this period of change than is the " Satire of Rogues." Religious satire in a broad sense had existed, as we have seen, since the days of Walter Map. It is the expression of a salient English characteristic, which has shown itself in the sometimes humorous, sometimes bitter gibes of the old Goliardic school; in the almost inarticulate wails of would-be reformers; in the strong arraignments of Langland; in the polemic protests of the Lollards.

[21] For a description of *The Twenty-five Orders of Fools* and of the *Quatern of Knaves* the present writer is entirely indebted to Professor Herford's *Studies in the Literary Relations of England and Germany in the Sixteenth Century.*

[22] Cf. *infra,* ch. VII, *passim.*

The Lollard satire represented far more than the traditional Satire on religious matters. It was a revolutionary attack on doctrines as well as on morals; a call for change of creed, as well as for a reformed morality. But these protests, powerful, searching, bitter as they were, failed in their object: Lollardry, with all its revolutionary doctrines, fell before the Lancastrian persecution in the earlier fifteenth century; and for a season the revolutionary voices were hushed. But only for a season. For the Lutheran satire of a hundred years later was the logical continuation of the Lollard cry for doctrinal reform. Under the impulse of Lutheranism from without, the embers of Lollardry were blown into flame. The religious satire produced by the radical puritans of this later time, which we call the Satire of the Reformation, added the more radical element to a renewal of the old plaints and of the old calls for moral and doctrinal reform.

Such was the satire of the religious revolutionists, the radicals. It had its antitype in the satire of the extreme conservatives. The voice that spoke in the time of Wycliffe *against* Lollardry, the voice that rejected reform and defended the old order, was still heard, opposed utterly both to Lutheranism and to the gentler, more gradual reform proposed by the men of the New Learning.

Besides both of these partisan varieties, there was a long line of religious reformers who, since the days of Walter Map, had spoken in English satire—had spoken in the Goliardic verses, in *Piers Plowman,* in the work of Lydgate and of Gower. This line of moderates was represented now by Skelton and the great scholars of the English Renaissance, who voiced the medium between Lutheranism and extreme conservatism. Save Skelton, they spoke mainly in prose; and it was of course in prose—the usual vehicle of religious disputation—that the religious spirit of the time largely found expression.

But from 1526, when Tyndale's translation of the *New Testament* was introduced into England, on to the close of Henry VIII's reign, the Reformation was an increasingly powerful and vigorous movement, with both opposition and support unsparing and outspoken. As a natural result, we find in this period a considerable amount of verse-satire both for and against the movement. As might be expected, such satire possesses very little literary merit. It is vituperative rather than critical; it deals in invective rather than in true satire; it is interesting only for the light it casts upon the religious temper of the time. As has been said, the Satire of the Reformation, strictly so-called, is distinguished from the previous religious satire—except that of the Lollards—in that it deals distinctly with the doctrines of the Lutheran Reformation. The satire of the reformatory party, not content with merely ridiculing or abusing clerical immorality and ecclesiastical corruption, attacks the very doctrines and polity of the Church—the Mass and all that it implied, shrines, images, pilgrimages, celibacy of the clergy, and all else against which the reformers made a stand. Although preluded in tone and much of its subject-matter by the Lollard satire, it is quite unconscious of literary tradition, and whatever heritage it has from the past is certainly not one of literary form.

Only two verse-Satires of this period rise into eminence. One is *The Satire of the Three Estates* by Sir David Lyndsay, the Scotchman; the other, *Rede Me and Be Nott Wrothe,* by two Franciscan friars, Roy and Barlow. Both Satires represent the radical or even revolutionary religious party, though Lyndsay, as we shall see later, stands in a class apart. Before we discuss *Rede Me and Be Nott Wrothe,* it is necessary to review briefly a series of events that led up to the poem and largely gave it motive, and without a knowledge of which it is hardly explicable.

The New Learning, which in England took a religious turn, had for one of its effects the translation of the Bible. It was to be expected that all attempts to bring the Bible home to the people should by scholars and reformers like More be looked upon as revolutionary and savoring of the Lutheranism that was just then invading England. And such was the case. William Tyndale, himself a scholar and reformer, met with opposition not only from the conservative clergy, but from scholars of the New Learning as well. He was forced to flee from English persecution, and to finish in Germany his translation of the New

Testament. In 1526 six thousand copies were surreptitiously introduced into England. All these were eagerly bought up by a people long hungry for religious truth. The translation was unauthorized; conservatives, led by the prelates, cried out against it. It savored of Lutheranism; and thus even the more liberal placed upon it their ban. At Oxford, it had found a generous welcome, and certain heretical young scholars, opponents of pilgrimages and image-worship, held secret meetings to discuss the new teaching and read the new translation. All this was discovered by the conservative ecclesiastics, keen-scented for heresy. Consequently, at the instigation chiefly of Cuthbert Tunstal, the Bishop of London, with Wolsey's consent, six of these young Oxford scholars in penitential dress, carrying lighted faggots, were forced to join in a procession through the streets of London. At St. Paul's Cross they stopped, and were led thrice around a blazing pile of books, into which they cast their faggots. This blazing pile was composed of copies of Tyndale's translation of the New Testament, bought up or confiscated by the conservatives.[23] After the bonfire, a sermon against heresy was preached by Fisher, Bishop of Rochester. But the people did not take kindly to the spectacular exhibition: they called it a "burning of the word of God." This penitential procession made a tremendous stir in the religious world. It was only the small beginning of prolonged and bitter persecution, but it echoed in verse for many a day.

Skelton, or, as we would prefer to believe, some imitator of Skelton, dedicates to Cardinal Wolsey his piece of invective against these same six young heretics. It is in the Skeltonical meter, which was, unfortunately, quite as well adapted to such impotent vituperation as it was to the sledgehammer strokes of Skelton's best work. *The Replycacion*[24] extended through some four hundred lines of what professes to be argument, but is in truth mere vulgar abuse, without sense and without humor. Of its tone and style a few lines will suffice as illustration:

[23] So thorough was this confiscation that but *two* copies of Tyndale's translation have survived to the present day.

[24] *The Works of John Skelton,* I, 206.

"I saye, ye braynlesse beestes,
Why iangle you suche iestes,
In your diuynite
Of Luther's affynite,
To the people of lay fee,
Raylyng in your rages
To worshyppe none ymages,
Nor do pylgrymages?
I saye, ye deuyllysshe pages,
Full of such dottages,
Count ye your selfe good clerkes
And snapper in suche werkes?"

Certain references to Luther, Wycliffe, and "Lollardy lernyng" show the writer to be a conservative who sees in new translations of the Bible only Lutheranism and revolution —"sedition, privy conspiracy, and rebellion."

If the translation of the Bible had produced only a *Replycacion,* however, it would here demand little attention. But out of it and subsequent similar events grew the *Rede Me and be Nott Wrothe,*[25] greatest of English verse Satires of the Reformation period. Whether or not Tyndale was a Lutheran, the readers of his translation became largely identified with the party of religious revolution. Certainly there can be no doubt of the religious tenets of the authors of *Rede Me and be Nott Wrothe.* William Roy and Jerome Barlow were two English friars, Franciscan observants, and "Protestants," who had taken refuge in Strassburg from the persecution against Lutheranism already begun in England. Germany was being swept by the Reformation. Strassburg was the storm-centre. The Swiss cantons had formally abolished the Mass and had taken their stand unequivocally in favor of Lutheranism. But in Strassburg, a free city, the Mass, though morally dead, had not yet been buried by a formal abolition. This was to come a few months later. Just at this critical juncture, these two Protestant friars indited *Rede Me and be Nott Wrothe.* True, it was both written and printed abroad; but it was by Englishmen, for Englishmen, and about English affairs. In England

[25] *Arber's English Reprints,* vol. II, pp. 19–123.

reports of its publication went about in the autumn of 1528, and Wolsey, "the protagonist in this religious drama," ordered his agent Rynck to buy all the purchasable copies in Germany. Thus the edition was virtually destroyed, and the influence of the powerful Satire almost brought to naught. Had it been freely circulated in England, it might have worked a revolution, or at least have had results comparable to those effected in Scotland by its northern counterpart, *The Satire of the Three Estates;* for it comes right from within the fold, and is thus all the more unsparing and thoroughgoing in its denunciations and exposures.[26]

In form and in tone *Rede Me and be Nott Wrothe* presents nothing radically new. Its invective, sarcasm, ridicule, were shared by much other satire of the time; and the form, that of dialogue, was widely popular. Moreover, its subject-matter, wholly religious, is, so far as regards its attack on the ecclesiastical orders, that of religious satire for over three centuries preceding it. Wolsey was a constant target for contemporary English satire. Even what seem the distinctly reformatory—the Protestant—elements are not all new. Pilgrimages and shrines had been assailed by Langland. The celibacy of the clergy had long been a subject for controversy. Pardons and indulgences had for centuries been the objects of incessant attack. But the spoliation of the abbeys and the abolition of the Mass itself are, of course, of the Reformation alone; and, in the aggregation of all these various charges, the attack on the policy of the Church and its hierarchy, the substitution of the New Testament for the authority of the Church's propaganda, the call, not merely for reform in moral standards, but for radical changes in polity and doctrine,—all these mark this Satire as distinctly of the Protestant Reformation,—thus separating it fundamentally from all that has preceded it. In England it is a pioneer, and by far the greatest of its kind.

[26] Manuel's *Krankheit der Messe,* a poetic dialogue of great humor and power, had begun the Mass satire. From this source Roy and Barlow probably borrowed their idea; but, judging from the general inferiority of their Satire, the two frars had not read Manuel's dialogue. The mere idea, however, might well have reached them orally, since the country was full of it. See Herford, pp. 43-44.

In form, this Satire is simply a dialogue between two serving-men of a priest. Watkyn and Jeffraye recognize the fact that the Mass is actually dead and that consequently their master must soon be without employment—his occupation gone. What shall they, then, do for a living? This is a delicate question. While considering it, they fall inevitably into religious disputation, after the custom of their time. If the Mass is really dead, where shall it be buried,—in France, in Rome, or in England? Finally the shrine of St. Thomas at Canterbury is decided upon as the most fitting place of interment. Then, who shall perform the funeral ceremony,—Cardinal, Bishops, Secular Clergy, Monks, or Friars? As each class is considered, an opportunity is taken to expose its enormities; and these form the staple of the theme.

There is nothing dramatic in the dialogue. Watkyn is the simpler fellow: he relies on God's Word only, and to it he appeals. But he is acquainted with Protestant affairs on the Continent; and the first part of the dialogue deals largely with happenings in Germany. Jeffraye, shrewd, bitter, replete with common-sense, is fresh from England. He is thoroughly familiar with English ecclesiastical affairs and knows the craft and subtlety of the various religious orders. Throughout, he is the bolder of the two, and the principal speaker.

The work is dedicated with superb insolence to the "Cardinal of York." It opens with a piece of burlesque— a mock-lament for the Mass, supposedly spoken by a priest who bewails the death of that venerable dignitary and his own consequent loss of occupation. This consists of thirty-four seven-line stanzas *a b a b b c c;* the first six lines of five accents; the last, of four. This mock-lament is followed by the first part of the dialogue. In this the two Protestant friends discuss generally the doctrines of the church—celibacy of the clergy, the Mass, miracles, pardons, pilgrimages, shrines, the Pope, religious affairs in England. Both Watkyn and Jeffraye have heard much of miracles, but neither has ever seen one. Priests, they say, reverence these fables a thousand times more than they do the Gospel! But severe as is this indictment, their crowning piece of invective is reserved for the Pope. After finishing with the Pope, and assailing the celibacy of the clergy, Jeffraye strongly advocates the suppression of the monasteries. This is especially interesting, since the poem was written some years before monastic disestablishment went to such extremes under Cromwell. Jeffraye dwells upon the economic aspect of monastic land encroachments, thus making the only departure from a purely religious tone in the whole dialogue. "These monks turn lands into pasture, and let a dozen farms under one lease; hence one or two rich franklins occupy the rightful livings of a dozen men." Thus is thrown upon the land-owning clergy the entire burden of a wretched social phase for which they were but partially responsible.

With such advanced Lutheranism, naturally go abundant references to contemporary affairs. Chief among such references are the allusions to the reception of Tyndale's New Testament in England, and the action of the Bishop of London. The burning of the Testament at Saint Paul's Cross is dwelt upon at length. Eight stanzas in *rime royal,* filled with bitter invective, are addressed to Wolsey as the instigator of the sacrilege. With these contemporary references there are many personalities—and for these the present Satire is especially distinguished. Wolsey is of course the chief target for abuse. He is "the butcher," "the butcherly sloutche"; and, at the same time, the ruler of England, "greater than King or Queen." Every possible charge is alleged against his character, and not one virtue is allowed him. He is represented even as a traitor to his country. At last, after the Cardinal's character has been minutely analyzed, he is chosen as the fittest celebrant of the obsequies of the dead Mass.

But Roy and Barlow were not content with such large prey as the mighty Wolsey. Both on the Continent and in England, they singled out for that thorough and cordial mud-flinging in which they were such adepts, other conservatives, or even reformers, if over-cautious. Father Mathias, John Faber, Emfer, Dr. Eck, Murner, Erasmus, Thomas Winter (Wolsey's illegitimate son), Standish, and Cochlaeus, are all generously remembered. Of the last named, the chief Continental spy of the English prelates, Watkyn gives a very unflattering description; and to this Jeffraye replies,

> "Yf he be as thou sayst he is
> I warant he shall not mis
> Of a benefice and that shortly.
> For I ensure the oure Cardinall
> With wother bisshops in generall
> Love soche a felowe entierly."

After these bitter personalities and contemporary allusions follows a lament over the decline of spirituality among ecclesiastics, written in fifteen stanzas of *rime royal.* This lament forms an interlude. It might have been written by *Lydgate,* so remote, so general, so dull is it, and so little has it in common with the dialogue proper. This old-fashioned and lugubrious lament is followed by the second part of the dialogue, devoted to just as time-honored an assault on the clergy. In the manner sanctioned by every religious satirist since Walter Map, the two Franciscan brothers engage in a specific exposure of the misdeeds of the English ecclesiastics of the established Church. Jeffraye speaks, first paying his respects to the bishops:

> "As for preachynge they take no care
> They wolde se a course at an hare
> Rather then to make a sermon.
> To folowe the chace of wylde dere
> Passynge the tyme with ioly chere
> Amonge theym all is common.
> To playe at the cardes and dyce
> Some of theym are nothynge nyce
> Both at hasard and momchaunce.
> They dryncke in gaye golden booles
> The bloudde of povre simple soules
> Perisshynge for lacke of sustenaunce.
> Their hongery cures they never teache
> Nor will soffre none wother to preache
> But soche as can lye and flatter."—

The secular clergy are not spared; neither are the mendicant orders, nor the monasteries and the monks. Roy's own order, that of the Observants, is condemned utterly and at great length. The cry against plurality of benefices, especially strident in England at this time, is not wanting; but perhaps the only distinctly new charge against the clergy in this long and severe arraignment is that of betrayal of confessions. Hence, viewed merely as an attack on the clergy, the Satire, though lively and vigorous enough with its mingling of humor and invective, connects itself with its own perennial class, which had flourished through the three hundred years preceding the Lutheran reformation.

The tone of *Rede Me and Be Nott Wrothe* is marked by bitter invective, thoroughly English and at times as harsh as that of Skelton, but far superior to that of most religious satire. Yet there is much irony—the very antithesis of invective, tremendous sarcasm, and some telling burlesque. The satire carries a strange conviction of truth-telling, though the tone towards Wolsey has a ring of personal resentment.

Through all its thirty-three hundred lines of dialogue, *Rede Me and Be Nott Wrothe* employs a consistent verse-scheme, rhyming *a a b c c b,* with four accents to the line, regularly, but sometimes three accents. The verse is light, and suits the material. Its unity of theme and its consistent structure render the poem readable. Violent as it is, this polemic is not dull; and with its sufficient humor and thoroughly destructive tone, it very well merits the designation of Satire. It is the result of a spiritual revolution, and was well calculated to further that revolution, called forth as it was by a crying need and answering a popular appeal. Almost needless to say, in form, in matter, and in spirit, *Rede Me and Be Nott Wrothe* bears no trace of classical influence.[27] The allusions in the poem are so far unclassical that they relate wholly to contemporary religious affairs, after the manner of the polemic Satire. The Christian reaction speaks in every line, but nothing of the pagan Renaissance. What is old, is of the Middle Ages; what is new, is of the Protestant Reformation.

[27] See *supra,* p. 15 f.

Appearing about the same time with the *Rede me and Be Nott Wrothe,* and quite possibly by the same authors, is a Protestant tract that goes under the name of *A Proper Dialogue Between a Gentleman and a Husbandman.*[28] This somber and severe production seems to have been written for the purpose of giving to Protestantism the dignity of age by connecting it with Lollardry. An address to the reader in ten *rime royal* stanzas, very similar in every respect to the interlude in *Rede me and Be Nott Wrothe,* introduces us to the dialogue. This is opened by the gentleman. In several stanzas, written in *rime royal,* he relates his hard fortune at the hands of the clergy, and tells us how estates that are rightfully his have been given away by his ancestors in return for masses promised by the priests. The husbandman replies in the meter of *Rede Me and Be Nott Wrothe;* and this verse is retained throughout the remainder of the dialogue. If the gentleman has suffered the loss of his patrimony, the husbandman has been ruined by extortionate rents—a strange accusation, as the clergy were notoriously easy landlords. Complaints against the avarice of the clergy continue throughout the piece, developing mainly the theme of Roy and Barlow's Satire, but emphasizing the economic aspect. We are told of the hatred felt by the clergy for the New Testament in English, of the reasons for this hatred, and of the burning of the New Testament in London. Clerical immorality is touched upon, and the historical references carry us back to Sir John Oldcastle and the persecution of the Lollards under Henry V. The significance of the *Proper Dialogue* lies largely in the attempt to give historical continuity to the reformatory movement, but also in the insistence upon the economic aspect of monastic proprietorship. This latter is a note strangely at variance with the almost universal cry against the enclosures and evictions that multiplied so largely after the dissolution of the monasteries.

Doctor Double-Ale,[29] a highly humorous and at times vituperative Satire, written in five hundred and twenty lines of

[28] *Arber's English Reprints,* 2, 125.

[29] *Early Popular Poetry,* 3, 303 f.

Skeltonical verse, is distinctly of the Reformation, although it does not attack the doctrines of the church. Written probably between 1530 and 1545, this is virtually the ecclesiastical Satire of the Goliardic school, though more humorous and far more vital in its characterization. The writer, with exceeding unction and zest, limits himself to describing the character and habits of a priest who is a confirmed toper and who totally neglects his parochial duties. He is a great favorite with the ale-wives, whose chief customer he is, and he usually makes the round of all the ale-houses. When he sticks to one, there is trouble:

> "For sometime he wyll go
> To one, and to no mo,
> Then wyll the hole route
> Upon that one cry out,
> And say she doth them wronge,
> To kepe him all daye longe
> Ffrom commyng them amonge."

But *Doctor Double-Ale* satirizes only one order of the clergy. In the *Image of Hypocrisy,* written about 1533, we have a purely religious satire, attacking the whole ecclesiastical hierarchy. This ballad exists only in manuscript. Its two thousand five hundred and seventy-six Skeltonical lines furnish such a terrific arraignment of every clerical order and hurl such floods of vitriol upon the offending clergy that it becomes highly significant, and characteristic of its period. It must have been written by some extreme Protestant, and, though on the opposite side, corresponds in its tone to the Skeltonical *Replycacion.* Argument is here replaced by abuse and rank invective, which now and again loses itself in "sound and fury, signifying nothing." Such Billingsgate, imitating Skelton's worst features, is only too characteristic of this new period of religious strife. But *The Image of Hypocrisy,* while far too diffuse, is sufficiently entertaining.[30]

The poem is divided into four parts. Part I contains a general denunciation of the clergy. Their treatment of so-called heretics is dwelt upon:

[30] *Ballads from Manuscripts,* 1, 181; *The Works of John Skelton,* 2, 413.

" A fagott for his backe,
or, Take him to the Racke,
And drowne hymne in a sacke,
Or burne hymne on (a) stake.
lo, thus they vndertake
The trothe false to make."

Part II is directed against the Bishops, the Pope, and the Cardinals. The Pope is the Antichrist of Rome; the Sire of Sin; a Crocodile; the Devil's priest from whom all evils spring. Part III is against the preachers. " Now we have a knight (Sir Thomas More) with his apology for the prelacy. He helps to bring simple innocent men to death [here follows another reference to the persecution at Paul's Cross]:

" And so the innocent,
for feare to be brent,
Must suffer checke and checke,
his faccott on his necke,
Not for his life to quecke,
But stande vpp, like a bosse,
In sight at paules crosse."

Part IV attacks the many orders of the popish clergy, monks, and friars. " You are beasts of Belial, yet you would have us call you ' fathers angelical ' ":

" In Councells myschevous,
In musters monstrous,
In skulkings insidicious,
Vnchast and lecherous,
In excess outragious,—"

The *Image of Hypocrisy* in its form, as has been said, shows the baleful influence of Skelton. It is by far the most elaborate religious Satire of its time.

Some ten years later, toward the close of Henry VIII's reign, the Reformation tract known as *John Bon and Mast Person*,[31] a dialogue in one hundred and sixty-five lines, furnishes a fine contribution to the Reformatory satire of this period. The abundant humor of this argumentative dialogue furnishes a delightful contrast to the tone of most religious satire. John Bon, the ploughman, involves the parson in a

[31] *Early Popular Poetry*, 4, 3 f.

discussion about the Mass, in which, with apparent artlessness, he draws the priest into all kinds of absurdities.

But the Satire of the Reformation was not one-sided, nor was invective the weapon of the Protestants alone. We find preserved in Dr. Furnivall's collection of manuscript ballads a poem representing the conservative side of religious controversy. Through forty-six six-line stanzas in the form of a popular ballad, the writer inveighs against the heresy which sprang from the devil and is infecting many of God's people.[32] "Luther is responsible for it all—that German dragon, who plots against all true Christianity, despises the priesthood, and strives to infect Englishmen with such damnable doctrines. These heretics contend that holy oil is no better than butter for anointing, that the clergy may marry, and stand for other abominable heresies that lead to damnation." Without humor and without literary merit as it is, the significance of this unmitigated invective lies in its popular tone and use of strictly contemporary material.

Skelton's influence again appears a few years later, towards the close of Henry's reign, in *A Poor Help,* some three hundred and sixty lines of invective against the Reformation.[23] The title of the poem is only too indicative of its nature; for while it reviews the various arguments of the reformers and attempts reply, its theme is without unity and its tone without humor. Had *The Image of Hypocrisy* ever been printed, one might think this a reply to that Protestant tract. "Will none in all this land take in hand these fellows, like the sand in number, who meddle with the gospel, and tell false tales against our holy prelacy, and the dignity of the holy church, saying it is but popistry and hypocrisy?"

The Reformation set in motion, however unwittingly, by Henry VIII, grew and expanded in the reign of Edward VI. What had been at first but a break with Rome, without any significant change of doctrine or polity, became rampant Lutheranism a few years later under the fostering care of Archbishop Cranmer and the Duke of Somerset. From the litera-

[32] *Ballads from Manuscripts,* 1, 275.
[23] *Early Popular Poetry,* 3, 249 f.

ture of the time, it is very apparent that these violent religious changes were unwelcome to a vast majority of the people. The Mass, which had been abolished, the monasteries, which had been supressed, the Catholic doctrines, which had been swept away by Lutheranism, all were still held dear by the conservatives, who constituted a very respectable minority of the people. However dominant the Protestant party might be at Court, it was by no means so influential among the people at large. Religious conditions were far from settled; the Reformers still found it necessary to contend vigorously against a powerful and active opposition. It is not strange that under these conditions the satire both for and against the Reformation should continue through the reign of Edward VI. It was merely a continuation of what preceded it, and presented nothing new in either subject-matter or in literary form.

Sometime in this period *A Ballad of Luther, the Pope, a Cardinal and a Husbandman,* in which each character speaks three eight-line stanzas, utters a plea for the reformers.[34] The Cardinal and the Pope, are, of course, satirized, while Luther and the Husbandman get the best of the argument. The Husbandman praises God, who has given a fall to those extortionate wolves, the Roman clergy. Luther addresses the Pope as Antichrist, who has usurped political power and juggled with God's word, has flattered the prince but threatened the peasant. The Pope does not excuse his deeds, but claims he is above both law and scripture:

> " As for scripture, I am above it;
> Am not I God's hye vicare?
> Shulde I be bounde to followe it,
> As the carpenter his ruler? "

Protestantism became the fashion at the court of Edward VI. Religious discussion was a favorite way of passing the time. Concerning matters of faith, courtiers spoke with as much assurance as expert theologians. Edward's corrupt court was thronged with members of the nobility,—" upstarts," who moved in the passing show and professed the Protestant faith merely because it was fashionable. Under a surface of religi-

[34] *Percy's Reliques* (1847), p. 117 f.

ous zeal lay an abyss of corruption. How superficial and insincere was the religious tone of the court, the reaction a few years later under Queen Mary only too plainly showed.

It is with such conditions as these that *Little John Nobody*[35] deals, in eight eight-line stanzas of alliteration and rhyme, written probably towards the end of the reign of Edward VI. The author passes along and finds one making a song about the condition of the Faith. This man says his name is John Nobody, and he dare not speak out. "Gay gallants pretend to discuss the Gospel as sage as Solomon. It is meet, to be sure, that all should have the Gospel in mind; but is it meet that all should discuss it and still live in lust?"

"For bribery was never so great, since born was our Lord,
And whoredom was never les hated, sith Christ harrowed hel,
And poor men are so sore punished commonly through the world,
That it would grieve any one, that good is, to hear tel.
For al the homilies and good books, yet their hearts be so quel,
That if a man do amisse, with mischiefe they wil him wreake:
The fashion of these new fellows it is so vile and fell;
But that I little John Nobody dare not speake."

Not without humor and rather effective in form, *Little John Nobody* is interesting as a side-light cast on the religious condition of the times by some cynical contemporary.

Of such quality is the verse satire of the English Reformation. It was an age of revolution, not only in religion and politics, but in literature as well. Old forms were disregarded and thrown aside. Religious satire of any period shows contempt for literary form, and it rarely possesses literary merit. It is didactic and reformatory. It abuses rather than ridicules, prefers invective to humor, and would rather knock a foe down with a cudgel than pierce him with a rapier. All these characteristics appear in the satire of the period from 1520 to 1550. Such work can have but little value as a contribution to the Satire, and is interesting only in the light it casts upon the religious temper of its period, and its exhibition of the English tendency to speak freely and vigorously upon religious matters.

[35] *Ibid.*, p. 119.

CHAPTER VII

Sir David Lyndsay and the Satiric Play

Sir David Lyndsay.—His life.—Lyndsay the man.—His poetry.—His satire.—Lyndsay as a satirist of the Reformation.—The Reformation in Scotland.—Lyndsay's *The Dream.—The Complaint.—The Testament of the Papingo.*—His minor Satires.—*A Satire of the Three Estates.*—Its subject-matter.—Its tone.—Its first part.—Its abstractions.—The interlude.—Realism and Burlesque in *The Three Estates.*—The second part.—John the Common Weal.—The didactic element in *The Three Estates.*—Its effect.—Lyndsay's contribution to the Satire.—Dramatic satire in England.—The Interludes and Moralities.—Confusion of terms.—Religious and social satire.—Satire of low life.—Satire in the Miracle Plays.—Skelton's *Magnyfycence.*—Heywood's Interludes.—Their burlesque elements.—Bale.—His Moralities.—His *Kyng Johan.*—Other Moralities and Interludes.—*Nature.—Respublica.—New Custom.*—Incidental satire in other plays.—Lost polemic plays.—Elizabethan dialogues.—Value and significance of this dramatic satire.

I

The work of Sir David Lyndsay, Scotchman and Reformer, while little influencing subsequent satire in English, is still extremely significant. Above all others writing in English, Lyndsay is generally accepted as the distinctive satirist of the Reformation. His work shows a combination of the qualities of Gower, Dunbar, and Skelton: of Gower, in moral earnestness; of Dunbar, in burlesque humor; and of Skelton, in power of invective. While no great attention can be paid here to the history of satire north of the Border, yet Lyndsay, in his own period, is so great a figure that the same reasons which led to some mention of Dunbar must make us pause for consideration of this vigorous and versatile satirist.[1]

The life of Sir David Lyndsay covered sixty-five years, from 1490 to 1555, a stormy and momentous epoch in the

[1] The *Poetical Works of Sir David Lyndsay,* ed. Laing, 2 vols., Edinburgh, 1871.

history of Scotland—the reigns of James IV and James V and the regency during the minority of Mary Stuart. Lyndsay's life was as eventful and busy as the times in which he lived. Poet as he was, poet-laureate of the Scottish court, he was yet—as Lyon King of Arms, head of the college of heralds, play-fellow of James V, ambassador to various kingdoms,—even more a man of affairs than a man of letters. Lyndsay lived through the disaster of Flodden, French intrigues during the reign of James V, the vacillating regency of the Duke of Albany, the feud of the Douglasses against the Hamiltons, and the murder of Cardinal Beaton. He witnessed the continual border wars with England, saw Scotland rent with domestic discord, welcomed the introduction of the New Testament, and deplored the martyrdom of Patrick Hamilton. He went as ambassador to Charles V in 1531, and again in 1535; as ambassador to France in 1536. He participated in the marriage ceremonies of James V, first to Magdalene of France, then to Mary of Guise; represented his native town of Cupar as a member of Parliament; became the friend of John Knox, and encouraged him to preach, though himself always a Catholic; and, finally, died in 1555, beholding the dawn of a better day for Scotland.

Lyndsay as man, sterling, strong, courageous, lover of Scotland, hater of immorality, hypocrisy, and oppression, friend of the common people and born reformer, is far more interesting than Lyndsay as poet; but the qualities of the man himself and the times in which he lived interest us here only so far as they are mirrored in Lyndsay's satirical verse. Given the man and the times, it was inevitable that Lyndsay's poetry should be intensely practical and show little imaginative quality. And such it is, being almost wholly didactic and satirical. With a copious vocabulary and an almost fatal fluency in rhyme, but devoid of the high imaginative qualities that mark the true poet, he is inspired by a reformatory purpose. And in this respect Lyndsay stands in strong contrast to Dunbar, both as man and as satirist. Dunbar's satirical verse, as we have seen, was born of no such motive, for it was but the comment of a man of the world upon the life around him, without the idea of making that world better in any degree. Lyndsay, without Dunbar's poetical genius, is far more earnest and sincere. He apparently writes with but one motive: to destroy the wrong and upbuild the right. In his earnestness and practicality, he reminds us of the English Gower; but he is unlike Gower in that a copious humor illumines everything he writes.

Lyndsay wrote for the common people, and he earned a popularity perhaps accorded to no other Scottish poet save Burns. His style and vocabulary are suited to the popular taste. The coarseness that colors so much of his verse made a popular appeal. Whatever may be the literary qualities of his work, there resulted from this popular appeal a tremendous effectiveness. This work shows no literary inheritance, not a shadow of classicism—thoroughly native to the man and to the soil, it springs spontaneously from public needs to rectify public abuses. Lyndsay was the voice of all Scotland as no Scottish poet had ever been before.

The range of his satirical material is remarkably wide and varied. As he looks about him over his native land, threatened by foreign foes, rent by domestic discord, oppressed by a selfish nobility, with corruption permeating every estate of the realm, Church and State in the grasp of unscrupulous prelates and ministers, the reformatory spirit within him is stirred to utterance. It speaks sometimes in direct satire, sometimes in invective, sometimes in burlesque, arraigning and rebuking a thousand abuses in church, society, and state. Lindsay's direct satire is keen, his invective scorching, his burlesque exceedingly humorous. While almost wholly of historical interest, his satirical and didactic poems become invaluable as a criticism of his times.

We have said that Lyndsay is known as the satirist of the Scottish Reformation. If this means that he attacked the fundamental creed and polity of the church, the epithet is largely misapplied. It is true he assailed every imaginable form of clerical abuse, arraigned entire the Roman hierarchy, ridiculed pilgrimages, penances, and image worship. But Skelton had done the same; and this was the common material of a host of Lyndsay's satirical predecessors. In Lyndsay' poetry there is no attack on the creed or the Mass, no advocac of the abolition of popery such as marked the distinctive Satir of the Reformation, as seen for instance in *Rede me and b Nott Wrothe*. In the *Satire of the Three Estates,* howeve the polity of the church is called into question; and there i reason to believe that had Lyndsay lived ten years longer hi satire would have been as distinctly of the Protestant Refor mation as any written in English. Even as it is, his satiri cal verse contains so many allusions to the ecclesiastical af fairs of this epoch that it cannot be well understood or ap preciated without reference to the Scottish Reformation.

The Reformation in Scotland was mainly due to a con dition of the church even more scandalous than that exist ing at the same time in England. Those evils that had af fected the church for generations were growing intolerable The sale of benefices, corrupt morals of the clergy, plura livings, undue interference of churchmen in State affairs, ha generated an anti-clerical spirit that in Lyndsay's time wa beginning to find determined expression. The Reformation then, arose from an attempt not so much to secure doctrina reform or to keep out Papal influence, as to purify the churc from within. The clergy, presumptuous and arrogant, re sented popular criticism, and persecuted their accusers by fire Such persecution resulted in still more widespread and bitte accusations and calls for reform. Finally, opposition to Frenc influence gave the Scottish Reformation a political bearing that probably did more than anything else to speed the caus of the reformers.

There can be no doubt that Lyndsay, at least as much a any man in Scotland, was in sympathy with this reformatory spirit. His verse is one great cry for reform, echoing with the nation's social, political, and religious strife. His literary work begins with *The Dreme* in 1528 and ends with *The Monarchie* in 1553; though his strictly satirical work closes with the *Satire of the Three Estates,* about 1540. Most of his poems are medleys of satire and didacticism. *The Dreme,* written in eleven hundred and thirty-four lines, in Chaucerian stanzas, and addressed as an exhortation to the young King James V, comprises a vision of Hell, Heaven, and Scotland. In the good old medieval fashion, the poet dreams, and is conducted by Dame Remembrance into Hell, where he sees Popes, Emperors, and Kings, conquerors who are despoilers of other people's property, cardinals and archbishops in their prelatical robes, abbots, and "false, flattering friars." After the voyage through hell and the empyrean, the poet looks upon Scotland, and inquires the cause of her poverty and distress. He is told by his guide that these arise from the unpatriotic and selfish conduct of the great nobles. John the Common Weal, who is about to leave his country, explains his reasons for departure and his own ragged habit, by further reflections upon the state of the realm. His comments are very direct and severe. The spiritual estate, eaten with vice, disdains him; the nobility are careful only of their own ends. In this allegorical form of narrative, though Lyndsay indulges in no personalities, his political satire on the general condition of Scotland is very fearless and direct. Never were abstractions more effective. The figure of John the Common Weal gives dignity to the poem, which forms a worthy prelude to the *Satire of the Three Estates.*

Political satire and social satire are combined in *The Complaynt of Schir David Lyndesay to the Kingis Grace* (1529). This is a didactic poem, written chiefly in tetrameter verse, reflecting largely upon the vices of the clergy, and advising the king as to the religious, political, and social disorders of the country. Severe, without humor, but with a mighty strength of attack, it is very much alive, as witness this one stanza on the corrupt practices of the temporal and spiritual lords:

> "Thay lordis tuke no more regaird,
> But quho mycht purches best rewaird:
> Sum to thair friendis gat benefyceis,
> And uther sum gat Byschopreis.
> For every lord, as he thocht best,
> Brocht in ane bird to fyll the nest;
> To be ane wacheman to his marrow,
> Thay gan to draw at the cat harrow.

The proudest Prelatis of the Kirk
Was faine to hyde thame in the myrk,
That tyme, so failyeit wes thair sycht.
Sen syne thay may nocht thole the lycht
Of Christis trew Gospell to be sene,
So blyndit is thair corporall ene
With wardly lustis sensuall."—

Following *The Complaynt to the King,* religious and social satire are combined in *The Testament and Complaynt of our Soverane Lordis Papyngo,* a partly didactic and partly satirical poem, in Chaucerian stanza, on court follies and clerical irregularities. The *Testament,* an old literary form, had time and again on the Continent been used for satirical purposes. In English, though " Testaments " galore had appeared through the preceding two centuries, Lyndsay seems the first to employ the form as a vehicle for satire. The parrot, or " papingo," appeared frequently as a court bird in the European literature of the Renaissance. Skelton in his *Speke Parrot* makes the wise bird the mouth-piece of his satire. Now, for the first time, a poet uses the form of the *Testament* together with the parrot as the vehicle of his satire, and we have the *Testament of the Papyngo.* We are reminded of Skelton's *Speke Parrot,* for the present poem is very much the same kind of medley.

After her first epistle—a purely didactic epistle—to the king —to whom she leaves her " trew unfeinyeit hart," the Papingo indites a second to the courtiers, a grave admonition against the perils of the court and a homily on the reverse of fortune and the fall of pride, as illustrated in the unhappy deaths of the last four Scottish kings, the career of Wolsey, and the death of Angus. The religious satire begins with the last part of the poem and runs through seventy-six stanzas in the form of an allegory. The dying parrot wishes confessors, and the Magpie, who is a regular canon and prior, the Raven, a black monk, and the Kite, a friar, come to her side. The parrot is suspicious of them all: she has seen the Kite steal a chicken. But she has to accept them as religious counsellors and executors, since she can do no better. Before dying, she sets forth the reasons why she holds the clergy " so abominable," and recounts the growth of the corruption of the priesthood and the sensuality and avarice of the church. *The preaching of the begging friars alone preserves faith among the clergy.* After this long and severe rebuke, the parrot makes her will and testament, sending unto her "Soverane Kyng" her heart. To the owl she leaves her green dress; to the pelican, her beak; her voice to the cuckoo, and her eloquence to the goose. Her bones she orders to be burnt with those of the phœnix; the rest of her she leaves to the officiating clergy, whom she now appoints her executors. She dies, and after this event her friends of the clergy fight fiercely over her remains.

Though characteristically without personalities, the *Papyngo* forms one of Lyndsay's strongest attacks on clerical corruption. The form and conception are trite enough, but the added vitality and strength mark a new era in the Satire.

Genuinely satirical, with abundant humor, is *Ane Supplicatioun in Contemptioun of Syde Taillis,* written in 1536. This is in the form of an epistle to the king; in length, one hundred and sixty-four lines of rough tetrameter verse—"The cause the matter bene so vile, it may nocht have an ornate style." The *Supplication* is a rather coarse but really humorous attack on fashions in dress, a light but genuine little piece of social satire.

We have again in *The Complaynt of Bagsche the Kingis auld Hound,* a court Satire against the vices of the courtiers; in *Kitteis Confessioun,* a frank Satire on the confessional; in *Ane Descriptioun of Pedder Coffeis,* an exposure of the tricks of the peddler of that time. Finally, in *The Monarchie* (1554), an elaborate poem in 6333 lines, we find, among much else, an advocacy of the vernacular for poetical, religious, and legal purposes; and an attack on pilgrimages and the worship of images, on corruption at Rome, on rack-rents of the lords and barons, on the injustice of both civil and ecclesiastical courts, and on the extravagant dress of women.

But for our present purpose, all of Lyndsay's previous work forms merely the introduction to his *Satire of the Three Estates,*[2] written at some uncertain date, but produced before

[2] The full title is *Ane Pleasant Satyre of the Thrie Estaitis in commendatioun of Vertew and vituperatioun of Vyce.*

king and court at Linlithgow in 1540. It is a very long Morality, written in Scottish vernacular verse, the only specimen of its kind from north of the Tweed. The *Satire* is not only Lyndsay's most elaborate but in every respect his most significant work, uniting in itself every phase of material and tone that characterizes his minor productions.

The range of its subject-matter is well nigh universal. The social aspect of this subject-matter is highly significant: it is the woes of the people. Pauper describes in homely language his unjust treatment by laird and vicar and his present miserable lot; while John the Common Weal, a dominating figure, reviews all the religious, political, and social abuses of Scotland. Again, the political phase of the subject-matter shows us two of the "Three Estates" selfish and ambitious, bound by their vices, the lords thinking only of oppressing the poor, and the prelates thinking only of high living. Furthermore, from the religious point of view, Lyndsay wishes to change somewhat the polity of the church as well as to reform its morals. He unsparingly attacks bishops, cardinals, and friars along the old lines, but with added vigor and earnestness, and especially inveighs against plural livings and absentee clergy. In addition to all this, the *Satire of the Three Estates* has a moral aspect in its treatment of the vicious condition of all classes of society from king to peasant; while the abstract vices are satirized by personification in such figures as those of Flattery, Sensuality, and Deceit. One reads in every line of the *Satire* the reformatory purpose that inspired it and the deep moral earnestness that spoke through it.

The *Satire of the Three Estates* as a whole admirably illustrates the transition from the medieval religious play to the Elizabethan drama. In its vast number of separate characters and variety of topics there is much that is commonplace, as well as unique and powerful. With its genuine satire, invective, didacticism, and burlesque, it forms a strange medley—a "cross between the old morality, the interlude of Heyward, the modern play, and systematic satire." Though primarily constructive and thoroughly reformatory in its purpose, the *Satire* has abundant humor, and its often conventional and commonplace material is yet rendered unique by Lyndsay's masterful treatment. "Its satirical commonplace" declares itself—the corruption of the clergy was no new theme for satire,—but its local and contemporary elements, such as the wars on the Border, the rapacity of the nobility, are new and are native to the soil. All topics are treated effectively, because treated with an eye on the object, not generally, but specifically. Medieval in literary form, showing no classical influence, the *Satire* is still distinctly of the Renaissance in realism and close observation of life. The figures of Pauper and John the Common Weal embody a strength of characterization that makes Lyndsay akin to Langland and Skelton.

The first part of the *Satire of the Three Estates,* like the old morality, introduces such conventional figures as Wantonness, Sensuality, Falsehood, Deceit, Good Counsel, Dame Verity, and Flattery; but even here we find incidental satire, when Wantonness addresses Rex Humanitas and hits fiercely at the immorality of the clergy.[3] Then, too, Flattery clothes himself as a *friar*. The friars, he says, are free at every feast; and God has given them such grace that Bishops put them in their places to preach throughout the diocese,

> "And thocht the corne war never sa skant,
> The gudewyfis will not let Freiris want."

But, as an almost entirely new note in the morality,[4] just here at the beginning is introduced the satire of the Reformation. The vices warn Humanity against Dame Verity, because she bears in her hand that heretical and proscribed book, Tyndale's New Testament, which had recently crossed the water into Scotland, caused the martyrdom of young Patrick Hamilton, and was soon to overthrow the Established Church. Flattery sees Verity:

[3] *Works,* 2, 121.

[4] Not *entirely* new, apparently; Professor A. H. Thorndike of Columbia University calls my attention to Collier's account of a Morality in Latin and French, acted before Henry VIII and Wolsey by the Boys of St. Paul's school in 1528. The Morality introduced Luther and his wife, and ridiculed the Reformation. The play is no longer extant.

> "Quhat buik is that, harlot, into thy hand?
> Out, walloway! this is the New Test'ment;
> In Englisch toung, and printit in England:
> Herisie, herisie! fire, fire! incontinent."

Again and again, through this part of the play, Lyndsay reverts to his favorite theme, the gross immorality of every order of the clergy. The satire is dramatic, indirect, tinged with irony and a rather bitter humor. Sensuality, when expelled by Divine Correction from the court of King Humanitas, announces her intention of proceeding to Rome, where she is sure to find hospitality among the princes of the church:

> "My Lord, I mak yow supplicatioun,
> Gif me licence, to pas againe to Rome;
> Amang the princes of that natioun,
> I lat yow wit, my fresche beautie will blume,
> . . . .
> War I amang bischops, and cardinals,
> I wald get gould, silver, and precious clais:
> Na earthlie joy, but my presence, availis."

Chastity, too, banished from the court, seeks refuge among the clergy, but meets with a cold reception. The lady prioress, whom she first approaches, scornfully bids her begone. She passes on to the lords of the spirituality, then to the Abbot and the Parson, all of whom order her off on pain of punishment. These figures of the Abbot, the Parson, and the Spiritual Lords, form an addition to the conventional figures of the old Morality, and connect the *Satire of the Three Estates* with that newer dramatic form, the Interlude.

In the interlude which binds together the first and second parts of the play, this religious satire passes into social, in the figures of Diligence, the Pauper, and the Cardinal. Pauper is a typical figure, that of the Scottish peasant, and his tale of woe is that of the common people of Scotland. In his talk with Diligence, Pauper tells how he had supported his old parents with one horse and three cows. His parents died and then his trouble began, for the laird took the horse for a fine, the vicar took the best cow when the father died, and another on the death of the mother; the wife died for sorrow, and thereupon the vicar took the third cow. Now Pauper with his bairns has to beg for a living.

Pauper's sombre note is changed for one of ludicrous burlesque in the speech of the Pardoner, who is made to satirize himself as a social, rather than as a religious, personage. Lyndsay's Pardoner is a blood brother to Heywood's[5] and Chaucer's.[6] He too speaks at great length, advertising his wares, and making permanent contribution to the universal satire on public imposters. He cordially commits to the Devil the wicked New Testament, those that translated it and those that read it, Martin Luther, Bullinger, and Melancthon, and all their crew. His motley assortment of relics includes the horn of a criminal cow, and a cord that hanged a malefactor. So ends the interlude.

In the second part of the play we have the Morality again. The Three Estates—the spiritual lords, the temporal lords, and the burgesses—from whom the Satire takes its name, figure here as bound by vice and given over to every manner of corruption. Strangely in contrast with these abstractions is the intense realism of the figures and speeches of Pauper and John the Common Weal. This satire is realistic enough and permeated with abundant humor, as when Pauper complains of the injustice and delays of the Consistory courts. For his mare, drowned by a neighbor, he seeks redress from the Consistory:

> "They gave me first ane thing, thay call *Citendum,*
> Within aucht dayis, I gat bot *Lybellandum,*
> Within ane moneth, I gat *ad Opponendum,*
> In half ane yeir, I gat *Interloquendum,*
> And syne, I gat, how call ye it? *ad Replicandum:*
> Bot, I could never ane word yit understand him;
> And than, thay gart me cast out many plackis,
> And gart me pay for four-and-twentie actis:
> Bot, or thay came half gait to *Concludendum,*
> The Feind ane plack was left for to defend him:
> Thus, thay postponit me twa yeir, with thair traine,
> . . . .
> Bot I got never my gude gray meir againe."

[5] See *infra,* p. 213.

[6] See *supra,* p. 101.

John the Common Weal represents the well-being of Scotland. When asked by Temporality to name his enemies, he inveighs against strong beggars, fiddlers, pipers, pardoners, and especially complains of feuds among the lords. The friars, too, come in for wholesale condemnation. But this is not all: severe judgment on the poor, while the rich escape through bribery; faults in both consistory and secular courts; the tributes of rack-rent and heriot, which fall so heavily on the poor cotter—all these furnish material for reprehension in the mouth of John the Common Weal:

> "Grandmerces, then, I sall nocht spair.
> First, to compleine on the Vickair:
> The pure Cottar, lykand to die.
> Haifand young infants, twa, or thrie;
> And hes twa ky, but ony ma,
> The Vickar must haif ane of thay,
> With the gray frugge, that covers the bed,
> Howbeit, the wyfe be purelie cled;
> And gif the wyfe die on the morne,
> Thocht all the bairns sould be forlorne,
> The uther kow, he cleiks away,
> With the pure cot of raploch gray."—

So far the material of the *Satire,* while often didactic, has been largely destructive in its criticism. All the abuses in every estate of the realm have been catalogued, and rebuked in direct satire, abused in invective, or ridiculed in burlesque. But now the reformatory and constructive element begins to preponderate, and the purpose that gave birth to the *Satire of the Three Estates* becomes apparent. The satirist has rehearsed the evils that permeate the realm, and finally, in the person of John the Common Weal, proposes a remedy. Parliament must pass a reform bill, which will take cognizance of the abuses in the Three Estates, that is, in the spiritual, the political, and the social worlds. All temporal lands are to be "set in few" unto virtuous men that labor with their hands. Lords shall make answer to the crown for the thieves on their estates who oppress the poor. Law courts are to be provided for the northern counties; nunneries are to be abolished; temporal cases are to be removed from the jurisdiction of ecclesiastical courts—

> "Let Temporall men seik Judges temporall,
> And spirituall men to spiritualitie."

Benefices shall be given only to "men of good erudition, above suspicion of vice, and qualified right prudently to preach, or to teach in famous schools." Because ignorant priests have brought the Church into reproach, no Bishop shall henceforth allow any except educated men to teach. No prelate shall purchase a benefice from Prince or Pope, nor any priest serve two benefices, nor any bishop two bishoprics. That they may the better care for souls, every bishop shall remain in his diocese, and every parson in his parish. No money shall from this day forth be sent to Rome, for that our substance is thus consumed for bills and processes. As priests for the most part lack the gift of chastity, we will grant them license to marry and live all their lives in chaste and lawful wedlock.

Such is the *Satire of the Three Estates,* rich in invective, burlesque, and didacticism; in elements of the satirical and of the reformatory; in an immense range of material, and a wide variety of tone. Medley as it is, frequently anything but satirical, it still remains in its entirety a great Satire and a genuine contribution to the literature of its kind.

It is interesting to know that, partly owing to the fact that the times were ripe for Lyndsay's satire, partly owing to the vitality and force of its presentation of abuses, the *Satire of the Three Estates,* together with Lyndsay's other satirical verse, became a tremendous motive power in contemporary Scotland. Sir William Eure tells us that after the representation at Linlithgow, "The king did call upon the Bishop of Glasgow, the Chancellor Dunbar, and the other bishops, exorting them to reform their manner and fashion of living." James, indeed, seems to have encouraged Lyndsay's attacks on the clergy. Probably to this friendship of the king, Lyndsay owed his immunity from persecution on the part of the church. His onslaught against clerical morals was far more determined and vehement than any that had brought, or was to bring, to the stake other critics unprotected by the royal favor.

This, however, was only one reason for Lyndsay's immunity. The *Satire* had its comic side, and served as a source of amusement to the very classes whom it reprehended. Long ago in France Rûtebeuf had, through similar comic effects, secured a similar immunity;[7] and Lyndsay, as did Rabelais, probably adopted the broad and indecent as an expedient to secure his own personal safety as well as to insure a popular hearing.[8]

Lyndsay's genuine and permanent contribution to satire lies rather in the tone than in the form of his work. His form was one that was already decadent; it was medieval and outworn, and could not well have any influence on the development of the formal Satire. But Lyndsay's wide range of material and variety of tone render his satirical work typical of almost all preceding satire in English. Still more than this, his style, realistic, vital and popular, and his spirit, aggressive and fearless, mark, as does the work of Skelton, a new era in satirical writing. In this respect Lyndsay's satire is, indeed, not of the Middle Ages, but of the Reformation.

II

But, while *The Satire of the Three Estates* is by far the finest as well as the most elaborate specimen of the early satiric play in English, that genre was not the property of Scotland alone. South of the Border the English Moralities and Interludes, produced between 1500 and 1560, were attempting what Lyndsay attempted—a survey and criticism of the religious, social, and even, to a less degree, the political conditions of their time. Their attempts were sporadic, confused, often almost chaotic, but nevertheless significant, and worth consideration as dramatic satire.

It is well known that any treatment of the Moralities and Interludes of this period is rendered difficult by several facts. The drama itself was in a chaotic condition: various forms

[7] Lenient, p. 52 f.

[8] I have seen this suggestion somewhere, but cannot find the reference.

existed side by side, often melted into one another, and frequently became indistinguishable. The Miracle Plays continued to be presented long after the Elizabethan play had taken formal shape in tragedy, comedy, and history-play. The terms " Morality " and " Interlude " seemed to have been used interchangeably; and, from the mere title, one never knows what to expect from a pre-Elizabethan play. *The Interlude of Youth* is a mere Morality; the Interlude *Respublica* is a religious polemic; the Morality *Albion Knight* is a political polemic; the Interlude *King Darius* is a pseudo-history play. Thus the confusion seems to increase with the investigation.

This confusion is one not merely of title, but also of methods. Very few plays of this period are clearly defined in scope and purpose. Nothing is more common than to find burlesque and didactic moralizing, the ideal and the real, inextricably mingled in the same play.

Its apparent lack of progress, of improvement in form and style, is another characteristic that marks the drama in England from the beginnings of the Renaissance to the rise of the " regular drama." The older criticism that developed the Miracle play, the Morality, the Interlude, and the history-play, in beautiful order, each type from the one preceding, is abundantly refuted by the most cursory reading of the plays themselves.

But it is here our purpose merely to call attention to the satirical element in this anomalous drama. Broadly speaking, the satire found in the Moralities and Interludes is of two kinds—religious and social. The social satire is of a clearly pronounced type. That picturing of low life which came into English satire as far back as *The Vision of Piers Plowman*, which was continued by Skelton in his *Elynour Rummynge*, and which was exemplified so largely in the satire on Fools and on Rogues, is vastly elaborated in the later Moralities. This satire on low life grew more realistic and graphic as the power of characterization increased in the drama. The didactic element in the later Moralities is often so overshadowed by it that the dramatist seems to have forgotten his original didactic intent. The scenes from low life are presented simply for their own sake, with all their vulgar realism—so low has the later Morality fallen from its original and high estate.

Together with this comic portrayal of low life, often mingled with it, one may find here and there in the plays of all types a religious satire which is mainly the direct outgrowth of the Reformation. Some of these plays, notably Bale's *Kyng Johan* and *Respublica,* are professed religious polemics; in many others, such as *Lusty Juventus* and two or three of the Interludes of Heywood, religious satire is informal and incidental.

But dramatic satire in England has left its traces even in the Miracle Plays. What Collier terms "the earliest specimen of dramatic satire in the language" occurs in the twenty-sixth pageant of the Coventry plays, where Satan describes himself as a gallant of the time and has his fling at contemporary dress and manners. Religious satire crops out in the Twenty-eighth Towneley ("Juditium"), when the three devils read over their lists of the wicked, describing every kind of sinner, and the devil "Tutivillus" refers to himself as a "master Lollar." Such traces, however, are so rare as to render them practically negligible. It was not until realism, characterization, observation and criticism of actual life, came into the drama that satire began to play in it an appreciable part.

Amid a host of anonymous playwrights of this our present period three known writers stand out conspicuously: Skelton, Heywood, and Bale.

Skelton's one extant play, the Morality *Magnyfycence,*[9] is a cross between the old Morality with its severe abstractions and the new type with its growing realism. It is so far from being primarily satirical, that its satirical content is proportionally slight and of a very general nature—glimpses of characterization, as in Folly; general allusions to the low life of London with concomitant vulgarity of speech; and the speeches of Counterfet Countenaunce, such as,

> "Counterfet prechynge, and beleue the contrary;
> Counterfet conscyence, peuysshe pope holy;
> Counterfet sadnesse, with delynge full madly;
> Counterfet holynes is called ypocrysy."—

Courtly Abusyon is really the lying, false courtier, and might

[9] *Works,* I, 225–310.

well have figured in *The Bouge of Courte.* As he speaks to Magnyfycence, he utters the most telling satire of the play:

> "What sholde ye do elles? are not you a lorde?
> Let your lust and your lykynge stand for a lawe."

One wonders whether Magnyfycence himself, a vague, shadowy figure, relying on his own power and wealth and falling so disastrously, does not perhaps stand for the whole of the New Nobility. But whatever satire *Magnyfycence* contains is, beyond these specific passages, very difficult to determine.

A more striking figure in the drama than Skelton is John Heywood, though perhaps the purely satirical element in his humorous Interludes has been exaggerated. Of Heywood's six dramatic pieces, three are in no wise satirical; but the three about to be named, though, in all likelihood, written primarily to amuse, contain more or less intentional satire.

A Mery Play between John the Husband, Tyb the Wife, and Sir John the Priest,[10] is a dramatized *fabliau* in that it holds up to ridicule the credulous husband, the unfaithful wife, and the wily ecclesiastic. *The Pardoner and the Friar*[11] is a burlesque dialogue in which the Pardoner's elaborate speech is of a kind with those found in Chaucer, Lyndsay, and *Cock Lorell.* Both Pardoner and Friar are rank imposters. Here the humorous element far outweighs the purely satirical, though the burlesque on ecclesiastical types is the old satire which began at least with the Goliards.[12] The Pardoner again figures in that most amusing of Heywood's Interludes, *The Four P's.*[13] Pardoner, Palmer, Pedler, and Pothecary, here indulge in satire both direct and indirect, as each makes himself ridiculous and in turn holds up to ridicule his opponent in the absurd contest that forms the action of the piece.

Wit, humorous situations, and glimpses of characterization render these three Interludes worthy of the honorable place

[10] *Quellen des weltlichen Dramas in England vor Shakespeare,* ed. A. Brandl.

[11] *Dramatic Writings of John Heywood,* ed. Farmer.

[12] See *supra,* p. 40 f.

[13] *Dramatic Writings,* ed. Farmer.

they hold in the history of the English drama; but it is difficult to determine their exact satirical content. They are humorous burlesques, written primarily to amuse a courtly audience. In their subject-matter there is nothing new. Heywood was himself a Catholic; and, if his Interludes be of satirical intent primarily, they are probably quite unrelated to the Reformation.

The five extant plays of John Bale, bishop of Ossory, are at the opposite pole from the Interludes of Heywood. While more or less polemic, Bale's plays can be termed satirical only by the broadest application of the word. An outgrowth of the Reformation as they are, the little real satire they contain is of course religious and militant.

In *The Temptacyon of our Lorde*[14] the first speech of "Baleus Prolocutor" advocates the use of the "Word of God" as an authority in matters of religion and a means of defense against the assaults of the devil. More plainly satirical are a few lines of Satan's last speech: False priests and bishops, even the "Vicar of Rome," shall worship the devil, and Christ may worship whom He will! Apart from these passages, this Morality is wholly didactic.

God's Promises,[15] a setting forth of the doctrine of justification by faith, is even more innocent of satire than the preceding. *The Three Laws of Nature, Moses, and Christ, Corrupted by the Sodomites, Pharisees, and Papists,*[16]—not an easily accessible play,—is, according to Professor Herford, a biblical plot made to serve as a vehicle for Protestant tenets. Its abstractions, such as Ambition, Avarice, and others, are monks and priests in disguise.[17] *John Baptyste*[18] is in its controversial elements very similar to the preceding.

It is, finally, to *Kynge Johan*[19] that we must look for Bale's contribution to dramatic satire. This play, written about 1546, is, first of all, a distinct product of the Reformation, a religi-

[14] *Fuller's Worthies Misc.*, I, ed. Grosart.
[15] *Dodsley's Old Plays,* ed. Hazlitt, 1, 285 f.
[16] *Anglia,* V, 137 f.
[17] Herford, pp. 133, 134.
[18] *Harleian Misc.*, I.
[19] Cam. Soc. Pub., vol, 2, ed. Collier.

ous polemic, not a true Chronicle play. Bale seized upon the bare fact that John had been opposed by the Pope and by the French, and thus transforms the miserable, lying, treacherous knave into a hero; he turns Stephen Langton into a seditious traitor; and presents his other historical characters so faintly that the reader feels no surprise when he finds each character "the double of an abstraction." The use of the mere Morality for polemic purposes was not new—the *Satire of the Three Estates* preceded *Kyng Johan* by several years; but the introduction into the Morality of actual historical personages, each of whom at the same time represents an abstract quality—as Langton, Dissimulation; Pandulph, Private Wealth; the Pope, Usurped Power,—this was quite new and, in its peculiar way, strikingly effective.

To detail the story of the play would here be supererogatory, since Professor Morley furnishes an elaborate synopsis in the eighth volume of his *English Writers,* and Professor Ward a detailed analysis in his *History.* It would be equally superfluous to enter upon any criticism of the literary quality of the play or to discuss its place in the history of the English drama. It is enough to say that *Kyng Johan,* anomalous as it is in its general scheme, absurd in many of its details, yet attains as a whole considerable dignity and power.

Lyndsay's influence is apparent in the idea of the "three estates"—here given as Commonalty, Nobility, and Clergy; and England appears in the role taken in Lyndsay's play by John the Commonweal. Aside from this, Bale perhaps owes little to Lyndsay, and his play is not comparable to the *Satire of the Three Estates* in range of subject-matter or in variety of tone and style. That *Kyng Johan* is indebted to Kirchmeyer's *Pammachius* for its general plan is asserted by Professor Herford, who furnishes interesting parallels between the two plays.[20] We are here concerned only with the satirical content of the play; and it cannot be denied that Bale's scorn of "popery" finds expression that is often surprisingly vigorous. The tone of *Kyng Johan* as a whole, however, is moralistic and sombre rather than satirical. Bale was a man

[20] Herford, pp. 136, 137.

of one idea. His attack is direct and unsparing, without subtle thrust or lambent humor. Sarcasm and invective are his ready weapons; his satire is the satire of utter scorn that will not condescend to play with the object of its contempt. As Dissimulation unveils his own methods and shamelessly exposes the practices of the Church, Bale's voice may be heard in the stinging indictment. Sedition's speech as a Pardoner, analogous to the burlesques in Chaucer, Lyndsay, Heywood, and *Cock Lorell,* shows the vulgarity of speech to which the bishop of Ossory could descend when bent upon his prey. Treason's plain speeches show how much the Church includes of Mosaic and of pagan rites and how little of Christ—

> "Nothynge at all, but the epystle and the gospell,
> And that is in Latyne that no man shoulde it knowe."

It is quite possible that one single burlesque speech in any one of Heywood's Interludes accomplished more for the Reformation than all the sarcasm and scorn and vulgarity of Bale's *Kyng Johan.* Yet the play is in itself a prophecy and a link in a chain—a prophecy of a time, little more than a generation distant, when the drama of England was to show what satire could achieve in a dramatic form; a link in a chain, because it is but one of a long and mighty series of religious satires more or less dramatic, stretching down from the time of Langland and Chaucer, and also one of the many Protestant polemics of its own tempestuous period.

Apart from the work of Skelton, of Heywood, and of Bale, we must turn to the mass of mainly anonymous Moralities and Interludes of the present period for further evidences of dramatic satire.

In such well-known plays as *The Castle of Perseverance; The Nice Wanton; Mind, Will, and Understanding; Mankind,* and *Everyman,* satire is practically absent. In the equally well-known *Lusty Juventus* the satire of the Reformation appears in the speech of Hypocrisy, who asserts that he has set up, as snares for the innocent, all the trappings of Rome:

> "Holy cardinals, holy popes,
> Holy vestments, holy copes,

Holy hermits, holy friars,
Holy monks, holy abbots,
Yea, and all obstinate liars,"—

and so on, through the list of all that was antipathetic to the Lutheran. In *Hick Scorner,* where the satire is wholly incidental, the speeches of Freewill and of Imagination give pictures of low life, and so connect with the Satire on Rogues.

Into *Nature,*[21] which is in form a true Morality, new elements have entered. Some of its personages are more than mere abstractions, they are types; and here and there through the play are glimpses of low life portrayed with vivid realism and genuine humor. The two speeches of Pride, distinct Satires on the dress and manners of the young gallant of the period, suggest Wynkyn de Worde's *Treatise of this Gallant.*[22] Gluttony, Wrath, Man, and other characters in *Nature,* join in producing a series of brief but telling sketches of life in the author's London. It is practically impossible in such a play to dissociate the satirical from the purely humorous elements.

The Morality *Albion Knight,*[23] which exists only as a fragment, was written some time between 1540 and 1566, and perhaps satirizes political conditions in the early years of Henry VIII. While the fragment extant does not deal with the Reformation, it is probable that the play as a whole reviewed the entire conditions of its time. The fragment shows nothing new, and, coming after Bale and Lyndsay, is of no especial significance.

In 1553 *Kyng Johan* found its answer in *Respublica,*[24] distinctly a Catholic polemic. *Respublica* marks a religious reaction. But, while it is evidently an answer to the Protestant polemics, it is remarkable in that it makes no attempt to defend the ecclesiastical practices attacked by the Protestants, and is in no sense theological. On the contrary, it attempts to portray the economic condition of the country towards the close

[21] Ed. Brandl, *Quellen d. welt. Dramas.*

[22] See *supra,* p. 170 f.

[23] *Anonymous Plays,* 2d Series, ed. Farmer, pp. 117 to 132.

[24] "*Lost*" *Tudor Plays,* ed. Farmer.

of Edward the Sixth's reign—England ruined by Protestant domination. People, though rather a comic character, who speaks in dialect, is very much in earnest as he complains of his sad lot. Avarice, Insolence, Oppression, and Adulation, Protestant ministers of state under Edward VI, through the disclosure of their own frauds, reflect severely upon the maladministration of Edward's reign. Though tedious, diffuse, rather colorless, *Respublica* contains a few touches of real power.

The Protestant side again finds an advocate in *New Custom,*[25] an odd mixture of true Morality and sheer burlesque. Burlesque satire, directed against "popery," appears in the speeches of Hypocrisy and of the "popish priests," Perverse Doctrine and Ignorance. New Custom and Light of the Gospel are both ministers of the Reformed Faith, whose cry is "Give the people light through reading the New Testament and preaching from its texts."

While its epilogue declares that the school Interlude *Jack Juggler*[26] (1553?) contains a double meaning and has great contemporary significance, and while Professor Gayley builds on this epilogue a plea for the satiric quality of the play, it is difficult to see in it anything more than amusing burlesque. Satire so completely hidden can hardly be effective. This same obscurity envelops the Interlude *Godly Queen Hester,*[27] written perhaps before 1530. Possibly the career of Wolsey is sketched in the downfall of Haman, but the treatment of the theme is anything but satirical.

In *The World and the Child*[28] occurs a satiric dialogue between Manhood and Folly. The speech of the latter connects with the Satire of Fools, as might be expected, but in one of its phases it is also vaguely reminiscent of Piers Plowman[29]—for Folly, in his relations with various classes of society, is a welcome guest in the nunneries, and has for many years dwelt

[25] *Anonymous Plays,* 3d Series, ed. Farmer, pp. 157–202.
[26] *Ibid,* pp. 1–40.
[27] *Anonymous Plays,* 2d Series, ed. Farmer, pp. 245–287.
[28] *Dodsley's Old Plays,* ed. Hazlitt.
[29] See *supra,* p. 75.

with the friars, who crowned him king! Also mildly anti-papist are the speeches of Iniquity, the Vice in the Interlude *King Darius*,[30] printed in 1565.

The Four Elements[31] contains a trace of literary satire in the speech of the Messenger, who pleads for the English tongue as a vehicle for serious matter in place of the folly which now wholly employs it. The figure of Riot in *The Interlude of Youth*[32] reminds the reader of Skelton's Riot in the *Bouge of Court.* The Priest in *The Disobedient Child*[33] inveighs against drunken clerks. It is scarcely necessary to record the faint traces of satire, social, political, and religious, that occur in the other Interludes and Moralities of the present period. Professor Ward states that several polemic plays, no longer extant, were produced in the later days of Henry VIII.[34] These probably presented little variation on what has already been considered. Such controversial Moralities were continued on into the Elizabethan age. *Robin Conscience* and *The Endightment against Mother Masse* are satiric dialogues described by Professor Herford.[35]

Taken as a whole, the plays satirical either wholly or in parts, written between the beginning of the sixteenth century and the accession of Elizabeth, present no subject-matter that differs radically from that found in the undramatic satire of the same period. The satire on low life, a phase of social satire, was shared by forms other than the drama; the satire on religious questions, while it chiefly characterizes the plays, is also found in other literary forms. It is rather in their picturesque and vivid treatment, sometimes approaching the truly dramatic, that the Moralities and Interludes from *Magnyfycence* to *Albion Knight* surpassed other more or less satirical verse of their time. This fact again illustrates the statement made in the introductory chapter of the present book—that

[30] *Anon. Plays,* 3d Series, ed. Farmer, pp 41–92.
[31] *Dodsley's Old Plays,* ed. Hazlitt.
[32] *Ibid.*
[33] *Ibid.*
[34] Ward, *A History of English Dramatic Literature,* Vol. I, p. 136.
[35] Herford, p. 55; 63–6.

only when satire actually takes the form of the drama, or at least employs the general dramatic method, does it achieve its highest and most effective expression.[36] Religious satire was soon to fade from the drama; but out of these crude attempts at the satiric play, after cross-fertilization from foreign sources, were finally to come *The Alchemist, Volpone,* and *Bartholomew Fair.*

[36] See *supra,* p. 24.

CHAPTER VIII

Summary and Conclusion

The Church the chief object of medieval satire in England.—Attitude of various satirists towards the Church.—The Goliards, Wireker, Gower, Chaucer, The Lollards, Dunbar, Skelton, Lyndsay.—Religious satire a gradual growth.—Political Satire.—Its constant appearance from the reign of John to that of Henry VIII.—Its value.—The Moral Satire.—Its lack of interest and power.—The Social Satire.—Its growth.—Its significance and value.—The tone of medieval verse-satire in England.—Its chaotic form.—General relation of this medieval product to later satire in verse.—The New Satire of Wyatt and the Elizabethans.

I

With the great names of Barclay, Skelton, and Lyndsay comes the close and the summing up of medieval satire in England. Nothing could better illustrate the characteristics of the English people through these three centuries than the subject-matter, the tone, and the form, of this medieval product. Of the subject-matter, the religious aspect was the most significant feature. It speaks volumes for the wretched condition of the church in England, that for centuries this condition should have furnished the chief target for satirical attack. The immorality and ignorance of the clerical orders of every kind and degree, the sale of benefices, absentee clergy, plural livings, and other ecclesiastical corruptions, continue to furnish a perennial source of satire of every conceivable tone.[1] The Goliardic writers and Nigellus Wireker laughed at this clerical corruption; Gower wept over it; Chaucer satirized it in his inimitable pictures of contemporary life. The Lollards, sometimes abusing and sometimes ridiculing clerical immorality, did not confine themselves to this one theme, but demanded reforms in church doctrine as well as in the morals of the

[1] Satire against the clergy was the common property of medieval Europe. The English product is inferior to that of the Continent, at least in humor. See Schneegans, Lenient, *passim*.

clergy. Dunbar treated the subject largely in burlesque; Barclay reverted to the generalized lament; Skelton scolded, stormed, and abused; and Lyndsay arraigned clerical corruption with an effective mingling of ridicule and invective. The "Satire of the Reformation" sums up every phase of this religious subject-matter, enlarging on the scope of its predecessor, the Lollard satire of a century previous, and calling for reform in the morals, the doctrine, and the polity of the Church, with a voice sometimes harsh with invective and abuse, sometimes laughing with ridicule, but often effective, because earnest and sincere.[2]

This Religious Satire was a gradual growth. Through three centuries it became more comprehensive in its material, more outspoken and bitter in its tone. At last its purpose was effected, very differently from the expectations and desires of many of its exponents. Reform from within failed. Only radical methods from without could attain the object aimed at by almost every British satirist from Walter Map to Sir David Lyndsay.

With the Reformation, this distinct variety of satire of course died away, though its echoes continued through the Elizabethan period, until ecclesiastical polity and doctrine were settled once and forever, and the clergy ceased to offer so inviting a target for satirical shafts.

While this Religious Satire was a gradual growth, the Political Satire of the Middle Ages is an even more significant and distinct product of development. From the beginning, the political Satire shows the English interest in public affairs. It is far more inclined to personalities than the Religious Satire, and exhibits much more contemporary color. It begins with the *sirventes* against King John,[3] and again appears in the weak and disastrous reign of Henry III and the turmoil of the Barons'

[2] In mere bulk, the satire of the Reformation in England cannot compare with the analogous product in France; while in humor, literary power, general effectiveness, it falls far below that of France and that of Germany.

[3] See *supra*, p. 48 f.

War.[4] It fills the reign of Richard II with a strident cry against the weakness of the king and the corruption and incompetentcy of his ministers.[5] It speaks again through the long and troublous reign of Henry VI and the Wars of the Roses;[6] and finally culminates in the early part of the sixteenth century with the numberless and virulent attacks against the great ministers Wolsey and Cromwell, who, in the eyes of the people, represented wickedness in high places.[7] Usually direct and severe, such satire embodies little humor, but great vigor of expression. It is characteristic of English conservatism, that through the entire range of this political satire England's kings are usually spared, while upon royal ministers is laid the entire blame of maladministration. As the English people gained in power to govern and to express themselves, their political satire grew from small beginnings into one of the most powerful instruments ever wielded for the expression of the people's rights. In Skelton's bitter attacks on Wolsey[8] and in Lyndsay's vigorous calls for political reform in Scotland,[9] the Political Satire of medieval England culminates in a type replete with vitality and contemporary interest.

This contemporary interest is fatally lacking in what may be termed the Moral Satire, the most prevalent but least effective variety of its kind in medieval literature. It is only too apt to be abstract and dull, for it is entirely free from personalities and exhibits but little contemporary color. On the contrary, it delights in a maximum of that "satirical commonplace" which more or less characterizes every variety of the medieval Satire, and is so fatal to permanent interest and power.[10] This didactic Satire on the virtues and vices is so apt to invade the domain of other varieties that very few medieval English satirical poems are entirely free from its influence. Yet, as in the poems of Gower, it is frequently found quite by itself.

[4] See *supra*, p. 50 f.
[5] See *supra*, p. 82 f.
[6] See *supra*, p. 126 f.
[7] See *supra*, p. 172 f.
[8] See *supra*, p. 150 f.
[9] See *supra*, p. 204 f.
[10] See *supra*, p. 32.

Though perennial, it suffered a loss of vigor upon the advent of the greater individuality and realism of the Renaissance, when attention to actual life and its details became necessarily fatal to the dull abstractions of medievalism. The Satire on *The Seven Deadly Sins* survived till the Elizabethan period, but passed into something far more interesting through its greater attention to contemporary life.

Far removed from the vague and ineffective generalities, the didacticism and dullness, of the Moral Satire, is the Social Satire on themes concrete and contemporary. In its beginnings, this variety connects itself with the Moral Satire on the one hand and with the Religious Satire on the other. Indeed, at first it is largely identical with these varieties. But gradually a type is developed, dealing with purely social themes, such as the condition of the people, and suggesting their aspirations. Far back in the thirteenth century we see this type exemplified in the long poem on *The Times of Edward II.*[11] Langland illustrates it, too, with increased vividness and power.[12] The long anonymous poems of the reign of Henry VIII again exemplify it, for *Vox Populi, Vox Dei*[13] is also of this kind. It is ever the voice of the people, sure and strong. Of humor there is little enough; the touch is heavy; the purpose distinctly reformatory. At last the type culminates in Lyndsay's powerful and vivid sketches of "Pauper" and "John the Commonweal."[14] While pathetic, there is yet something splendid, something epic, in this voice of a nation struggling upward to the light. In such an aspect, this Social Satire, crude and formless as it often is, assumes a considerable measure of dignity and power.

In this sombre and earnest type we find little real characterization and little genuine social satire of the lighter and more interesting kind. This was to come later. Yet satire of this kind also had its early beginnings. It manifests itself first in the *genre* pictures of Langland. It attains its best estate in the

[11] See *supra,* p. 64 f.
[12] See *supra,* p. 76 f.
[13] See *supra,* p. 173 f.
[14] See *supra,* p. 206 f.

delightful contemporary sketches of Chaucer. But it is most characteristically a product of the Renaissance, with its humor, realism, and treatment of actual life. The *Elynour Rummynge*[15] of Skelton is of this type; while a host of anonymous productions of the new period embody the same spirit. Even Barclay, when he forgets himself, indulges slightly in real social satire; Dunbar glories in it; Lyndsay exemplifies it finely in the *Satire of the Three Estates.* Subvarieties of this kind are the so-called Fool Satire and Satire on Rogues,[16] which picture low life with humor and a certain amount of characterization. With the growth of the Renaissance comes an increase of contemporary detail, of local color, in the Social Satire. In this respect it offers an analogy to the growth of the drama through the earlier and more abstract Moralities to the later Moralities and Interludes with their humorous character-studies. Gradually this new Satire tends to displace the earlier, heavier, and more generalized type, and looks forward to the Social Satire of the Elizabethan classicists, and even beyond—to the Satire of Pope. It is the greatest variety of its kind. Having all the essentials of life within itself, it needs only the classical influence[17] from without to develope finally into a form highly representative of the period in which it flourishes. It is ever tending toward the dramatic, striving to fulfill the true function of the Satire—the picturing and the criticism of contemporary life.

II

Such, in brief, is the *subject-matter* of the medieval English Satire. In regard to the *tone* of this product little remains to be said. Its weapon is mainly invective, with few traces of genuine humor.[18] This lack of humor may perhaps be explained by the didactic and reformatory purpose that inspired this medieval product, which arose as a popular mode of expression and not as a literary genre. Yet its pessimistic tone

[15] See *supra,* p. 149.
[16] See *supra,* p. 177 f.
[17] See *supra,* p. 15 f.
[18] See *supra,* p. 8.

is somewhat relieved by religious hopefulness: the world is not all bad; certain social classes are often exempted from the general censure. The didactic and constructive element appears in the representation of the ideal, as in *Piers Plowman*. Finally, with all its lack of individuality and self-revelation, with all its invective, didacticism, and dullness, the medieval verse-Satire in England still remains at its best estate a product dignified through its earnestness and sincerity.

III

Varied as is the subject-matter of this medieval Satire in England, it is perhaps in *form* that the greatest variety occurs. The form was, indeed, almost chaotic; for we must remember that through these centuries the Satire was not a recognized genre. Even the name "Satire" itself was rarely used, and then only with the vaguest reference to the classics. The verse-form might or might not be stanzaic, as suited the whim of the writer. The poem might be of any length, in any meter. And the method was almost as varied as the form of verse. This method might be that of direct address, as in the *Poem on the Times of Edward II;* again it might be narrative, as in *Piers Plowman;* dramatic, as in the *Satire of the Three Estates;* or it might be the method of the popular ballad, as in *Richard of Cornwall*. The characteristic style is diffuse and free from allusions of any kind. The Protean forms are bound together only by the unifying spirit of destructive criticism.

IV

Such is the typical medieval English Satire before the time of Wyatt—a poem embodying political, religious, and social subject-matter; in tone didactic, severe, of little humor, of much invective; employing mainly the method of direct attack, with little individuality and little picturing of contemporary life; practically formless, yet through the centuries very gradually but distinctly tending to evolve from its chaotic condition into a recognized literary genre.

The relation of this protoplasmic medieval product to the more finished form of the late seventeenth century cannot be treated here. It is more than possible, however, that the native English qualities of this early Satire passed in some measure into the Elizabethan imitations of Horace and Juvenal; and, through these, bequeathed to the finished Satire of a century later a breadth of interests, a wide range of subject-matter, and a vigorous form of expression. These qualities, combined with those derived from the Classics, finally made the genre not a mere exotic imitation but a type thoroughly native to the soil. This happy blending of English and Classical qualities appears partly in the Satires of Sir Thomas Wyatt (c. 1540); it appears again and perhaps more fully in the imitative experiments of the Elizabethans; but it is best illustrated in the work of Dryden and of Pope.

With the year 1540 was reached the end of an era in the history of the English Satire. A new age began when Wyatt turned for his inspiration to Horace and to Alamanni. Some of the anonymous and elaborate Social Satires were yet to be written; but the Medieval Satire, though still dominant, was on the decline. With the work of Wyatt a new species appeared—a Satire of classical origin,—quiet, polished, reflective, individual, in almost every detail contrasting strangely with that spontaneous, uncouth, didactic, generalized product embodied in English verse-satire before the Renaissance.

BIBLIOGRAPHY.

The following list gives all editions of texts used as a basis for the foregoing study; all works, critical or otherwise, which are actually cited in the text of this volume or in its foot-notes; the principal critical studies which have proved of value; those histories of England and of English literature, etc., which have furnished the historical background and the connecting links for the present work; and, finally, histories of foreign literatures, ancient and modern, which have been found serviceable. The most important omissions from the list are as follows: texts of foreign writers, ancient and modern, which in part form the basis for the conclusions reached in Chapter I (the theory of the Satire); many critical studies of various literary genres, such as the Fable, the Beast-Epic, the Allegory, the Epigram, etc.; and a great number of essays, magazine articles, etc., on the Satire and on satire in general, which proved of little practical value.

Alden, R. M. *The rise of Formal Satire in England under Classical Influence.* Philadelphia, 1899.

Alliterative Poem on the Deposition of King Richard II. Ed. T. Wright. Cam. Soc. Pub., vol. 3. London, 1838.

Altenglische Dichtungen des Ms. Harl. 2253. Ed. K. Bödeker. Berlin, 1878.

Altenglische Legenden. Ed. C. Horstman. Heilbronn, 1881.

Altenglische Sprachproben. Ed. E. A. F. Maetzner. Berlin, 1878.

Ancient Songs and Ballads, from the reign of Henry the Second to the Revolution. Ed. J. Ritson. 2 vols. London, 1829.

Anecdota Literaria; a collection of short poems in English, Latin, and French, illustrative of the literature and history of England in the thirteenth century. Ed. T. Wright. London, 1844.

Anglo-Latin Satirical Poets and Epigrammatists of the Twelfth Century, The. Ed. T. Wright. 2 vols. London, 1872 (*Roll Series*).

Anonymous Plays. Ed. J. S. Farmer. 1st Series (1550–1553), London, 1905; 2d Series (1528–1561), London, 1906; 3d Series (1550–1565), London, 1906.

Archæologia: or Miscellaneous Tracts Relating to Antiquity. Published by Society of Antiquaries of London. 59 vols. London, 1770–1906.

Aubrey, W. H. S. *Rise and Growth of the English Nation.* 3 vols. London, 1895–99.

Babuder, Giacomo Cav. *L'Eroicomica e Generi Affini di Poesia Giocosa-Satirica.* Capodistria, 1896.

Bale, John. *Johan Baptyste.* Harleian Miscellany, I.

Kynge Johan. A Play in Two Parts. By John Bale. Ed. J. P. Collier. Cam. Soc. Pub., vol. 2. London, 1838.

The Temptacyon of our Lorde, by John Bale. Ed. Rev. A. B. Grosart, 1870. *Fuller Worthies Library,* vol I.

Ballads from Manuscripts. Ed. F. J. Furnivall. 2 vols. Printed for The Ballad Society, London, 1868–1872.

Barclay, A. *Certayne Egloges.* Spenser Soc. Pub., 1885.

The Cytezen and Uplondyshman: An Eclogue by Alexander Barclay. Ed. F. W. Fairholt. Percy Soc. Pub., vol. 22.

The Ship of Fools, Translated by Alexander Barclay. Ed. T. H. Jamieson. 2 vols. London and Edinburgh, 1874.

Becker, E. J. *A Contribution to the Comparative Study of the Medieval Visions of Heaven and Hell, with Special Reference to the Middle English Versions.* Baltimore, 1899.

Bédier, J. *Les Fabliaux; études de littérature populaire et d'histoire littéraire du moyen âge.* Paris, 1895.

Bibliothek der Angelsächsischen Poesie. Ed. C. W. M. Grein and R. P. Wülker. Leipzig, 1894.

Brandt, S. *Narrenschiff.* Ed. F. Zarncke. Leipzig, 1854.

ten Brink, B. *Chaucer. Studien zur Geschichte seiner Entwicklung und zur Chronologie seiner Schriften.* Münster, 1870.

Geschichte der englischen Literatur. Berlin, 1877.

Brooke, S. A. *English Literature from the Beginning to the Norman Conquest.* New York, 1898.

Chambers, E. K. *The Mediæval Stage.* 2 vols. Oxford, 1903.

Chaucer, G. *Complete Works.* Ed. Rev. W. W. Skeat. 6 vols. Oxford, 1894.

Cock Lorell's Bote: A Satirical Poem. Ed. E. F. Rimbault. Percy Soc. Pub., vol. 6.

Collier, J. P. *The History of English Dramatic Poetry to the Time of Shakespeare and Annals of the Stage to the Restoration.* 3 vols. London, 1831.

Courthope, W. J. *History of English Poetry.* 4 vols. New York, 1895–1903.

Creizenach, W. *Geschichte des Neueren Dramas.* 3 vols. Halle, 1893–1903.

Dodsley's Old English Plays. Ed. W. C. Hazlitt. 15 vols. London, 1874–6.

Dressel, J. P. R. *Zur Geschichte der Fabel.* Berlin, 1876.

Dunbar, W. *Poems.* Ed. J. Small. Scottish Text Soc. Pub., vols. 2 and 4. 1893.

Early English Poems and Lives of Saints. Ed. F. J. Furnivall. Transactions of the Philological Soc., 1858, Part II.

Epigrammatists, a Selection from the Epigrammatic Literature of Ancient, Mediæval and Modern Times. Ed. Rev. H. P. Dodd. London, 1870.

Excerpta Historica or, Illustrations of English History. Ed. S. Bentley. London, 1833.

Fischer, A. *Kritische Darstellung der Lessingischen Lehre von der Fabel.* Halle, 1891.

Flögel, C. F. *Geschichte der Komischen Literatur.* 4 vols. Liegnitz und Leipzig, 1784.

Fraustadt, F. *Über das Verhältnis von Barclays "Ship of Fools" zur lateinischen, französischen und deutschen Quelle.* Breslau, 1894.

Gairdner, J. *The Houses of Lancaster and York.* London, 1875.

Garnett, R. *History of Italian literature.* New York, 1898.

Gingeuène, P. L. Histoire littéraire d'Italie. 9 vols. Paris, 1824.

Gower, J. *Complete Works.* Ed. G. C. Macaulay. 4 vols. Oxford, 1899–1902.

Green, J. R. *History of the English People.* 4 vols. New York, n.d.

Gubernatis, A. de. *Storia della Satira.* Milan, 1884.

Haessner, M. *Die Goliardendichtung und die Satire im 13. Jahrhundert in England.* Leipzig, 1905.

Hammond, E. P. "*London Lickpenny.*" *Anglia,* vol. 20.

Henryson, R. *Poems.* Ed. D. Laing. Edinburgh, 1865.

Herford, C. H. *Studies in the Literary Relations of England and Germany in the Sixteenth Century.* Cambridge, 1886.

Heywood, J. *Dramatic Writings.* Ed. J. S. Farmer. London, 1905.

History of Reynard the Fox, The. W. J. Thoms. Percy Soc. Pub., vol. 12. London, 1844.

Hoccleve's Works, The Minor Poems. Ed. F. J. Furnivall. Early Eng. Text Soc. Pub., Extra Series 61. London, 1892.

Julleville, L. P. de. *Histoire de la Langue et de la Littérature française.* 8 vols. Paris, 1896–99.

Krapp, G. P. *The Legend of St. Patrick's Purgatory: its later literary history.* Baltimore, 1900.

Latin Poems Commonly Attributed to Walter Mapes, The. Ed. T. Wright. Cam. Soc. Pub., vol. 16.

Lenient, C. *La Satire en France au Moyen Age.* Paris, 1893.

La Satire en France au XVIe Siecle. Paris, 1886.

Lessing, G. E. *Anmerkungen über das Epigramm.* Sämtliche Werke. 20 vols. Stuttgart, 1882–5. Vol. 15.

On the nature and history of the Fable. *Ibid.,* vols. 1 and 2.

Loiseleur-Deslongchamps, A. S. A. *Essai sur les fables indiennes et sur leur introduction en Europe.* Paris, 1838.

"Lost" Tudor Plays (1460–1566). Ed. J. S. Farmer. London, 1907.

Lounsbury, T. R. *Studies in Chaucer, His life and Writings.* 3 vols. New York, 1892.

Lydgate, J. *A Selection from the Minor Poems.* Ed. J. O. Halliwell. Percy Soc. Pub., vol. 2.

Lyndsay, Sir D. *Poetical Works.* Ed. D. Laing. 2 vols. Edinburgh, 1871.

Mead, W. E. *The Prologue of the Wife of Bath's Tale.* Pub. of the Mod. Lang. Ass. Am., vol. 16; N. S., vol. 9.

Minot, L. *Poems.* Ed. J. Hall. Oxford, 1887.

Monumenta Franciscana. Ed. J. S. Brewer. London, 1858 (*Roll Series*).

Morley, H. *English Writers; an Attempt towards a History of English Literature.* 11 vols. London, 1887–95.

Müller, K. O., and Donaldson, J. W. *History of the Literature of Ancient Greece.* 3 vols. London, 1858.

Old Ballads from Early Printed Copies. Ed. J. P. Collier. Percy Soc. Pub., vol. I.

Old English Miscellany, An. Ed. Rev. R. Morris. Early Eng. Text Soc. Pub., vol. 49.

Owl and the Nightingale, The. Ed. T. Wright. Percy Soc. Pub., vol. 11, London, 1843.

Ibid., ed. J. E. Wells. *Belle-Lettres Series,* 1907.

Paris, G. *La Littérature française au Moyen Age.* Paris, 1905.

Petersen, K. O. *On the Sources of the Nonne Prestes Tale.* Boston, 1898.

Pierce the Ploughman's Crede. Ed. Rev. W. W. Skeat. Early Eng. Text Soc. Pub., vol. 30. London, 1867.

Piers the Plowman and Richard the Redeless by William Langland. Ed. Rev. W. W. Skeat. 2 vols. Oxford, 1886.

Poem on the Times of Edward II, A. Ed. Rev. C. Hardwick. Percy Soc. Pub., vol. 28. London, 1849.

Poetry of the Anti-Jacobin. Ed. C. Edmonds. London, 1890.

Political Poems and Songs Relating to English History, Composed during the Period from the Accession of Edw. III. to that of Rich. III. Ed. T. Wright. 2 vols. London, 1859 (*Roll Series*).

Political, Religious, and Love Poems. Ed. F. J. Furnivall. Early Eng. Text Soc. Pub., vol. 15. London, 1866.

Political Songs of England, from the Reign of John to that of Edward II, The. Ed. T. Wright. Cam. Soc. Pub., vol. 6.

Quellen des weltlichen dramas in England vor Shakespeare. Ed. A. Brandl. Strassburg, 1898.

Rambeau, A. *Chaucer's "House of Fame" in seinen verhältnis zu Dante's "Divina Comedia." Englische Studien,* vol. 3, p. 209.

Reliques of Ancient English Poetry. Ed. T. Percy, D.D., Bishop of Dromore. London, 1847.

Reliquiæ Antiquæ. Ed. T. Wright and J. O. Halliwell. 2 vols. London, 1841.

Remains of the Early Popular Poetry of England. Ed. W. C. Hazlitt. 4 vols. London, 1864.

Rey, A. *Skelton's Satirical Poems in their relation to Lydgate's Order of Fools, Cock Lorell's Bote, and Barclay's Ship of Fools.* Bern, 1899.

Richard Rolle de Hampole. *The Pricke of Conscience.* Ed. R. Morris. Philological Soc. Pub., 1863.

Robert of Brunne. *Handlyng Synne.* Ed. F. J. Furnivall. Early Eng. Text Soc. Pub., O. S., nos. 119 and 123.

Robertson, J. G. *History of German Literature.* New York, 1902.

Root, R. K. *The Poetry of Chaucer, A Guide to its Study and Appreciation.* Boston and New York, 1896.

Roy, W., and Barlow, J. *Rede Me and be Nott Wrothe.* Ed. E. Arber. London, 1871. (*Arber's English Reprints, vol. II.*)

Schneegans, H. *Geschichte der Grotesken Satire.* Strassburg, 1894.

Select Epigrams from the Greek Anthology. Ed. and trans. J. W. Mackail. London, 1906.

Select Pieces of Early Popular Poetry. Ed. E. V. Utterson. 2 vols. London, 1817.

Skelton, J. *Poetical Works.* Ed. Rev. A. Dyce. 2 vols. London, 1843.

Social England. Ed. H. D. Traill. 6 vols. New York, 1895–97.

Stubbs, W. *Early Plantagenets.* London, 1876.

Taine, H. A. *LaFontaine et ses Fables.* Paris, 1888.

Teuffel, W. S. *History of Roman Literature.* 2 vols. London, 1873.

Ticknor, G. *History of Spanish Literature.* 3 vols. New York, 1854.

Trevelyan, G. M. *England in the Age of Wycliffe.* New York, 1899.

Turner, S. *The History of England during the Middle Ages.* 5 vols. London, 1830.

Warburton, W. P. *Edward III.* London, 1876.

Ward, A. W. *A History of English Dramatic Literature.* 3 vols. London, 1899.

Wine, Women, and Song. Medieval Latin Students' Songs, now first translated into English verse, with an essay by John Addington Symonds. London, 1889.

Wolff, E. *Reinke de Vos und satirische-didaktische Dichtung.* Stuttgart, n.d.

Wright, T. *History of Caricature and of Grotesque in Literature and Art.* London, 1875.

INDEX.

Absalom and Achitophel, 32
Addison, 6, 10; satiric essays, 7
Aelfric, references to heaven and hell in his prose, 53
Aeneas Silvius, 165
Aeschylus, 25
Aesop, 27, 136; *King Stork and King Log*, 32 n.
Against Evil Women, 139, 140
Against Women Unconstant, balade, 116
Alamanni, 227
Albion Knight, 211, 217, 219
Alchemist, The, 7, 112, 220
Alchemy, satire against, 112f., 166
Allegory, the satiric, 28; in *Speculum Stultorum*, 45; in *Piers Plowman*, 70–9; in *The House of Fame*, 114–6
Anglo-French satire, 36, 37; songs against King John, 48f.; against papal tax, 49f.; against monastic clergy, 57f.; against public fraud, 59
Anglo-Latin satire, 39; *Speculum Stultorum*, 43–6; *De Vita Monachorum*, 46; *Entheticus*, 47
Anglo-Latin satirists and epigrammatists, 17 and n., 36, 39; Wireker, 43f.; Neckham, 46; John of Salisbury, 47.
Anti-Jacobin, The, satire of, 5
Apocalypsis Goliae, analysis of, 40
Archilochus, 11, 23
Aretino, Pietro, 30
Ariosto, Satires, 7, 18
Aristophanes, 6, 24, 25, 33; plays, 7, 14, 18; *The Frogs*, 24
Art of Cookery, The, 21 n.
Art of Love, The, 21 n.
Art of Preaching, The, 21 n.
Awdelay, John, 54, 181

Bale, John, 212; *Temptacyon of our Lorde*, 214; *God's Promises*, 214; *Three Laws*, 214; *John Baptyste*, 214; *Kynge Johan*, 214–6; his satiric method, 216, 217
Ball, John, doggerel rhymes, 82
Ballad of Luther, the Pope, A Cardinal and a Husbandman, A, 195
Ballads, politico-satirical, 4; of Civil War and Protectorate, 4, 7; in Wars of the Roses, 130, 131 n.
Ballat of the Fenȝeit Freir, 137, 141
Bansley, Charles, 177
Barclay, Alexander, 5, 178, 180, 222, 225; *The Ship of Fools*, 155–64; *Eclogues*, 164–6; idea of satire, 156; characterization, 159; satiric methods, 159f.; remedy for follies, 160f.; pictures of real life, 161f.; lack of poetry, 162; influence of classical satire upon, 162f.; medieval ethics, 163; individualizing tendency, 163f.; his English heritage, 164; subsequent influence, 164; his court-satire, 165; literary satire, 165; Mantuan and Aeneas Silvius, 165f.; influence of *Eclogues*, 166
Barlow, Jerome, 185
Bartholomew Fair, 220
Batrachomyomachia, The, 20, 23, 25, 26
Battle of Lewes, The, 50
Beast-Epic, The, 7; as parody, 26f.
Beast-Fable, The, 27f., 109
Bede, *Vision of Furseus* and *Vision of Drihthelm*, 53
Beggars and Idlers, satire against, 73, 180f.
Bel Acueil, in *Roman de la Rose*, 104
Bembo, epigrams, 17
Benedictines, the, 39
Béranger, songs, 7, 37

Bernard de Rovenac, *sirventes* against Henry III, 49
Berni, 8, 20 n., 30
Bertrand de Born, *sirventes,* 37
Bertrand de Born, the younger, *sirvente,* 48
Bishop Golias, 1, 38
Bishops of Bath, Norwich, Winchester, Rochester, and Ely, satire against, 48
Blickling Homilies, 35
Boccaccio, 106, 109
Boccalini, 33
Boileau, 5, 6, 16; Satires, 7; *Le Lutrin,* 22
Boothe, William, bishop of "Chester," satire against, 128, 129
Bouge of Court, The, 144, 145, 213, 219; as court-satire, 146; analysis of, 146f; origin of name, 146 n.
Brandt, Sebastian, 119, 147 n., 155, 158
Buchanan, George, epigrams, 17; as satirist of the Reformation, 32 n.
Burchiello, Domenico, 20 n.
Burgundy, Duke of, defection, 124; satire against, 125
Burlesque, as a prose genre, 7; as a poetic genre, 7; as a satiric method, 18f.; in the Middle Ages, 25f.; Goliardic burlesque, 40f.; in *Speculum Stultorum,* 45; in *Satire on the Men of Stockton,* 83; in *Council of London,* 88; in ballads on siege of Calais, 125; in parody of the Mass, 129; in Chaucer, 98–117, *passim;* in Dunbar, 136–43, *passim;* in Cock Lorell, 179f.; in Heywood, 213f.; in *New Custom,* 218
Butler, Samuel, 1, 5, 7, 14; *Hudibras,* 3, 18, 22, 23, 28
Byron, George Gordon, 1, 4, 8, 14; *Don Juan,* 7, 23, 28; burlesque poetry, 18; *Vision of Judgment,* 22; *English Bards and Scotch Reviewers,* 33
Calais, siege of, satiric ballads, 125
Cambridge, Richard Owen, *Scribbleriad,* 22
Candide, 7
Canning, George, 1; *Knife-Grinder,* 21
Canon's Yeoman's Tale, The, analysis of, 112f.
Canterbury Tales, The, 98, 99, 100; satire in General Prologue, 100–103; *The Pardoner's Tale* and prologue, 103f.; prologue to *Wife of Bath's Tale,* 104f.; envoy to *Clerk's Tale,* 105; interlude before *Monk's Tale,* 105; *Merchant's Tale,* 109; *Nun's Priest's Tale,* 109f.; *Friar's Tale,* 111; *Summoner's Tale,* 111f.; *Canon's Yeoman's Tale,* 112f.; *Sir Thopas,* 113f.
Caporali, Cesare, 33
Caricature, 18
Castle of Perseverance, The, 216
Catullus, epigrams, 17
Cervantes, 7, 14; *Don Quixote,* 7; *Viaje al Parnaso,* 33
Champion des Dames, 72
"Character" writers, 163
Chansons des Gestes, parodies of, 25f.
Chaucer, Geoffrey, 1, 5, 162, 207, 213, 216, 221, 225; *Friar's Tale,* 7; *Sir Thopas,* 26; *Nun's Priest's Tale,* 27 n.; *House of Fame,* 28; influence of Jean de Meung, 72; his satiric poetry, 98–117; general character of his satire, 98; point of view, 99; his satiric methods, 100; indebtedness to *fabliau,* 107; his *fabliaux,* 109–12; his place in the history of English satire, 117; influence upon immediate successors, 118
Churchill, Charles, 1, 6, 10
Cistercians, the, 39
Classes, Social, satire against, 74, 84, 94; on classes represented by individuals, 100–17, 166, 179; rise of "Class satire," 66f.
Classical Latin Satire, The, 3, 10 n.;

evolution of, 15; description of, 15f.; burlesque element, 23; moral and social elements, 33
Clergy, the, satire against, 40f., 44f., 46, 58, 59, 65f., 74f., 81, 84, 94, 100, 111, 132, 142, 151f., 172, 189f., 191, 192, 201, 202, 205, 206, 208, 213, 219.
Clerk's Tale, The, envoy to, 105
Cleveland, John, 1, 4, 5
Cochlaeus, 188f.
Cock Lorell's Bote, 101, 163, 213, 216; analysis of, 178f.
Cognizances of the Nobles, in *Richard the Redeless,* 95, 96; reasons for use in satire, 126, 127; in Wars of the Roses, 130
Colyn Cloute, by Skelton, 145; analysis of, 150f.
Complaint of the Plowman, The, analysis of, 89f.
Complaynt of Bagsche the Kingis auld Hound, The, 203
Complaynt of Schir David Lyndesay to the Kingis Grace, The, 201
Confessio Amantis, satire in prologue, 94
Confession of Golias, The, 40f.
Conquest, the, effect on English satire, 36
Consistory Courts, satire against, 56f., 75, 135, 203, 207
Copland, Robert, 180
Coppeta, Francesco, burlesque sonnets, 20
Council of London, the, trial of Wyckliffe, 87
Council of London, The, Satire, 83; analysis of, 87f.
"Court-satire," in Dunbar, 139; in Skelton, 146–8; in Barclay, 165; in Lyndsay, 202, 203
Cowper, William, 1
Cratinus, 24
Cromwell, Thomas, 172; satire against, 173, 223
Cytezen and Uplondyshman, The, analysis of, 166

Dame Sirith, 108, 109
Dance of the Sevin Deidly Synnis, The, 141
Dante, 114
"Daw Topias," possible author of anti-Lollard Satire, 91
De Casibus Virorum Illustrium, 106
De Conjuge non Ducenda, 41, 122, 175, 176
De Cruce Denarii, 41
Defence of Women, The, 176 n.
DeFoe, Daniel, lampoons, 7; satiric pamphlet, 14 n.
De Mundi Miseria, 41
De Nummo, 41, 42
Deslongchamps, 27
Dialogue, the satiric, 7, 13
Dialogue, The, Occleve's, 176
Dialogue between the Body and the Soul, 53
Disobedient Child, The, 219
Divine Comedy, The, as a vision of Heaven and Hell, 53; relation to *The House of Fame,* 114
Dit d'Aventure, 25f.
Doctor, the, as a satiric type, 102f.
Doctor Double Ale, 191f.
Don Juan, by Byron, 7, 23, 28
Don Quixote, 5, 7
Donne, John, 1, 16
Dreme, The, 200
Drunkenness, satire against, 77, 192, 219
Dryden, John, 1, 2, 5, 6, 13, 36, 227; *Mac Flecknoe,* 11, 14, 33; burlesque poetry, 18; *Absalom and Achitophel,* 32
Dunbar, William, 57, 134, 155, 177, 197, 198, 222, 225; satiric poetry, 136–43; character and times, 136; nature and genesis of his satire, 136f.; range of his satire, 137; humor, 138; form of his satiric poems, 138; sum of characteristics as satirist, 143
Dunciad, The, 20, 22, 31, 33

Eclogue, the satiric, of Barclay, Googe, Spenser, and Gay, 4; Barclay's, 164–6

Edward I, King, satire in reign of, 56–63
Edward II, King, satire in reign of, 63–8; satire against, 67f.
Edward III, King, satire in reign of, 68–79; satire against, 70
Edward IV, King, satire in reign of, 132f.
Edward VI, King, satire in reign of, 173–77, 194–6; economic troubles, 173; growth of Reformation, 194f.; Protestantism at court, 195f.
Elegy, the, 1
Elegy on a Lap-Dog, 21
Eleven Pains of Hell, The, analysis of, 54–5
Endightment against Mother Masse, The, 219
English Bards and Scotch Reviewers, 33
Epicharmus, 23
Epigram, the, 7; Elizabethan and Augustan, 4; relation to the Satire, 17f.; Greek epigram, 17; Martialian, 17; place in history of the English Satire, 17f.
Erasmus, 6, 10, 14, 144; *Praise of Folly,* 7
Essay, the satiric, 7
Eubeus of Paros, 23
Everyman, 216
Exhortation to the Nobles and Commons of the North, An, 173

Fable, the satiric, 4, 7; of Marie de France, 7; of Gay and Prior, 7; of LaFontaine, 7; Beast-Fable, 27f.
Fabliau, the, 5, 7; influence upon Chaucer, 107; in France, 107, 108; not primarily satirical, 108; in England, 108, 109; various *fabliaux,* 108–12; in dramatic form, 213
Fabliaux di Cognaigne, li, 55, 58f.
Farce, the French, 7
Fashions, satire on, 56, 170, 171, 203, 217
Fastnachtspiel, the, 7 n.
Fescennine Verses, 12
Fischart, 14, 18
Fischer, 27
Flemings, the, satire against, 125
Flyting of Dunbar and Kennedie, The, 141
"Fool Satires," 46, 119f., 155–64, 211, 218, 225
Folengo, Teofilo, *Orlandino* and *Maccaronea,* 18, 20
Four Elements, The, 219
Four P's, The, 101, 213
Fox and the Wolf, The, 27n, 109
Franc, Martin, 72
France, satire against, 69
Franco, Matteo, 20 n.
Fraser, Sir Simon, 61
Fraud, satire against, 59, 121, 139
Friar, the, as a satiric type, 101
Friar's Tale, The, 7; analysis of, 111
Friars, the, as objects of satire, 44f., 65, 75, 81, 87, 88, 101, 111, 132, 142, 189, 201, 205, 208; ministerial work, 52; spiritual degeneration, 57, 59
Frogs, The, 24
Froschmeuseler, the, 26

Gargantua, 7
Gautier of Sens, 38 n.
Gaveston, Piers, satire against, 67f.
Gay, John, satiric fables, 4; parodies, 20f.
Geburt Jesu, 175
"General Satire on all Classes of Society, A," 42
Gifford, William, 1, 5, 11, 16; Satires, 3
Godfrey of Winchester, epigrams, 17 and n.
Godly Queen Hester, 218
God's Promises, 214
Goethe, *Reineke Fuchs,* 27
Golden Targe, The, 136
Goldsmith, Oliver, 33 n.
Goliardic satire, 5; origin, nature, and history, 37f.; examples, 40f, 47f., 50, 67

Goliards, the, poetry, 36, 213, 221; origin, 37
Gongora, 20 n.
Googe, Barnaby, eclogues, 166
Gower, John, 47, 98, 100, 144, 182, 197, 221, 223; *Vox Clamantis,* 83–5; *Tripartite Chronicle,* 85; *On the Reign of Rich. II,* 93f.; *The Search for Light,* 94; prologue to *Confessio Amantis,* 94
Grotesque, the, in satire, 18
Guillaume de Digulleville, *Le Pelerinage de la Vie Humaine* and *Pelerinage de l'Ame,* 53

Hall, Joseph, 1, 16
Handlyng Synne, analysis of, 62f.
Hegemo Thasius, 23
Henry III, *sirventes* against, 49; satire in reign of, 49–56
Henry IV, King, satire in reign of, 85, 118–24; conspiracies against, 123; no satire against, 123f.
Henry V, King, satire in reign of, 124–6; no satire against, 124
Henry VI, King, satire in reign of, 126–32; political events in reign of, 126f.
Henry VIII, King, satire in reign of, 168–73, 177–94; social changes, 168f.; dissolution of monasteries, 172; "The Pilgrimage of Grace," 172; vagabondage, 177f.; the Reformation and religious parties, 181f.; translation of the Bible, 182f.
Henry of Huntingdon, epigrams, 17 and n.
Henryson, Robert, fables, 27, 134–6
Heywood, John, 216; epigrams, 17; Interludes, 101, 204, 212, 213
Hick Scorner, 217
Hipponax, 23
Homer, 6, 11
Horace, 6, 8, 11, 14, 15, 23, 32, 33, 98, 99, 227; Satires, 7; "Appian bore," 23
House of Fame, The, 28, 103; analysis of, 114–6; relation to *The Divine Comedy,* 114; satire in, 116; personal element, 116
How Dunbar was desyrd to be ane Freir, 137, 138; analysis of, 142
How myschaunce regneth in Ingelond, 132
How the Plowman learned his Pater Noster, 80 n.
Hudibras, 3, 7, 18, 22, 23, 28
Hunt, Leigh, 33
Hutten, Ulrich von, 6; dialogues, 7, 14; use of travesty, 20; *Phalarismus,* 31
Hwon holy chireche is vnder uote, 53
Hye Way to the Spyttel Hous, The, analysis of, 180f.

Image of Hypocrisy, The, analysis of, 192f.
In Vice most vicius he excellis, 141
Innocent III, pope, 47
Interlude of Youth, The, 211, 219
Interludes, satire in, 211; confusion with Moralities, 211; pictures of "low life," 211; Heywood's, 213f.; other Interludes, 216–19, *passim*
"It may wele ryme, etc.," 119

Jack Cade's Rebellion, 130
Jack Juggler, 218
Jack Upland, origin, 90; analysis of, 90f.
Jean de Meung, satire in *Roman de la Rose,* 71f.; influence upon Langland, 71f.; upon Chaucer, 72; upon Satire on Woman, 175
Jeste des Dames, La, 175
John, King, 47; *sirventes* against, 48f.
John Baptyste, 214
John Bon and Mast Person, 193
John de Wethamstede, 130
John of Bridlington, 70
John of Gaunt, 85
"John the Common Weal," in Lyndsay's satire, 201, 204, 207, 215, 224
Jonson, Ben, 7, 112

Judges, satire against, 56, 75
Juvenal, 5, 6, 8, 9, 10 n., 15, 24, 33, 176, 227; Satires, 7, 23

King, William, 21 n.
King Darius, 211, 219
King Henry VI, 127
Kirchmeyer, 215
Kittei's Confessioun, 203
Knife-Grinder, The, 21
Krankheit der Messe, 186 n.
Kyng Johan, 212, 214–6

LaFontaine, 5, 27, 136
La Secchia Rapita, 7, 20
Lampoon, the 7
Land of Cokaygne, The, 39, 55, 58
Langland, William, 1, 5, 98, 100, 148, 180, 181, 186, 205, 216, 224; *Piers Plowman,* 70–9; *Richard the Redeless,* 95f.
Langton, Stephen, 47, 215
Lapps and Greenlanders, primitive satire among, 30 n.
Latin Poems Commonly Attributed to Walter Mapes, 38
Le Lutrin, 7, 22
Lenvoy a Bukton, 116f.
Lenvoy de Chaucer a Scogan, 116
Lessing, fables, 27
Letter of Cupid, The, 176
Literary Satire, The, 33
Little John Nobody, 196
Lollards, the, satire for and against, 85–92; persecution of, 90
London Lickpenny, analysis of, 121f.; authorship, 121 n.
"Low Life," satire on, 148, 149, 179, 212, 217
Lowell, J. R., 4; *Fable for Critics,* 33
Lucian, 6, 14; dialogues, 7; epigrams, 17; use of travesty, 19
Lucilius, Latin satirist, 15, 23
Lucilius, Greek epigrammatist, 17
Lusty Juventus, 212, 216
Lutel Soth sermun, A, 51f., 55
Luther, 32 n., 151, 185, 207; satire against, 194, 205 n.
Lydgate, John, 46, 158, 159, 164, 170, 182, 189; satirical poems, 119–21
Lyndsay, Sir David, 1, 5, 32 n., 101, 134, 135, 136, 137, 167, 183, 213, 216, 217, 221, 222, 223, 224, 225; life of, 197f.; as man and as poet, 198f.; genesis of satiric poems, 199; range of material, 199; as satirist of the Reformation, 200; satiric poems, 200–10; immunity from persecution, 209; contribution to the Satire, 210; influence upon Bale, 215
Lyric, the, 1

Maccaronea, 18
Mac Flecknoe, 11, 14, 22, 23, 31, 33
Magna Charta, 67
Magnyfycence, 212f., 219
Manciple, the, as a satiric type, 102
Mankind, 216
Manner of the World Nowadays, The, 170
Mantuan, eclogues, 164f.
Manuel, 186 n.
Manuel des Peschiez, 63
Map, Walter, 1, 4, 37, 38, 47, 151, 181, 189, 222; Goliardic poems sometimes attributed to him, 40f.
Margites, 23, 25
Marie de France, fables, 7, 26, 27, 136
Martial, epigrams, 7, 17
Mass, the, satire against, 185–90, 193, 219
Menander, 25
Merchant's Tale, The, 109
Merry Play between John the Husband, Tyb the Wife, and Sir John the Priest, A, 213
Miller, the, as a satiric type, 102
Mind, Will, and Understanding, 216
Minnesingers, the, satire, 37 n.; love poetry, 175
Minot, Lawrence, 63, 125; songs, 68f.
Miracle Plays, satire in, 212
Miseriae Curialium, 165
Mock-Epic, the, 21f.

Mock-Heroic, the, 4, 7, 18, 21f., 22
Molière, satiric comedies, 7, 24
Monarchie, The, 200, 203
Monk, the, as a satiric type, 100
Monks, the, satire against, 40, 43f., 46, 58, 59, 65, 81, 87, 100, 189, 191
Monk's Tale, The, 106, 107; interlude before, 105; interlude following, 106–7
Moralities, satire, 211; confusion with Interludes, 211; low life, 211; various Moralities, 216–9, *passim*
More, Edward, 176 n.
More, Sir Thomas, 144; epigrams, 17
Morgante Maggiore, 7, 18
Mother Hubberd's Tale, 27
Murner, 32 n.

Narenschiff, the, 119, 147 n., 155; relation to *The Ship of Fools,* 156
Nature, 217
Neckham, Alexander, 46, 85
New Custom, 218
Nice Wanton, The, 216
Novel, the satiric novel, 7
Nowadays, analysis of, 169f.
Nun's Priest's Tale, The, 27 n.; analysis of, 109f.

Occleve, Thomas, poem on Oldcastle, 91f.; appeal to Henry V, 122; ballade on interment of Rich. II, 122; *The Letter of Cupid,* 176; *Dialogue,* 176
Ode, the, 1
Of Men Lif that wonip in Lond, 59
Old English Miscellany, An, 54
Oldcastle, Sir John, 91, 124, 191
Oldham, John, 10
On the Council of London, 19 n.
Order of Fair Ease, The, 39
"Order of Fair Ease, The," 58
"Order of the Ass, The," 45 n., 84
Orlandino, 18
Owl and the Nightingale, The, 57
Ovid, 85

Pain and Sorrow of Evil Marriage, The, 176
Pammachius, 215
Pantcha-Tantra, the, 27
Papal Court, satire against, 47f., 203
Pardoner, the, as a satiric type, 101, 103f., 179, 207, 213, 216
Pardoner and the Friar, The, 101, 213
Pardoner's Tale, The, analysis of, 103f.
"Parnassian poems," 4, 33
Parody, as a satiric method, 20; Goliardic parodies, Ch. 11, *passim*
Persius, 15
Personal Satire, The, 30f.
Personal satire, against King John, 48f.; anti-Wyckliffite clergy, 88; Oldcastle, 91f.; King Rich. II, 95f.; Bushey, Scrope, Greene, Bagot, Ver, 95f.; House of Lancaster, 123; Duke of Burgundy, 125; Say and Daniel, 127f.; Suffolk, 127–30; Boothe, 128; Donald Owre, 141; Friar Damian, 141; Wolsey, 150–55, *passim,* 185–90, *passim;* Thomas Cromwell, 173; Father Mathias, etc., 188; Luther, 194; the Pope, 195, 214.
Petrarch, 20
Phaedrus, 27
Pierce the Plowman's Crede, 89, 90; analysis of, 80f.
Piers Plowman, 1, 28, 94, 148, 182, 211, 218, 226; analysis of, 70-9; authorship, 70 n.; influence of *Roman de la Rose,* 71; allegorical form, 72; personifications, 73; satire against idlers, social classes, 74; civil and ecclesiastical courts, 75; clergy, 75; constructive element, 76; *genre* pictures, 76f.; contemporary allusions, 77; humor, 78; place in history of English Satire, 79; influence, 80; imitations of, 80f.
"Pilgrimage of Grace, The," nature and causes, 172; in satire, 173
Pilgrimages, Shrines, and Image

Worship, satire against, 77f., 203
Pitt, Christopher, 21 n.
Peasants' Revolt, the, causes, 81, 82; in satire, 83f.
Play, the satiric, 7, 13
Plowman, the, as a type, 75, 81f.
Poem on the Times of Edward II, A, 169, 224, 226; analysis of, 64–6
Poema Morale, 53
Political Satire, the, in general, 31f.; in medieval England, 222f.
Poor, the, satire on oppression of, 65, 135f., 170, 174, 188, 206f., 208
Poor Help, A, 194
Pope, Alexander, 1, 6, 7, 11, 14, 16, 32, 36, 98, 225, 227; epigrams, 17; burlesque poetry, 18; *Dunciad,* 20, 22, 31, 33; Satires, 7, 11
Praise of Folly, The, 7, 13
Pricke of Conscience, The, 62; analysis of, 63
Prior, Matthew, satiric fables, 4
Proper Dialogue Between a Gentleman and a Husbandman, A, 191
Prophecy of Golias, The, 41
Prophecy of John of Bridlington, 69f.
Proud Wives Pater Noster, The, analysis of, 176f.
Pulci, *Morgante Maggiore,* 7, 18

Quatern of Knaves, 181 and n.

Rabelais, 6, 14, 18, 210; *Gargantua,* 7
Ragguagli di Parnaso, 33
Ragman Roll, 122, 175
Raoul de Houdin, *Songe d'Enfer* and *la Voie de Paradis,* 53
Rape of the Lock, The, 22
Rede Me and Be Nott Wrothe, 185–90, 191; authorship, 185; genesis, 185; confiscation by Wolsey, 186; relation to *Krankheit der Messe,* 186 n.; form, 187; subject-matter, 187; personal satire, 188; tone, 190; verse-form, 190
Reformation, Satire of the, 181–96, 200, 205–9, 214–6, 217f., 219
Religious Satire, The, 221f.
Renart le Contrefait, 26
Replycacion, The, 184f., 192
Respublica, 211, 212, 217f.
Retaliation, The, 33 n.
Reve, the, as a satiric type, 102
Richard II, King, 85; satire against, 95f.; satire in reign of, 80–117
Richard of Cornwall, Earl, ballad against, 50f.
Richard of Cornwall, English ballad, 51, 226
Richard the Redeless, analysis of, 95f.; authorship, 95 n.
Richert, French *fabliau,* 107
Robene and Makyne, 134
Robert Mannyng, *Handlyng Synne,* 62f.
Robin Conscience, 219
Rogues, satire on, 178–81, 211, 217, 225
Rollenhagen, 26
Roman de la Rose, the, 5, 28, 46, 104, 146 n., 175
Roman de Renart, 7; cycle of, 26f.; as source of material, 109
Roman de Rou, 82 n.
Romance, metrical, parody of, 25, 113f.
Roy, William, 185
Ruin of a Realm, 171f.
Rûtebeuf, 210
Saint Patrick's Purgatory, 54

Satire, the, 1; gradual development, 2; confusion of terms, 2; satire, Satire, and the satiric spirit, 3; classical Latin Satire, 3; Anglo-Latin Satires, 4, 5; the Lollard Satire, 4; allegorical Satire, 4; Satire on Woman, 4; Satire of the Reformation, 4; on Rogues, 4; "Parnassian" Satire, 4; rise and progress in England, 4f.; foreign influences, 5; perennial life, 12; the Satire in prose, 13; methods of expression, 14; the grotesque and the burlesque Satire, 18f.; distinction between Satire and other genres, 29f.; division into groups,

30f.; the Personal Satire, 30f.; Greek lyric Satires, 30; the Political Satire, 31; the Moral and Social Satire, 32; the Literary Satire, 33

Satire, definition, 3; Goliardic, 4; Trouvère, 4, 36; Civil War, 5; grotesque and burlesque, 18f.; Greek, 23f.; among Lapps and Greenlanders, 30 n.; in Anglo-Saxon literature, 35; schools, 36; in sermons, 52f.; in Visions of Heaven and Hell, 53f.; lack of political satire in reign of Ed. II, 64f.; rise of class-satire, 66f.; in *fabliaux*, 107f.

Satire, objects of: alchemy, q. v.; astrologers, 162; beggars and idlers, q. v.; bishops, 48, 172; celibacy, 105; chivalry, 140; social classes, q. v.; clergy, q. v.; consistory courts, q. v.; courts, q. v.; drunkenness, q. v.; fame, 116; fashions, q. v.; fortune, 116; France, 69; fraud, q. v.; inconsistency, 119; judges, q. v.; Lollards, q. v.; low life, q. v.; marriage, 116f.; Mass, q. v.; metrical romance, 113f.; money, 41f.; papal court, 47f., 203; peddlers, 203; persons, see "personal satire;" pilgrimages, etc., q. v.; politics in Scotland, 140; oppression of the poor, q. v.; public manners, 132f.; Reformation, q. v.; rogues, q. v.; rumor, 116; scholasticism, 62; Scotch, q. v.; Seven Deadly Sins, q. v.; sins of the city, 166; social parasites, 42; society in general, 42; tailors, q. v.; the times, q. v.; vices in abstract, 94, 132; woman, q. v.

Satire on Edinburgh, 140

Satire on the Men of Stockton, A, 83

Satirical spirit, the, nature and working, 6f.; destructive element, 8; humorous element, 9; exaggeration, 9; reformatory purpose, 10; *stimuli*, 10; instruments, 11

Satirists, great English, 1; Elizabethan, 5; Restoration and Georgian, 5

Satyrical Ballad, A, 121

Savary of Mauleon, 48

Scaliger, J. J., epigrams, 17

Scarron, *Virgile Travesti*, 7, 19

School-House of Women, The, 176

Scotch, the, Satire against, 61, 125

Scribbleriad, The, 22

Scrope, Richard, Archbishop of York, 123

Sermon joyeux, 7

Seven Deadly Sins, satire against, 94, 171, 224

Sheffield, John, Earl of, 33

Shepherd's Calendar, The, 166

Shepherd's Week, The, 20

Ship of Fools, The, 155, 178, 180; analysis of, 156–64; variations from *Narrenschiff*, 156; moral character, 157; literary character, 157; popularity, 157; pictures, 158; form, 158; classes of Fools, characterization, 159; satire against classes and religious satire, 160; constructive element, 161; bookish origin, 161; pictures of real life, 161f.; poetic quality, 162; influence of classical satire, 162f.; medieval ethics, 163; English elements, 164; subsequent influence, 164

Showing and Declaring the Pride and Abuse of Women Nowadays, 177

Silli, the 24, 25

Simon de Montfort, Earl, 50

Simonides of Amorgos, 23

Sir Thopas, 26, 98, 113

Sirvente, 4 and n., 5, 36, 37 and n., 48f., 222

Skelton, John, 1, 4, 5, 46, 57, 134, 162, 170, 173, 182, 192, 193, 194, 197, 202, 205, 210, 211, 212f., 216, 219, 221, 222, 223, 225; Satires against Wolsey, 31 n.; Satires, 143–55; use of satire, 144; life, 144f.; meter, 145; heritage, 145f.; attitude toward Wolsey, 150; sub-

ject-matter, 151; qualities as satirist, 154f.; *Replycacion,* 184f.; *Magnyfycence,* 212
"Social Parasites, The," 42
Society, generalized Satire against, 42
Song against the Friars, 88f.
Songe d'Enfer, 53
Songs, against French and Scotch, 4; of Béranger, 7
Sottie, the, 7
Speculum Stultorum, 20 n., 28, 43–6, 58, 72
Speke Parrot, 149f., 171, 202
Spenser, Edmund, 27, 166
Suckling, Sir John, 4, 33
Suffolk, William de la Pole, Duke of, 126–9, *passim*
Summoner, the, as a satiric type, 101f., 111
Summoner's Tale, The, 111f.
Supplicatioun in Contemptioun of Syde Taillis, 203
Swift, Jonathan, 1, 6, 8, 9, 10, 11, 14, 18, 31, 33; *Gulliver's Travels,* 7; grotesque satire, 18
Syr Peny, 122

Taill of the Dog, the Scheip, and the Wolf, 135
Taill of the Wolf and the Lamb, The, 135
Tailors, satire against, 55, 140
Tale, the satiric, 7, 13
Tale of Threscore Folys and Thre, A, analysis of, 119f.
Tassoni, 7, 20
Telȝouris and Sowtaris, The, 138
Temptacyon of our Lorde, The, 214
"Testament," the, as a literary form, 202
Testament and Complaynt of our Soverane Lordis Papyngo, The, analysis of, 202f.
Testament of Cresseid, The, 134
Theophrastus, 162
Thistle and the Rose, The, 136
Three Laws of Nature, Moses, and Christ, The, 214
Tidings from the Session, 137; analysis of, 138f.
Times, the, generalized Satire on, 93, 120, 132, 149f.
Timon of Phlius, 24
Town Eclogues, 20
Travesty, 19
Treatise of this Gallant, 217; analysis of, 170f; relation to *Speke Parrot,* 171
Tripartite Chronicle, analysis of, 85
Trivia, 20
Trouvères, 4, 36, 37, 175
Tua Mariit Wemen and the Wedo 137, 140, 177
Tunning of Elynour Rummnyg, The, 149, 211, 225
Turnament, The, by Dunbar, 137, 138, 140
Turnament of Totenham, The, 123 n.
Twenty-Five Orders of Fools, The, 181
Tyndale, William, 182, 183, 184, 205

Ulrich of Würtemberg, Duke, 31

Viaggio in Parnaso, 33
Viaje al Parnaso, 33
Virgil, 164
Virgile Travesti, 7, 19
Vision of Furseus, 53
Vision of Judgment, A, by Byron, 22
Vision of St. Paul, 54
Vision of Tundale, 54
Vision of Thurcill, The, 54
Visions of Heaven and Hell, origin, 53; in France, 53f.; in Middle Ages, 54; in England, 54; relation to the Satire, 55
Visions of the Monk of Evesham, 54
Vita de Mecenate, 33
Volpone, 220
Voltaire, 7, 14
Vox Clamantis, analysis of, 83–5
Vox Populi, Vox Dei, 224; analysis of, 173f.

Wace, 82 n.
Wars of the Roses, satire, 130–1, 223; popular ballads, 131 n.

We lordis hes chosin a chiftane mervellus, 140f.
Why Come Ye Not to Court, 145; analysis of, 152–4; qualities as satire, 154
Wife of Bath, the, as a satiric type, 103, 104, 105
Wife of Bath's Tale, The, prologue to, 104f.
Winchelsea, Lady, 33
Wireker, Nigellus, 4, 84, 85, 100, 164, 221; *Speculum Stultorum,* 4, 20 n., 28, 43–6
Wither, George, 33, 84
Wolsey, Thomas, Cardinal, 150–55, *passim;* 172, 173, 184, 186f., 202, 218, 223
Woman, satire on, 41, 104, 105, 110, 116, 122, 140, 171, 175–7
World and the Child, The, 218f.
Wulfstan, homilies, 35; references to heaven and hell, 53
Wyatt, Sir Thomas, 1, 3, 4, 5, 16, 144, 226, 227
Wyckliffe, John, 71, 85–92, *passim;* 151, 185

Xenophanes of Colophon, 24

Young, Edward, 1, 16